ON BECOMING RESPONSIBLE

ON BECOMING
RESPONSIBLE

Michael S. Pritchard

 UNIVERSITY PRESS OF KANSAS

© 1991 by the University Press of Kansas

Published by the University Press of Kansas (Lawrence, Kansas
66045), which was organized by the Kansas Board of Regents and is
operated and funded by Emporia State University, Fort Hays State
University, Kansas State University, Pittsburg State University,
the University of Kansas, and Wichita State University

Library of Congress Cataloging-in-Publication Data
Pritchard, Michael S.
   On becoming responsible / Michael Pritchard.
     p. cm.
   Includes bibliographical references and index.
   ISBN 0-7006-0444-8 (alk. paper)
   1. Moral development. I. Title.
  BF723.M54P75 1991
  170—dc20   90-41613
                                      CIP

British Library Cataloguing in Publication Data is available.

Printed in the United States of America
10 9 8 7 6 5 4 3 2 1

The paper used in this publication meets the minimum requirements of the American
National Standard for Permanence of Paper for Printed Library Materials Z39.48-1984.

For my mother, Elenore, who has been there
from the very beginning

Contents

Preface

The face of moral philosophy has changed greatly since my graduate school years at the University of Wisconsin, when analysis of "the language of morals" was in the forefront. At some point I became dissatisfied with this analysis. Who, I asked myself, uses moral language—and what must they be like if they are to use it meaningfully and with understanding? Attempting to answer these questions led me into the then unfashionable area of moral psychology—an area that blurs distinctions between philosophical and psychological inquiry.

Fortunately, several of my teachers encouraged my interdisciplinary explorations. Gerald MacCallum introduced me to the writings of Herbert Fingarette, which led to my interest in the social psychopath. William Hay introduced me to Arthur Murphy's *Theory of Practical Reason* (1965), which continues to have a powerful influence on my thinking. Marcus Singer, my dissertation advisor, encouraged me to wrestle with John Rawls's article "The Sense of Justice" (1963), which introduced me to literature on moral development. I am grateful to all three of my former teachers for their support of my early attempts to find a place for reason and sentiment in moral life.

My work over the years has been generously supported by the National Endowment for the Humanities. I have benefited from participation in five NEH seminars. Seminar directors Theodore Mischel, Gene Outka, Alasdair MacIntyre, Gareth Matthews, and Jonathan Bennett have all played important roles in helping me develop and articulate various views expressed in this book. I have also learned much from the many participants in those quite wonderful seminars.

I am indebted to the many colleagues, students, and friends who have helped me shape my ideas. I could not name them all. However, I am especially grateful to Judith Andre, David Conway, John Dilworth, Joseph Ellin, Pamela Grath, Robert Hannaford, James Hood, Richard Pulaski, Wade Robison, Gregory Sheridan, and Laurence Thomas. I owe a special debt of gratitude to Matthew Lipman for opening my eyes to the remarkably rich philosophical life of children.

Although each is substantially revised and expanded, several chapters draw heavily from my previous publications. Chapter 3 draws from "Psychopathology, Responsibility, and Understanding," *The Monist*, October 1974, pp. 630–645. Chapter 4 draws from "Reason and Passion: Reid's Reply to Hume," *The Monist*, April 1978, pp. 282–298. Chapter 5 draws from "Human Dignity and Justice," *Ethics*, July 1972, pp. 299–313, Chapter 6 draws from "Rawls' Moral Psychology," *Southwestern Journal of Philosophy*, February 1977, pp. 59–72. Chapter 7 draws from "Cognition and Affect in Moral Development: A Critique of Kohlberg," *Journal of Value Inquiry*, Winter 1984, pp. 35–49. Chapter 9 draws from "Self-Regard and the Supererogatory," in *Respect for Persons*, edited by O. H. Green (Tulane University Press, 1982), pp. 139–151. I wish to thank the editors of these publications for permission to include relevant portions of these publications.

I wish also to thank Western Michigan University for its summer fellowship and sabbatical leave support of my work on various parts of this book over the years. Finally, I thank Kate Torrey, former editor-in-chief at the University Press of Kansas, for suggesting that I needed a sabbatical leave to complete the book; and I thank Cynthia Miller, current editor-in-chief, and the rest of the staff for their constant encouragement and support.

1
Introduction

Although we may find it difficult to explain what we think morality is, we are all familiar with it. We have this familiarity by virtue of being moral agents. We are confronted daily with what we take to be instances of unfairness, fairness, cruelty, kindness, selfishness, generosity, and so on. We are also familiar with what eighteenth-century British moralists such as Joseph Butler, David Hume, Adam Smith, and Thomas Reid called *moral sentiments*—resentment, indignation, guilt, shame, pride, sympathy, compassion, benevolence, and the like. Related as they are to our self-respect, sense of dignity, sense of justice, respect for others, and concern for others' well-being, the moral sentiments constitute an essential part of our moral sensibilities.

This book is a philosophical exploration of such familiar features of moral life. Just as the philosophical study of logic presupposes and makes use of our logical sensibilities, the philosophical study of morality presupposes and makes use of our moral sensibilities. However, since the study of both logic and morality is essentially normative, our sensibilities must be subjected to critical examination. This raises a question of circularity because we must employ our logical and moral sensibilities in their very appraisal.

In the case of logic, at least at an everyday level, this does not seem to pose a serious problem. It is not clear that we have any practical alternative to employing basic and familiar norms of consistency and deductive inference. The study of logic is useful in helping us to recognize instances of the use and violation of these norms. Logical paradoxes such as "the sentence you are now reading is false" are puzzling, but their resolution (or irresolution) does not threaten to undermine everyday logical norms.

In the case of morality, matters may seem quite different. Basic moral norms, it may be objected, are much more variable and conflicting. But this can be overstated and misleadingly characterized. Some moral theories are imperialistic, each advancing one basic moral principle from which all other moral considerations can be derived. It is true that one cannot consistently adhere to more than one of these theories; one cannot be a thoroughgoing utilitarian *and* an egoist or a utilitarian *and* a Kantian, and so on. Each of these options is a unified theory that attempts to provide a comprehensive, coherent grounding for morality. At most, only one of these theories can prevail, so they invite conflict. Yet much of this conflict occurs at a level of thought that seldom touches the moral lives of ordinary moral agents. Thus, if all moral judgments must ultimately be grounded in, say, the principle of utility, most moral thinking is done without attending to its grounding. Of course, there are times when we do employ utilitarian criteria, but this falls far short of embracing a general moral theory. As most utilitarians themselves acknowledge, our moral concerns are seldom explicitly bound up with utilitarian thinking.

For the conflict we find among general moral theories to generate comparable conflict at the level of practical judgment, we must first acknowledge the need for the kind of moral thinking to which these theories aspire. I am not convinced of this need, my own inclinations being more pluralistic. We can consistently appeal to self-interest, utility, and respect for persons on one and the same occasion, or selectively on different occasions. Each of these kinds of considerations (and many others) may have appropriate places in our moral thinking. Furthermore, we may know that this is so, even in the absence of an overall moral theory that puts everything in its place.

In this regard, the analogy with logic still holds. We may know that affirming the antecedent, denying the consequent, and hypothetical syllogism are reliable patterns of deductive reasoning without having a comprehensive, coherent logical theory that grounds their reliability. Most of us do not have such a theory. Yet we all know that "the ground is wet" follows deductively from "if it is raining, the ground is wet; and it is raining." Confident affirmation of this pattern of inference does not depend on confirmation by a general logical theory. If anything, any logical theory that commands our respect must acknowledge that such confidence is warranted. The use of such everyday patterns of inference is necessary for the confirmation of any logical theory.

At this point the comparison of morality to logic seems to weaken. Is there anything in moral thought that has an indispensability comparable to the basic patterns of deductive inference with which we are all familiar? This is a fair, and troublesome, question. However, we must be clear that the answer does not depend on the availability of a comprehensive, coherent moral theory. The absence of a comprehensive, coherent logical theory does not leave us without logical resources. We do not think our cupboards are bare—that we cannot confidently and reliably employ logical thinking. Even if we hope someday to construct a comprehensive, coherent logical theory, any plausible theory will have to respect the logical sensibilities that enable us to initiate the search. Similarly, we should not despair at the lack of consensus about comprehensive, coherent moral theories. They cannot all be right; perhaps none are. But whatever assessment we make of the candidates requires us to make use of moral sensibilities we acquire prior to theorizing at this level.

Having said this, we still must acknowledge that the analogy between our logical and moral sensibilities is rather weak. Familiar patterns of deductive inference live comfortably together, and they have more to do with structures, or forms, of thought than with any specific content. Furthermore, these patterns both facilitate and constrain logical thought. Familiar patterns of moral thought, on the other hand, frequently come into conflict. The demand for fairness, for example, may conflict with the demand that we not harm others. This does not mean that such conflicts cannot be reasonably resolved, but even when we are confident that they can, we have nothing as decisive as rules of deductive logic to rely on.[1]

There is another possible contrast. Truths of logic, at least deductive logic, are commonly thought to have a kind of timeless necessity. "If A implies B and B implies C, then A implies C," on this view, is a necessary truth. It in no way depends on anyone's having the capacity to apprehend its truth. Science, too, is often viewed, in principle at least, as expressing truths that in no way depend on anyone's having the capacity to apprehend them. Such truths are not characterized as having the kind of necessity attributed to logical truths, but they are regarded as having a kind of independent status.

Whether such views are defensible, or even tolerably clear, is a matter of some controversy. I will not venture further into this metaphysical thicket. What I wish to emphasize is that morality is very dependent on our moral sensibilities. Briefly put, the point is this. Whatever we should say about science, logic, or the "external world," without moral sensibilities there is no moral world where moral truths can reside. Morality has to do with how we should live our lives. As such, it is preeminently practical and, as Arthur Murphy (1965) puts it, "addressed to whom it may concern." That is, morality is addressed to those who have moral sensibilities.

Without an audience of such agents, morality simply has no applicability. If there is moral "objectivity," it is not independent of how we are naturally and socially constituted. If this is right, then to gain any serious hearing, a moral theory must respect our moral sensibilities, as well as other concerns that give our lives meaning and coherence. This, I take it, is the central thrust of Bernard Williams's (1981; 1985) recent attacks on impersonal utilitarian and Kantian moral theories. What must be explained is how any such impersonal theory can reasonably gain a foothold in an individual's life. Thus, philosophical reflection should proceed from the ground up. I am skeptical about whether this will yield a comprehensive, coherent moral theory. However, the skepticism does not extend to the groundings that any such theory must respect.

In exploring the groundings of morality, I will pay special attention to the development of moral concerns in the lives of children—something that is not often done in philosophical writings. However, I believe that focusing on how morality enters the lives of children helps us more clearly address fundamental questions about the nature of moral agency, the role of reason in morality, why we should be moral, and what it is reasonable to expect from moral theories. In addition, I believe that philosophical reflection on the moral lives of children is important in its own right. In recent years moral philosophers have begun to pay attention to the important work being done by psychologists in the area of moral development.

My general thesis is basically Humean. Whatever grounding morality has in our lives must essentially involve our "passions." Reason alone is insufficient. My sympathies are basically with Thomas Reid, for whom Hume was a favorite stalking-horse. Reid tries to rescue morality from being a "slave of the passions" by insisting that it must include certain elements of rationality. Reason alone may not yield morality, but neither will passion alone. *Sentiments*, for Reid, are a combination of reason and affect, involving judgment and feeling.

Among contemporary moral theorists, P. F. Strawson looms largest in the early chapters. His essay "Freedom and Resentment" (1968) is pivotal to almost everything I say there. A fundamental thesis of his essay is that, although there is no external, rational justification of morality, there is "a general structure or web of human attitudes and feelings" that is a given in human societies (1968, p. 94). These attitudes and feelings express our moral concern and regard for one another, and they provide a grounding for morality. Reactive attitudes and feelings are our natural responses to good and ill will others have for us. Although, according to Strawson, this general structure of attitudes and feelings cannot itself be rationally justified (it is nonrational rather than irrational), reason has a significant role to play *within* it. Within this broad framework of attitudes and feelings "there is endless room for modification, redirection, criticism, and justification" (1968, p. 94).

It is within this context that moral development and moral education should be discussed. For example, according to Joseph Butler (1730) and Thomas Reid (1788), resentment is expressed by "brute animals" as well as by human beings. Only in humans, however, can resentment become a *moral* sentiment. Similarly, dispositions of sympathy and caring in very young children later take on moral form. Current cognitive-developmental moral theories such as Lawrence Kohlberg's (1981) are right to emphasize the importance of the development of patterns of logical thought, although they tend to underestimate the importance of affect in moral development.

An adequate theory of moral development must be, at least in part, a theory of the development of the moral sentiments. This is the explicit concern of Chapters 6–8, which explore the theories of moral development of John Rawls (1971), Lawrence Kohlberg (1981; 1984), and Carol Gilligan (1982). My sympathies lie mainly with Gilligan's critique of Kohlberg, which charges his theory with underestimating the role of affect and personal relationships and with overestimating the role of impartial principles of justice and utility. The tension between Kohlberg's view of morality as impersonal and Gilligan's more personal view is more noted than resolved in the literature on moral development. However, it provides the major theme of much recent philosophical literature, particularly the writings of Bernard Williams (1981; 1985), Samuel Scheffler (1982), and Thomas Nagel (1986). A major question is whether impersonal theories such as utilitarianism can acknowledge the importance of personal integrity. Further reflection on the significance of moral sentiments casts serious doubt, I believe, on whether utilitarianism identifies the sole, or even the most basic, grounding of our status as moral agents.

Chapter 2, "On Becoming a Moral Agent," provides background for understanding some of my misgivings about utilitarianism. I explore Reid's account of differences between "brute animals," moved only by the strongest desire at any given moment, and moral agents, who by virtue of their rational capacities can achieve some measure of "self-government." Reid's discussion of the acquisition of first principles, their role in moral reasoning, and the continuing need for moral education are highlighted. Especially noteworthy is Reid's claim that moral knowledge is not the special province of moral philosophers or metaphysicians. It is the business of all of us and therefore ought to be within the reach of every moral agent. Reid emphasizes that we have firmly embedded attitudes and feelings prior to any moral theorizing we might undertake. Very few of us look at morality through the eyes of a moral philosopher or a metaphysician. Nevertheless, if we do have moral knowledge, it must be accounted for by the moral philosopher or metaphysician. Furthermore, a steady eye must be focused on those attitudes, feelings, and rational capacities that enable ordinary moral agents to have that knowledge.

I support Reid's view by considering a variety of examples of moral thinking (including attitudes and feelings) by children which suggest they have a good grasp of moral concepts, even though they lack a comprehensive theory of morality and even though they, like all of us, have much more to learn about morality. Chapter 2 has the dual purpose of showing that the moral agency of children is typically underestimated and that the importance of comprehensive moral theories is often overestimated by philosophers. What is important is that children develop a somewhat stable set of dispositions to respond in morally sensitive ways to a broad range of concerns and interests.

In Chapter 3, "Accountability, Understanding, and Sentiments," I consider the social psychopath as a limiting case. Psychopaths are clinically characterized as lacking moral sentiments entirely. While they have an "intellectual" understanding of moral principles and concepts, they lack what Strawson would call a "participant" understanding. I conclude that, lacking the requisite kind of understanding, they are not moral agents. Moral discourse is addressed to moral agents, not psychopaths. Problems about what morality requires of us, and why, are to be dealt with from within morality by those with moral sentiments rather than from a detached, external standpoint. But, as Strawson says, morality as a whole neither has nor needs an external, rational justification.

Chapter 4, "Reason and Resentment," develops Strawson's thesis that our morally reactive attitudes provide a grounding for morality that allows room for reasoning within morality. At the same time, these reactive attitudes are a natural, ineluctable feature of human beings living in society. I illustrate Strawson's central thesis about reactive attitudes by considering, in detail, Butler and Reid's account of resentment and its relation to reason. This account is then juxtaposed with Hume's view that "reason is, and ought to be, the slave of the passions." Although Reid treated Hume as his stalking-horse, close examination reveals that their views are similar in fundamental respects. The thesis that reason and sentiment are inseparable—and essential to morality—is supported.

Chapter 5, "Integrity, Dignity, and Justice," shows that regard for human dignity is solidly grounded within Strawson's general structure of attitudes and feelings—even though no rational proof of the claim that we have dignity is available. I find support for this thesis by exploring relationships between personal integrity and such attitudes and feelings as resentment, indignation, guilt, shame, self-respect, and respect for others, particularly as these are expressed through one's sense of justice.

Chapters 6–8 explore the theories of moral development of John Rawls, Lawrence Kohlberg, and Carol Gilligan. In his *Theory of Justice* (1971), Rawls points out that the plausibility of any particular moral theory depends in part on our capacity as moral agents to take its offerings seriously in thought and conduct. In support of his own theory of justice, he presents an account of how our sense of justice develops, stressing the central importance he attaches to the development of moral sentiments, especially those related to self-respect and self-esteem. A weakness of his account, however, is that his psychological principles of reciprocity do not provide full support for his view of justice as respecting all persons. They require supplementation with a psychological principle of sympathy. Kohlberg, too, tries to give an account of moral development culminating in universal respect for persons, but he seriously underestimates the role of sentiments in moral development. Insofar as he does discuss affective dimensions of moral development, he fails to show how the egoism he ascribes to very young children is transcended in later stages of development. The work of Carol Gilligan radically challenges Kohlberg's theory of moral development (and, to some extent, Rawls's). She claims that Kohlberg overemphasizes the notions of justice, rights, duties, and independence (autonomy) in his account. She argues for the importance of caring, responsibility, and interdependence. I conclude Chapter 8 with a discussion of the implications of the Kohlberg/Gilligan controversy for moral education.

Chapter 9, "Personal Morality," picks up on a puzzling contrast between first- and third-person appraisals of character and action that seems implicit in Gilligan's "different voice." Sometimes we make moral demands on ourselves that we do not make on others. Thus, we may have personal, moral ideals which we take seriously, but which we do not wish to impose on others. Some are satisfied merely to do what is minimally required as a matter of strict duty; others, however, are more directly responsive to the needs of the situation and give little thought to what is minimally required of them, unless they are aware of conflicting moral demands which cannot be fully satisfied. It is difficult to make a determination of where "strict duty" leaves off and something more enters in. Although the agents might see themselves as simply doing what needs to be done, third parties are likely to characterize them in terms of various praiseworthy virtues (for example, generosity, considerateness, conscientiousness). A difficulty is that, precisely because of their praiseworthiness, such virtues can be seriously altered, or even corrupted, through their self-conscious acknowledgment. (For example, John's generosity could become a form of self-flattery: "I do so much more than anyone has a right to expect from me!") Insofar as the virtues persons have constitute a part of their integrity, it is important to understand how these virtues may be expressed in their thoughts and actions without subverting that integrity.

Gilligan's critique of Kohlberg contains an implicit attack on the idea of autonomy. She raises the question of whether there is a fundamental conflict between autonomy and caring for others. No doubt some highly individualistic views of autonomy do conflict with the kinds of caring relationships Gilligan values, but in Chapter 10 I explore a view of autonomy that does not. Here Rawls is an ally. His account of one's sense of justice explicitly relies on love and friendship as essential to the development of self-respect and self-esteem that enables one autonomously to accept principles of justice. In the end, I advocate a combination of some of the views of Rawls and Gilligan in giving fuller psychological support for a principle of respect for persons.

Chapter 11, "Utilitarianism and Personal Integrity," returns to some of the concerns raised in Chapter 2 about what can reasonably be demanded of moral agents. Some of the personal, moral commitments and ideals one has might be directed to particular individuals, groups, institutions, or projects in ways that may not (in any obvious way) support general utilitarian ends. Furthermore, as Bernard Williams (1973) insists, we very likely have nonmoral, personal concerns, projects, or commitments that give our lives meaning. As such, they too constitute an important part of our personal integrity. Williams's worry about utilitarianism is that it might require us to abandon personal projects and commitments for the sake of general utility. Though acknowledging that tragic circumstances might reasonably require such sacrifices, Williams claims that utilitarianism makes unreasonable demands as well. He concludes that utilitarianism cannot take personal integrity seriously. Some utilitarians reply that opting for personal projects or commitments when greater good would result from abandoning them is self-indulgence.

Chapter 11 defends Williams against the charge of self-indulgence. An important part of this defense requires making a distinction between acting in ways that are consistent with, if not supportive of, personal integrity and acting for the sake of preserving or supporting personal integrity. However, for this distinction to help, it is also necessary to argue that moral agents are not ordinarily required to make direct comparisons between the overall consequences of sticking to their prior commitments and the alternatives that seem more likely to maximize good consequences.

Utilitarians are not necessarily wedded to the idea that our actual moral deliberations should refer explicitly to the principle of utility. Still, whether or not we are expected to make direct use of the principle of utility in making decisions, utilitarians maintain that whatever *moral* weight attaches to what we do is ultimately derivable from its utility. Samuel Scheffler (1982) joins Williams in rejecting this. He opts for an independent grounding of a personal moral perspective. At the same time, he argues that it is always morally permissible for one to act for utilitarian ends and also to opt for less than maximizing consequences. Scheffler sees no inherent problem of integrity for those who accept utilitarian ends; he supports what he calls an agent-centered *prerogative*. On the other hand, he can find no basis for claiming that there are any agent-centered *restrictions* that imply it may sometimes be impermissible, or wrong, to try to maximize good consequences.

I contend that, contrary to Scheffler, reasonable grounds can be given for agent-centered restrictions. Scheffler presents us with two "voices" of moral reasoning: a) the impersonal voice of a benevolent, ideal observer; and b) the personal voice of individuals pursuing their own ends. Unfortunately, although Scheffler does not want the personal voice to collapse into a form of egoism, he offers no clear guidelines that prevent this. I argue for a third "voice." Neither a) nor b) adequately represents the kinds of *interpersonal* concerns that I believe can be found in Strawson's general structure of attitudes and feelings. The interpersonal perspective I support emphasizes mutual respect and concern for the integrity and moral agency of persons. It focuses on what we can reasonably expect and demand from one another as loved ones, friends, acquaintances, members of local and wider communities, and as inhabitants of a shared world. It begins with moral agents living in a world with multiple sources of moral demand—but with no requirement that all these demands be ultimately grounded in a single demand (for example, to promote the greatest possible good).

No comprehensive, coherent moral theory emerges from my analysis; my sympathies are pluralistic rather than unitary. Nevertheless, I emphasize some values more than others. Respect for persons obviously plays a prominent role in my understanding of moral life. So does integrity. Chapter 12, "Why Be Moral?" asks what kind of regard for moral considerations a life of moral integrity requires of us. Here I argue, unfashionably, that it is not viciously circular to give moral reasons for being moral. In fact, I claim that we should expect this from someone with moral integrity and should encourage this in children. I connect this claim with the commonly held view that moral reasons should be overriding when there is a conflict between what morality requires of us and what we might otherwise want.

Bernard Williams (1985) suggests that, as we struggle with questions about how we should live, we seek a kind of *confidence* in our commitments that will survive critical reflection. We may seek such confidence in the form of propositions that express moral truths written in the skies, so to speak. We may attempt to step outside ourselves and dispassionately try to support these propositions from an external, objective point of view. However, as Strawson observes, no such attempt has yet succeeded, and with good reason. If external justification requires us imaginatively to strip ourselves of our moral sentiments so that we may view them "objectively," what resources will we be able to call on to conduct the examination? To do justice to the subject, we must employ our moral sensibilities, including, as they do, our sentiments. There is no neutral ground. If it is to be of any practical use for us, moral philosophy must be an "inside job," however much one may wish otherwise.

I do not regard this as a serious shortcoming. Once we acknowledge, with Strawson, that moral life falls within a general framework of human attitudes and feelings, we can get on with the business of exploring the endless room left for "modification, redirection, criticism, and justification." The confidence that can survive moral reflection is not grounded in an apprehension of a set of moral absolutes or a comprehensive, coherent moral theory. Rather, it is grounded in our moral *competence*—a competence based on fundamental moral dispositions that combine rational and affective capacities. Confidence in our competence is not confidence that all of our moral judgments are reliable; rather, it is confidence that we are morally equipped to strive to live reflectively, responsibly, and with integrity.

2
On Becoming a Moral Agent

By the name we give to it [the theory of morals], and by the custom of making it a part of every system of morals, men may be led into this gross mistake, which I wish to obviate, that in order to understand his duty, a man must needs be a philosopher and a metaphysician.
—*Thomas Reid*, Essays on the Active Powers of the Mind

Moral agency begins in childhood, so it is somewhat surprising that philosophical discussions of moral agency give so little attention to the moral development of children. If we do look at how morality develops in children, we quickly see that the process is not just an intellectual one. Basic feelings and attitudes are also fundamental. Noting this in children may remind us of the essential role feelings and attitudes play in the moral lives of adults as well—something that is often overlooked in our philosophical efforts to understand morality at its deepest level.

M. F. Burnyeat warns us of intellectualism, a one-sided emphasis on reason and reasoning—and, he adds, "a perennial failing in moral philosophy" (1980, p. 70). This is a fair warning. But Burnyeat risks erring in the opposite direction when he says, "The very subject of moral philosophy is sometimes defined or delimited as the study of moral reasoning, thereby excluding the greater part of what is important in the initial— and I think, continuing—moral development of a person" (1980, p. 70). Moral philosophy should not be confined to the study of moral reasoning, and Burnyeat is right to direct our attention to moral development. But his remark suggests a false dichotomy between moral reasoning and the initial moral development of a person.[1] In much that follows I will discuss in what respects they are not mutually exclusive.

Nevertheless, we are well advised to share Aristotle's response to intellectualism by, as Burnyeat puts it, "emphasizing the importance of beginnings and the gradual development of good habits of feeling" (1980, p. 70). Morality is not merely a matter of the intellect; good habits of feeling are equally fundamental. But at some point, even for Aristotle, reason and feeling must join in forming these habits. The basic question is where, and in what manner, this joining occurs. Recent explorations of the philosophical thinking of children suggest that this joining can occur much earlier than is commonly thought.[2] Whether this is something to be celebrated, as I am inclined to say, or ignored, as is the common practice, is another matter.[3]

Shakespeare's *Troilus and Cressida* reminds us that Aristotle insists that philosophy is not for the young. It mentions "Young men, whom Aristotle thought / Unfit to hear moral philosophy."[4] Aristotle's doubts focus on two apparent limitations of the young:

1. *Inexperience*: Children have inadequate acquaintance with, and understanding of, the context within which questions of moral character, conduct and judgment arise.
2. *Lack of rational principles*: Children are moved primarily by passions without real regard for rational principles.

These limitations suggest that we should not expect to find much of philosophical interest in conceptions of childhood—at least not in regard to morality. Children can be seen, basically, as lacking what (at least some) adults have. However, without simply dismissing Aristotle's observations, we may wonder if he underestimates children on both points.

THE PROBLEM OF INEXPERIENCE

If moral understanding requires a basic understanding of the social and political world of adults, then we can all agree that even older children are relatively inexperienced (as are many adults). But throughout childhood there are analogues to the complex social and political institutions characteristic of our adult world. Children's daily lives in schools and their participation in a variety of formally and informally structured social activities provide rich contexts for at least beginning to discuss moral aspects of political and institutional life. Thomas Reid's *Essays on the Active Powers of the Mind* (1788) offers a more optimistic view than Aristotle's about children's capacity for reflective moral thought.[5] Central to Reid's moral outlook is the idea that morality "is the business of every man; and therefore the knowledge of it ought to be within the reach of all"

(1788, p. 594). Given this general accessibility of moral knowledge, it is understandable that Reid maintains it is a "gross mistake" to suppose that "in order to understand his duty a man must needs be a philosopher and a metaphysician" (1788, p. 643).[6] Of course, this does not by itself imply that moral understanding is within the reach of children. However, since the scope of "every man" includes those who live in the least complex social arrangements, the importance of having experience with more complex social and political institutions and practices recedes.

Reid acknowledges that what are commonly understood as *moral systems* "swell to great magnitude." This is not because there is a large number of general moral principles, which, he says, are actually "few and simple." Moral systems swell because applications of these principles "extend to every part of human conduct, in every condition, every relation, and every transaction of life" (1788, p. 642). Given the wide reach of moral principles, it is clear that the limited experience of children restricts their ability to apply them. The same, to a lesser degree, is true of adults as well, since their range of experience, though more extensive, is also limited.

Still, this does not mean that adults, and even children, have no access to the general moral principles that moral systems apply to this array of circumstances. Furthermore, Reid maintains, moral systems are more complex and confusing than they need be for two reasons. First, they mix political and moral questions. Reid says, without explanation, that political questions belong to a different science that is "grounded on different principles." If he means that no moral issues require an understanding of politics for their resolution, he is surely mistaken. On this matter, most would side with Aristotle. If he means that principles of politics are separable from moral principles, many would challenge this, too. A more charitable interpretation of Reid's statement is that if we subtract from moral systems those elements that are peculiar to complex political systems, a significant core of morality remains. We can then ask how accessible this is to children and whether such accessibility contributes to their preparation for responsible adulthood. This interpretation eliminates much of Aristotle's first objection to philosophical discussion of morality with children—namely, their lack of experience in political life.

The second reason moral systems are more complex than they need be is that they mix the *theory* of morals with a *system* of morals. Reid says,

"By the Theory of Morals is meant a just account of the structure of our moral powers—that is, of those powers of the mind by which we have our moral conceptions, and distinguish right from wrong in human actions" (1788, p. 642). Reid admits that this is a complex and controversial area, among the most difficult in philosophy: "But it has little connection with the knowledge of our duty; and those who differ most in the theory of our moral powers, agree in the practical rules of morals which they dictate" (1788, p. 642).

Reid draws an analogy to the relationship between vision and the theory of vision. We can be very good judges of colors, for example, while lacking any knowledge of the anatomy of the eye. It may be argued that our visual powers can be improved somewhat by learning about the anatomy of the eye. Reid does not dispute this. Whatever the case may be, it seems clear that we can have excellent visual powers for at least ordinary affairs without any anatomical understanding of the eye. Whether we *see* some things differently when we gain this understanding is perhaps less clear than that we *judge* them differently. Reid himself says that the use of all the senses involves judgment; thus he thinks the comparison of our moral powers with visual, auditory, and tactile senses is stronger than might otherwise be supposed. Furthermore, he says only that the theory of our moral powers has "little connection" with knowledge of our duty, not that it has none. It is therefore with some plausibility that he concludes "a man may have a very clear and comprehensive knowledge of what is right and what is wrong in human conduct, who never studied the structure of our moral powers" (1788, p. 642).

Reid compares a system of morals to "laws of motion in the natural world, which, though few and simple, serve to regulate an infinite variety of operations throughout the universe" (1788, p. 642). However, he contrasts a system of morals with a system of geometry:

A system of morals is not like a system of geometry, where the subsequent parts derive their evidence from the preceding, and one chain of reasoning is carried on from the beginning; so that, if the arrangement is changed, the chain is broken, and the evidence is lost. It resembles more a system of botany, or mineralogy, where the subsequent parts depend not for their evidence upon the preceding, and the arrangement is made to facilitate apprehension and memory, and not to give evidence. (1788, p. 642)

An example will help clarify the contrast Reid is drawing. Utilitarianism illustrates the geometric model of moral systems.[7] It maintains that all criteria for moral judgment are derivable from the principle of utility, which commends the maximization of good consequences—variously interpreted by utilitarians in terms of happiness, some combination of intrinsic goods, or simply the satisfaction of preferences. We need not choose here from among these possibilities; for convenience, we can refer to utilitarianism in its popular form, as advocating the promotion of the greatest good for the greatest number. The point here is that any moral values—such as fairness, trustworthiness, truthfulness, loyalty, gratitude, benevolence, kindness, and compassion—derive their distinctively moral value from the contribution they make to overall utility. For example, "Why should I keep my promises?" must ultimately be answered in terms of whatever contribution promise-keeping makes to overall utility. Act-utilitarians allow us to appeal directly to the principle of utility in answering the question; rule-utilitarians tell us that we should answer the question by appealing to the moral rule that promises should be kept because of what the practice of promising is (the voluntary incurring of an obligation). But this practice is itself justified in terms of its utility.

In contrast, W. D. Ross's scheme of *prima facie* duties approximates the botanical or mineralogical model (1930). There are duties of fidelity, reparation, gratitude, beneficence, self-improvement, and not injuring others. Each of these has subcategories, but none is derivable from any other, nor does Ross attempt to derive them from some one, comprehensive moral principle, such as the principle of utility. A common criticism of Ross is that he provides no principled way of resolving conflicts among *prima facie* duties. Keeping a promise may cause injury. What should one do in that case? The principle of utility, say utilitarians, mediates such conflicts. However, even if this were conceded, much more would be needed to support a geometric model of utilitarian theory. To see this, suppose there are three, and only three, principles: A, B, and C. They stand in these relations to one another:

1. If A and B conflict, B should prevail.
2. If either A or B conflicts with C, C should prevail.

This prioritizing does not require us to say that A is derivable from B, nor that both are derivable from C. Reid illustrates this very concisely in saying that "unmerited generosity should yield to gratitude—and both to justice" (1788, p. 640).

We may disagree with the general sweep of Reid's rankings, but his example shows that in resolving conflicts a non-geometrical model permits priority rankings without grounding a ranked item in those ranked above it. In short, at the ground level, there is a plurality of fundamental kinds of moral considerations. The extent to which a nongeometric system embraces various ranking schemes is open to discussion and debate. Even if one kind of moral consideration (utility) is granted a mediating role in cases of conflict, other moral considerations can be equally fundamental in this sense. They carry moral weight in their own right at the most fundamental level of morality, weight that is not grounded in their contribution to overall utility, even if they have, as Reid acknowledges they do, great utility.

All of this has important implications for how we characterize moral development. On the botanical model, access to ground level moral understanding need not be an all-or-nothing affair. Its range and complexity can be a matter of degree. Understanding how different, ground level moral considerations are related to one another can be a matter for moral discovery (and dispute) without our having to say that those whose picture is incomplete have no understanding of morality at its most fundamental level.[8]

LACK OF RATIONAL PRINCIPLES

Still, it might be objected, this understanding has little bearing on the moral development of children. Consider what Aristotle says about our beginnings:

> For while one must begin from what is familiar, this may be taken in two ways: some things are familiar to us, others familiar without qualification. Presumably, then, what *we* should begin from is things familiar to *us*. This is the reason why one should have been well brought up in good habits if one is going to listen adequately to lectures about things noble and just, and in general about political (social) affairs. For the beginning (starting point) is "the *that*," and if this is sufficiently apparent to a person, he will not in addition have a need for "the *because*." (Burnyeat 1980, p. 71)[9]

Since Aristotle's lectures on moral philosophy concern "the *because*" and not just "the *that*," presumably the young are not ready for them. First there must be good habits of feeling concerning "the *that*." Only those with good habits will hear what reason has to say.

As for those who lack these habits, "the many," Aristotle says that arguments are of no use, "for these do not by nature obey the sense of shame, but only fear, and do not abstain from bad acts because of their baseness but through fear of punishment" (Burnyeat 1980, p. 75). It seems that Aristotle does not expect a large audience—even among adults. The many, it seems, are governed mainly by passion rather than by reason, so they are not suited for moral philosophy:

> For he who lives as passion directs will not hear argument that dissuades him, nor understand it if he does; and how can we persuade one in such a state to change his ways? And in general passion seems to yield not to argument but to force. The character, then, must somehow be there already with a kinship to virtue, loving what is noble and hating what is base. (Burnyeat 1980, p. 75)

If the many do live only "as passion directs," constrained by fear of punishment rather than shame, Aristotle's pessimism about the power of arguments is well founded.

I do not share his rather uncharitable view of the many, but I will not try to settle this issue here. Instead, I will focus on the relatively few who Aristotle thinks are properly brought up and thereby ready for lectures on moral philosophy. Why are they not like the many? Obviously, however accessible "the *that*" is, the few need strong guidance. They must become habituated to "the *that*"—but without reliance on "the *because*," for which they are neither ready nor needful. Without any direct guidance from reason, how are the few to accomplish this habituation? Consider what Aristotle says about temperance: "As the child should live according to the direction of his tutor, so the appetitive element should live according to reason. Hence the appetitive element in a temperate man should harmonize with reason; for the noble is the mark at which both aim, and the temperate man desires the things he ought, as he ought, and when he ought; and this is what reason directs" (Burnyeat 1980, p. 80).

Since, for Aristotle, children require the direction of a tutor, it is clear that their appetites are only weakly harmonized with reason. It is the appetitive element in a "temperate man," not children, that internally harmonizes with reason. For children, the harmony is external. It can be internalized only after they are habituated to doing "the *that*" required by reason; only then will they be ready for "the *because*" that bonds appetite and reason.

But if habit precedes reason, what causes behavior to conform to what reason requires? Here much depends on the available guides. Authority looms large in this picture, as do fear of punishment and shame. Authority figures such as parents and teachers may induce good behavior through the threat of punishment. If this were all, however, two problems would remain.

First, it is not clear how fear of punishment for falling short of the noble and just gets transformed into love for the noble and just. More plausibly, it would seem to work against this transformation by instead reinforcing a "morality" of power, authority, and fear. This problem will be pursued in Chapter 6. Here it need only be noted that there is considerable evidence that moral development depends less on the authoritative influence of parents, teachers, and others than theorists such as Freud and Piaget suggest (Damon 1988). If fear of punishment were the major factor in the development of the "morality" of the many, it seems that reasoning could still gain a significant foothold in the lives of children. Prudential reasoning about how to avoid punishment surely need not await children's readiness for "the *because*" of nobility and justice. Still, as I show in Chapter 12, exclusive reliance on such reasoning poses dangers for moral integrity. So, it would be desirable if reasoning more characteristic of moral integrity also has its origins in childhood. It is Reid's view that it does.

Second, if there is a ready explanation of how fear of punishment is transformed into love of virtue, why does such a change not work with the many as well as with the few? Aristotle does not seem to address this question. Shame presents problems as well. How is it that parents, teachers, and other authority figures can induce shame in children? Such shame requires that children care about disappointing authority figures in a way that is not reducible to fear of punishment, which suggests a kind of respect for authority distinct from fear of power or punishment. Perhaps this is related to a desire to emulate. But such a desire, in turn, seems to require a kind of admiration that makes little sense independently of "the *because*." Just *why*, we wonder, are parents, teachers, and other authority figures admired in this way? What do children see in them? To say that children see nothing in them, but simply fall in line through baseless admiration or blind obedience, is to fall prey to another perennial failing in moral philosophy—condescension to children, as well as to ordinary moral agents. By insisting that moral knowledge is everyone's business, not just that of philosophers and metaphysicians, Reid resists this condescension.

How fairly Aristotle can be accused of having a condescending attitude toward children is unclear. Burnyeat points out that, for Aristotle, habituation has its cognitive side:

> It turns out that Aristotle is not simply giving us a bland reminder that virtue takes practice. Rather, practice has cognitive powers, in that it is the way we learn what is noble or just. . . . [T]he ultimate goal toward which the beginner's practice is aimed is that he should become the sort of person who does virtuous things in full knowledge of what he is doing, choosing to do them for their own sake, and acting out of a settled state of character (1105a28–33). The beginner would hardly be on the way to this desirable state of affairs if he were not in the process forming (reasonably correct) ideas as to the nobility or justice of the actions he was engaged in; if you like, he must be on his way to acquiring a mature sense of values. (1980, p. 73)

This is promising. Still, it does not seem to go far enough. Burnyeat goes on to say that, for Aristotle,

> What you may begin by taking on trust you can come to know for yourself. This is not yet to know *why* it is true, but it is to have learned *that* it is true in the sense of having made the judgment your own, second nature to you—Hesiod's taking to heart. Nor is it yet to have acquired any of the virtues, for which practical wisdom is required (6.13; 10.8 1178a16–19), that understanding of "the *because*" which alone can accomplish the final correcting and perfecting of your perception of "the *that*." But it is a beginning. (1980, p. 74)

It goes beyond saying, "I have learned that it is just to share my belongings with others," when all this amounts to is that this is "the content of the instruction given by parent or teacher" (1980, p. 74).

But how far beyond this does it go? Not all the way to Aristotle's happiness, or *eudaimonia*. Should we agree that readiness for moral philosophy requires readiness to wrestle with *eudaimonia*? It is not clear why we should. Even if *eudaimonia* is a reasonable aim for a good life, it may not be the only object of a good life—and a good life may not be the only object of a moral life. Perhaps less lofty, but no less well grounded, moral ideas are available to children, as well as to the many. Let us consider some possibilities.

ILLUSTRATIONS

Young children have a very keen sense of fairness within their spheres of experience. Favoritism, taking more than one's fair share, not taking turns, and so on, are staple fare in the lives of children—in school, on the playground, and within their family structures. That they (like the rest of us) may more readily recognize unfairness in others than in themselves does not mean that they do not understand what fairness is. That they will later extend their conceptions of fairness to situations they cannot now understand (for example, taxation)—and that they will discover conflicts with other fundamental moral values—does not imply that they do not now have access to morality at its most basic level.

It might be argued that children begin with particular examples and only through unreflective habituation develop a sense of fairness. Even if this were so, some of the foundation seems well in place rather early on. Of course, children do learn from examples, but these provide them with only a starting point from which they may go on to deal competently with novel instances. Ronald Dworkin makes an important point in this regard:

> Suppose I tell my children simply that I expect them not to treat others unfairly. I no doubt have in mind examples of the conduct I mean to discourage, but I would not accept that my 'meaning' was limited to these examples, for two reasons. First, I would expect my children to apply my instructions to situations I had not and could not have thought about. Second, I stand ready to admit that some particular act I had thought was fair when I spoke was in fact unfair, or vice-versa, if one of my children is able to convince me of that later; in that case I should want to say that my instructions covered

the case he cited, not that I had changed my instructions. I might say that I meant the family to be guided by the *concept* of fairness, not by any specific *conception* of fairness I might have had in mind. (Dworkin 1977, p. 133)

If we think of particular moral conceptions as workable but somewhat inadequate renderings of basic moral concepts, then we can understand how we might learn from children as they wrestle with these concepts.

This way of looking at moral development differs in an important way from popularly accepted cognitive-developmental theories such as Jean Piaget (1932) and Lawrence Kohlberg (1981). Characteristically these theories claim that children's moral development goes through sequential stages, with each subsequent stage replacing inadequate concepts in the preceding stages. Concepts in different stages differ in kind, not simply degree. On this view, for example, "justice" for a very young child is understood primarily in terms of the threat of punishment for violating a rule emanating from authority figures. Later this conception of "justice" is displaced by one that emphasizes the fairness of reciprocal exchange ("You scratch my back, and I'll scratch yours"). Later still, this conception is displaced by a concept of reciprocal rights and duties that respect persons as ends-in-themselves.

At the same time that this stage theory of moral development emphasizes greater understanding with maturation, it implies that younger children live in a quite different moral world from adults, and it encourages a condescending attitude toward children's moral understanding. That there are striking moral differences between children and adults cannot sensibly be denied. However, there are ways of characterizing those differences that at the same time suggest even more striking similarities. Richard A. Shweder, Elliot Turiel, and Nancy C. Much (1981) present evidence that children as young as four have an intuitive grasp of differences among prudential, conventional, and moral rules. Characterizing young children as "intuitive moralists," they say, "Although four- to six-year-olds have little reflective understanding of their moral knowledge, they nevertheless have an intuitive moral competence that displays itself in the way they answer questions about moral rules and in the way they excuse their transgressions and react to the transgressions of others" (1981, p. 288). They continue:

In fact, at this relatively early age, four to six, children not only seem to distinguish and identify moral versus conventional versus prudential rules using the same formal principles (e.g., obligatoriness, importance, generalizability) employed by adults; they also seem to agree with the adults of their society about the moral versus conventional versus prudential status of particular substantive events (e.g., throwing paint in another child's face versus wearing the same clothes to school every day). (1981, p. 288)

Dworkin's example of children learning about fairness also suggests an alternative way of looking at moral development. It is developed in some detail by Gareth Matthews (1987), who emphasizes the importance of paradigms:

A young child is able to latch onto the moral kind, bravery, or lying, by grasping central paradigms of that kind, paradigms that even the most mature and sophisticated moral agents still count as paradigmatic. Moral development is then something much more complicated than simple concept displacement. It is: enlarging the stock of paradigms for each moral kind; developing better and better definitions of whatever it is these paradigms exemplify; appreciating better the relation between straightforward instances of the kind and close relatives; and learning to adjudicate competing claims from different moral kinds (classically the sometimes competing claims of justice and compassion, but many other conflicts are possible). (1987, p. 185)

On this view children as well as adults can be acknowledged to share some ground level understanding of morality. Although adults may typically have the upper hand in regard to breadth of experience and understanding, there is no warrant for entirely excluding children from the adult world of morality.

If the thought that young children might be capable of imaginative and provocative moral thought seems farfetched, consider an example provided by Matthews: "IAN (six years) found to his chagrin that the three children of his parents' friends monopolized the television; they kept him from watching his favorite program. 'Mother,' he asked in frustration, 'why is it better for three people to be selfish than for one?' (1980, p. 28).[10] This is not mere habituation of thought. It seems quite innovative and insightful, and Matthews suggests it may be an incipient challenge to utilitarian thought. Whether it could be a successful challenge need not be pursued here. However, what should be conceded is that Ian seems to have at least a rudimentary grasp of two fundamental moral concepts: fairness and selfishness. Furthermore, at least for Ian, these concepts are not derived from the concept of overall utility.

Matthews used Ian's remark as the basis for constructing a story for children. He then presented it to a group of eight- to eleven-year-olds. In Matthews's story, Freddie is watching his favorite program, *The Abbott and Costello Show*, when three younger children invade his home and take over the TV (Matthews 1984, pp. 92-93):

> Douglas, who acted as the leader of the group, walked calmly to the TV, reached for the knob, and switched the program to the Moomins.
>
> Freddie got up sadly and went out to the kitchen.
>
> "Why the sad face?" said Freddie's mother, as she filled the kettle. "I know they're younger than you, but they're nice kids, really. And their mum and dad are very old friends of your mum and dad. Please be nice to them."
>
> "But they want to watch the Moomins!" said Freddie in disbelief.
>
> "I'm sorry," said Freddie's mother; "I know you can't stand that program. But think of it this way. Three people are being made happy instead of just one."
>
> Freddie reflected a moment. "Mother," he said, slowly and deliberately, "why is it better for three people to be selfish than for one?"

Matthews wrote the story in such a way that the challenge to utilitarian thinking is made explicit. In addition, of course, the utilitarian voice is that of parental authority. However, none of the initial responses of the children picked up on utilitarian themes. David-Paul commented on the meanness of the three children; after all, they could have played together. He added: "They have to respect other people's rights as well. The Moomins are on almost every day." Martin commented that he would hate to have something like that happen to him. He concluded: "I mean, they could easily have watched what Freddie was watching." The children discussed whether either program could be watched on some other occasion. They recalled related examples from their own lives and constructed analogous imaginary examples. Still, says Matthews, "they found utilitarianism unattractive, and they were not inclined to search for any similarly high-level principle or theory to replace utilitarianism" (1984, p. 95). Finally, Matthews pressed the utilitarian case. "What about this argument," he asked, "that, if we let the three visitors have their way, three people will be made happy instead of just one?" Martin replied: "It's not really fair if three people get what they want and leave one person out. That one person will feel very hurt." The discussion then turned to very specific considerations, the types of programs involved, relationships among the children (relative ages, siblings or strangers), and whether one really wants others sharing the TV.

Despite further efforts, Matthews was unable to elicit utilitarian responses. He observes:

> Everyday ethics, like the common law, arbitrates disputes and conflicts of interest by appeal to cases, as interpreted, perhaps, by low-level "maxims," or "rules of law." This arbitration may succeed without anyone's having to show that the reasoning fits into some coherent system that will resolve all conceivable disputes. Of course, someone might insist that disputes resolved in this fashion are not resolved correctly unless the resolution can be shown to fall appropriately under some absolutely general principle or to fit properly into some universal system. (1984, p. 95)

However, despite the children's strong feelings about the case and their efforts to bring analogous situations to bear on this one, Matthews adds, "I was interested that none of my kids seemed attracted by the pull to general theory."

It might be suggested that the problem is that eight- to eleven-year-olds are too young to understand an appeal to general utility. Yet this is implausible, as a variation on Matthews's example should show. Suppose he told the children a story about a hermit writing into his will what to do with his modest life savings. He has no friends, but he wants to make sure that his money is put to use after he dies. Then the children are asked, "Should he give his money to a few rich people so that they'll be a little bit richer, or should he give it to a needy children's hospital?" Surely even very young children can entertain the thought that it would do more good, and for that reason would be preferable, to give the money to the hospital rather than to a few wealthy people. It is no objection that the children's thought might be mistaken, since the hospital might misuse the money or the wealthy might themselves put the money to more constructive use for others. The only issue here is whether young children can see that there are circumstances in which it is better to "make three people happy rather than one." It might be suggested that in Freddie's case the children simply do not see that more good is served by giving in to the three children, but this does not seem to be their concern. More prominent in their thinking is the issue of fairness, as well as the issue of rights. That is, they may resist the appeal to utility because they reject the idea that the "greater good" is the point at issue in this case.

A PHILOSOPHICAL REJOINDER

Philosophically speaking, what should be made of these illustrations of children's moral thinking? R. M. Hare (1981) would likely say that this is just what we should expect, not only from children but from ordinary adults as well. Hare distinguishes two levels of moral thinking, intuitive and critical. Everyday moral thinking is largely intuitive, reflecting moral dispositions that have become well established in the give and take of ordinary moral life. Those who have been "well brought up" will have moral dispositions whose everyday utility is very high. These will include dispositions to be fair, honest, trustworthy, considerate, civic-minded, and so on. Thus, without ever invoking the principle of utility in their everyday thinking, "well brought up" moral agents will employ dispositions that, in fact, promote utilitarian ends. This is the justification of these dispositions, as well as the justification of whatever well-grounded moral judgments issue from them.

Hare maintains that everyday moral dispositions and the moral judgments issuing from them operate primarily at the intuitive level. As long as we remain at this intuitive level of thinking, we cannot *justify* our moral judgments. Justification is available only at the critical level of judgment. Intuitions have no "probative force." For all we know, they may be sheer prejudice. Only critical thinking can sort out the wheat from the chaff.

At the critical level, however, we have only two resources: the logic of moral concepts and morally undifferentiated preferences. The fundamental logical concept for Hare is universalizability. Whatever we judge to be right or wrong in one case must be judged right or wrong in all relevantly similar cases. This excludes reliance on the identification of particular persons or circumstances (i.e., this specific individual in this specific situation). All preferences, without moral distinction, are then to be taken into consideration. Although no one can actually attain it, the ideal perspective assimilates all of these preferences to the collective preferences of a hypothetical superagent, an archangel, who then decides what is best from the standpoint of one whose preferences include all preferences. This standpoint represents, according to Hare, what from our individual perspectives is an essentially utilitarian outlook. What is best from the perspective of the archangel is, for us, the greatest good for the greatest number—determined impersonally and impartially.

Rather than discuss the details of Hare's argument here I only point out the implications of his view for ordinary moral agents.[11] Although Hare is confident that utilitarianism supports the everyday dispositions and intuitions of at least "well-brought up" individuals, their moral understanding is quite limited. The bottom line in the moral thinking of most people, most of the time, is decidedly nonutilitarian. Hare not only acknowledges this, he insists that this is just as it ought to be. Like Sidgwick (1907), he has serious doubts that many are capable of effective utilitarian thinking. Furthermore, many interpersonal relationships (especially those involving love and friendship) would be diminished, or even made impossible, if mediated by utilitarian thinking.[12] Hare's distinction between intuitive and critical levels of moral thinking may succeed in accommodating much of nonutilitarian everyday thinking within utilitarian theory, but it does so only at the expense of deflating ordinary moral understanding. Notice that, while ordinary moral agents are acknowledged to have reasons for the moral judgments they make—and that often these reasons are quite serviceable—they typically fall short of truly justifying reasons. Justifying reasons are, for the most part, one step removed from the thinking of ordinary moral agents.

Hare's comments on the principle of not punishing those who have not been duly convicted nicely illustrate what he has in mind. At the intuitive level, we typically have a retributivist response: It is wrong to punish people for something they have not done. Only the guilty deserve punishment.[13] At this intuitive level, there is no appeal to some more basic principle than that the innocent should not be punished. Hare remarks, "The retributivists are right at the intuitive level, and the utilitarians at the critical level" (1981, p. 163). Although the retributivist response is quite appropriate at the intuitive level, it does nothing to justify the claim that the innocent should not be punished. At the critical level, however, utilitarian considerations provide a justification: "It is proper and necessary for judges to sentence in accordance with the law, and sentence only those who have been duly convicted. But the reason why this is proper and necessary is that a legal system in which judges have not been brought up to treat this principle as in practice unbreakable is likely to be a bad system for nearly everybody subject to it" (Hare 1981, p. 163).[14]

Reid's response to this issue would likely be very different; this can be inferred from what he says about the perspectives of judges and those who suffer private injury: "The public good is very properly considered by the judge who punishes a private injury, but seldom enters into the thought of the injured person. And every man is conscious of a specific difference between the resentment he feels for an injury done to himself, and his indignation against a wrong done to the public" (Reid 1788, p. 427). Reid is here drawing a contrast between the perspective of a judge administering punishment for wrongdoing and the perspective of the person who is wronged. In Hare's case, the judge would be directly involved in the wrongdoing if an innocent person were punished. While not denying the importance of judges' concern for the public good, Reid would insist that there is another, equally fundamental, perspective—namely, that of the innocent person. Reid is unwilling to allow resentment at being wronged to be buried in the broader utilitarian concern for the public good. Quite apart from considerations of general utility, Reid insists that there is a moral objection to punishing the innocent. That such punishment would contribute to a bad system constitutes an additional moral objection.

Hare is convinced that, in all realistic situations, utilitarian considerations will oppose punishing the innocent. He is unimpressed by "desert island" counterexamples. Moral principles are for this world, not all imaginable worlds, however fanciful. However, Reid never challenges utilitarian thinking through the use of counterexamples. He seems as confident that there is no clash in outcomes between ordinary morality and utility as he is that there is no clash in outcomes between ordinary morality and real self-interest. Reid's concern is not simply with what conduct is commended or criticized but with why those commendations or criticisms are appropriate. Hare's utilitarian view is reductionistic; Reid's view is pluralistic.

To say that "knowledge of moral conduct" is accessible to all moral agents is not to say that they possess this knowledge. Reid insists that one can live an entire lifetime without recognizing even self-evident truths. Although he does hold that there are self-evident moral truths, he also insists that there is a great deal of moral confusion and thus a need for moral nurturing and education. The application of principles to actual circumstances often requires careful thought and deliberation. Hare might say to this that without reliance on his level of critical thinking we have little reason to believe that the thinking of ordinary moral agents is anything more than ungrounded intuition—which, for all we know, is sheer prejudice or bias. Reid's ultimate answer to this kind of challenge lies in his account of the moral development of children.

REID'S REPLY

Reid's account of moral agency begins with a contrast between human beings and "brute animals." Brute animals have no power of self-government—nor would we if we "had no power to restrain appetite but by a stronger contrary appetite or passion" (1788, p. 534). Some might object to the severity of this contrast. Even if Reid somewhat underestimates brute animals, this would simply bring them closer to moral agency than Reid suggests. Reid's fundamental claim is about the close relationship between the capacity for self-government and moral agency.

Next Reid observes that we naturally desire power, esteem, and knowledge. Their pursuit requires some degree of self-command, just as virtue does. Further, the desire to communicate knowledge is as natural as the desire to acquire it. We would not value power nearly as much as we do if we had no opportunities to show it to others. And the desire for esteem "can have no possible gratification but in society" (1788, p. 557). Reid concludes: "These parts of our constitution, therefore, are evidently intended for social life; and it is not more evident that birds were made for flying and fishes for swimming, than that man, endowed with a natural desire of power, of esteem, and of knowledge, is made, not for the savage and solitary state, but for living in society" (1788, p. 557). For Reid, nature's "intentions" reflect God's design and wisdom. However, much of what he is saying here could be given a naturalistic rendering—

say, in terms of natural evolution. That we are constitutionally suited for social rather than solitary life could still be maintained.

However our "natural constitution" is ultimately accounted for, Reid will insist that we have both benevolent and malevolent natural sentiments which are neither moral nor rational at the outset. They are shared, to some extent, with brute animals. Some natural sentiments are more distinctively human, such as gratitude for beneficence from others, pity and compassion toward the distressed, friendship, and even "public spirit, that is, an affection to any community to which we belong" (1788, p. 568). Each of these can take on moral forms, but they have premoral forms as well.

Reid's account of human sociability is decidedly more positive than that of Thomas Hobbes (1651), who emphasizes the natural aggressive tendencies of human beings—and the insecurities they cause in the absence of society (with civic rule). Life in a state of nature would be "nasty, short, and brutish." In contrast, Reid focuses on the loss of opportunities for sociability in the absence of society: "Without society, and the intercourse of kind affection, man is a gloomy, melancholy, and joyless being" (1788, p. 566).

In addition to natural, benevolent affections, there are natural, malevolent ones. Resentment receives the most attention from Reid. Brute animals react to harm and threats of harm with resentment—a defense mechanism. We share with them this capacity for sudden resentment. However, we are also capable of deliberate resentment, which requires "opinion of an injury" (1788, p. 567). Such an opinion supposes that the cause of harm is a responsible agent, rather than an inanimate object or animals that have no conception of right or wrong. Deliberate resentment also presumes that the agent causing harm acted voluntarily rather than from unavoidable necessity.[15] Clearly, the distinctions presupposed by deliberate resentment are possible only for rational agents. And only when such rationality shapes natural sentiments such as resentment will Reid acknowledge moral agency. It is also clear that the rational shaping of these sentiments begins in childhood.

Central to Reid's account of morality is that "we ought not to do to another what we should think wrong to be done to us in like circumstances" (1788, p. 590). Although this principle is similar to Hare's principle of universalizability, Reid regards it as a principle of justice, not simply as a feature of the logic of moral discourse. Furthermore, its acceptance is a necessary condition for being a moral agent: "If a man is not capable of perceiving this in his cool moments, when he reflects seriously, he is not a moral agent, nor is he capable of being convinced of it by reasoning" (1788, p. 590). Although Reid seems to be referring to adults in this passage, it is clear that he thinks even young children are capable of grasping the rudiments of this principle. His view is that "as soon as men have any rational conception of a favour and of an injury, they must have the conception of justice, and perceive its obligation" (1788, p. 654). Without specifying any particular age at which these conceptions originate, Reid adds: "The notions of a *favour* and of an *injury*, appear as early in the mind of man as any rational notion whatever. They are discovered, not by language only, but by certain affections of mind, of which they are the natural objects. A favour naturally produces gratitude. An injury done to ourselves produces resentment; and even when done to another, it produces indignation" (1788, p. 654).

That Reid intends to include children among those who have such conceptions is evident in the following passage:

One boy has a top, another a scourge; says the first to the other, If you will lend me your scourge as long as I can keep up my top with it, you shall next have the top as long as you can keep it up. This is a contract perfectly understood by both parties, though they never heard of the definition given by Ulpian or by Titius. And each of them knows that he is injured if the other breaks the bargain, and that he does wrong if he breaks it himself. (1788, p. 663)

While Reid acknowledges, with Hume, that justice does serve utilitarian ends, he insists that the moral obligation of justice "is inseparable from its nature, and is not derived solely from its utility, either to ourselves or to society" (1788, p. 655).

It is essential to realize that for Reid moral agency is the linchpin of any moral system. Bearing in mind that moral conduct is the business of all, we must be able to relate "the abstract notion of good and ill" to the particular circumstances in life that call for moral judgment and conduct (1788, p. 589). But this presupposes moral agents with certain kinds of sensitivities:

To reason about justice with a man who sees nothing to be just or unjust, or about benevolence with a man who sees nothing in benevolence preferable to malice, is like reasoning with a blind man about colour, or with a deaf man about sound.

But, if a man does not perceive that he ought to regard the good of society, and the good of his wife and children, then reasoning can have no effect upon him, because he denies the first principle upon which it is grounded. (1788, p. 590)

Again, Reid seems to be focusing on adults (more specifically, adult males). However, his main point has implications for children. Moral reasoning relies on first principles "whose truth is immediately perceived without reasoning, by all men come to years of understanding" (1788, p. 591). Although these principles are perceived without reasoning, they are rational principles because they can be grasped only by those with rational capacities. Whether monogamous or polygamous marital arrangements are to be preferred is to be determined by moral reasoning which must proceed from rational principles that express concern for the well-being of, and justice to, the specific parties affected. Although young children may not be prepared to reason their way through the monogamy/polygamy issue, they are capable of forming conceptions of justice, benevolence, and malice. Our moral conceptions, Reid says, develop gradually, just as our rational capacities do. Like the power of reasoning, the "seeds of moral discernment" do not appear in infancy, and they need careful cultivation: "They grow up in their proper season, and are at first tender and delicate and easily warped. Their progress depends very much upon their being duly cultivated and properly exercised" (1788, p. 595).

Even obvious truths, Reid says, are perceived only with "ripeness of judgment"; and this ripening of judgment happens, not simply with the passage of time, but "chiefly by being exercised about things of the same or of a similar kind" (1788, p. 641). Many obstacles lie in the way of clear thinking, and they are not simply a function of age. Seeing things clearly and steadily "requires an exertion of mind to which many of our animal principles are unfriendly" (1788, p. 641).

Reid points out the distorting effects of the passions. Our "love of truth" is often pushed aside by some passion, laziness, or aimlessness. We are blinded by the vehemence of our passions, their often hasty attribution of fault to others, and their prejudice in our favor. Reason has an essential role to play in harnessing the sentiments. Sometimes it results in their dissolution, but it may simply diminish their intensity. Reason also may sharpen or redirect their focus or in some cases rouse greater sentiment by bringing praiseworthy or blameworthy features of what has happened into clearer light.

According to Reid, a key difference between humans and brute animals is in how they relate to the past and future. Although brute animals can experience pleasure and pain, "they can take no large prospect either of the past or of the future, nor see through a train of consequences" (1788, p. 577). Thus, they lack the capacity for self-government, and "without self-government, that which is strongest at the time will prevail" (1788, p. 578). But self-government does not come easily, as "every man who maintains a uniform and consistent character, must sweat and toil and often struggle with his present inclination" (1788, p. 579). When does this struggle begin? Reid offers no timetable, but it is clear that he believes it is sometime in childhood—and that reason and instruction play an essential role: "Our first moral conceptions are probably got by attending coolly to the conduct of others and observing what moves our approbation, what our indignation. These sentiments spring from our moral faculty as naturally as the sensations of sweet and bitter from the faculty of taste" (1788, p. 641).

However, Reid also reminds us of our tendency to view human actions from partial and biased perspectives: "Prejudice against or in favour of the person, is apt to warp our opinion. It requires candour to distinguish the good from the ill, and, without favour or prejudice, to form a clear and impartial judgment. In this way we may be greatly aided by instruction" (1788, p. 641). When Reid insists that the development of conscience is a natural process, he is not denying the importance of the child's social environment. He says he is inclined to think that an infant reared outside of society "would hardly ever shew any sign, either of moral judgment, or of the power of reasoning" (1788, p. 641). Just as the power of vegetation in seed is dormant without heat and moisture, our rational and moral powers require instruction and example.

Morality is highly dependent on social interaction. According to Reid, it is through "natural signs," not reasoning, that "thoughts and sentiments are exchanged." This, he says, "is common to the whole species from infancy" (1788, p. 664). Though acknowledging that there is some degree of sociability among brute animals, Reid points out that they lack two social operations common to humans: "They can neither plight their veracity by testimony, nor their fidelity by any engagement or promise"

(1788, p. 664). In contrast, "children, as soon as they are capable of understanding declarations and promises, are led by their constitution to rely upon them. They are no less led by constitution to veracity and candour, on their own part. Nor do they ever deviate from this road of truth and sincerity until corrupted by bad example and bad company" (1788, p. 666).

Actually, says Reid, good faith and trust "are formed by nature in the minds of children, before they are capable of knowing their utility, or being influenced by considerations either of duty or interest" (1788, p. 666). When children do have the conception of right and wrong, their predisposition against lying and dishonesty is immediately transformed into moral disapproval. In regard to fidelity and trust, Reid adds, "In early years, we have an innate disposition to them. In riper years, we feel our obligation to fidelity as much as to any moral duty whatsoever" (1788, p. 666).

The following picture emerges from Reid's account of moral development. Utilitarian thought, insofar as it is embraced at all by ordinary moral agents, surfaces later than other rather stable affections, commitments, and concerns. Some of these are specifically moral; some are not. For our parents, children, friends, and communities we have natural benevolent affection, much of which is traceable to our natural sociability. The specific development of the social attachments of particular individuals is, of course, dependent on the actual social relations they enter into and the extent to which these relations are marked by reciprocal support.

For Reid, one of the functions of reason is to join one's past, present, and future in ways that contribute to leading a more or less coherent and meaningful life, a life marked by personal integrity. Moral integrity is only a part of a person's overall integrity, or wholeness. Frequently there are tensions between our nonmoral attachments and the moral demands that are pressed upon us. For example, as Reid points out, the special affection parents have for their own children is not originally grounded in any particular merit of their children, nor is it grounded in reason. There are times when this special affection may conflict with reasonable moral demands—for example, for a coach to treat all players fairly even when he is the father of one of the players who seems to want special favors.

However such conflicts are reasonably sorted out, moral theories must take into account the importance personal commitments and projects have to us. How moral theories take this importance into account is crucial. As we will see in Chapter 11, Bernard Williams (1973) thinks that utilitarian ways of handling personal integrity are woefully inadequate. One can only speculate about the extent to which Reid might have agreed with Williams on this matter, but I think the following projection can fairly be inferred from what he says.

Serious effort to "maintain a uniform or consistent character" is exerted well before an ordinary agent first encounters anything like standard utilitarian theories. Of course, as Hare and many other utilitarians insist, the vast majority of people who live morally good lives never do encounter such theories. This does not mean they live unreflective lives, although many might. It simply means that, from a utilitarian perspective, they do not lead deeply reflective moral lives—and it is, from that same utilitarian perspective, a good thing that they do not. Nevertheless, since Reid insists that ordinary moral agents are fully capable of understanding both what moral conduct requires and the reasons that ground those requirements, he may share some of Williams's concerns about utilitarianism. Reid would no doubt agree that any moral system that addresses the status of ordinary moral agents must stand in some reasonable relationship to their sense of themselves as moral agents and to the personal integrity that gives some meaning and coherence to their lives.

This does not mean that a moral system cannot reasonably demand that ordinary moral agents try to make integrity-affecting adjustments in their moral and personal lives. But moral agents can rightly insist that some regard for their integrity must be included in any such demand. One worry about utilitarianism is that it may require moral agents simply to disregard what matters most to their personal integrity in order to promote overall utility. Hare denies that this is likely to happen, but his denial requires him to take what, for Reid, borders on being a condescending attitude toward ordinary moral agency, including that in childhood. Hare's view implies that ordinary moral agents lack access to the justification of their most deeply held moral sentiments, beliefs, and commitments. That is, they are ignorant of the moral grounding of what they take to be most fundamental. As we have seen, Reid is unwilling to make this concession. In one sense, such a concession would leave the integrity of ordinary moral agents intact. However, it does so only by subtracting from the moral depth of that integrity. Before seriously considering making such a concession, Reid would need to be shown some good reason for accepting a moral system that entails this subtraction. He does not see one. In this, I think he is right.

To the suggestion that, without the benefit of Hare's critical level of utilitarian thinking, we have no reason to think our intuitions are more than sheer bias or prejudice, Reid offers a reply. A close look at how reason can enter into the lives of children as they develop moral sentiments reveals that, long before they entertain distinctively utilitarian thoughts, their moral integrity may be well established. To say that the intuitions issuing from their well-established moral dispositions may be mere bias or prejudice is arbitrarily to deny precisely what Reid claims to observe: namely, the various ways that children shape, refine, and modify their sentiments through the use of reason, independently of considerations of general utility.

Hare may still try to take refuge in the thought that his critical level of thinking does away with reliance on intuitions altogether. But Bernard Williams (1985, p. 105) points out that Hare actually relies on two. The first is, as Sidgwick insisted long ago, that "as a rational being I am bound to aim at good generally—so far as it is attainable by my efforts— not merely at a particular part of it" (1907, p. 382). Reid actually never challenges this intuition. However, he shares Williams's rejection of the second intuition on which Hare seems to rely, that "there are no other basic ethical considerations besides that first one" (Williams 1985, p. 105). This is the reductionist assumption of utilitarianism that all moral considerations are somehow derivable from, and dependent on, the principle of utility. This assumption allows Hare to relegate ordinary moral intuitions to a precritical, epistemologically secondary status.

Reid explicitly challenges this assumption. Although he never challenges utilitarianism through the use of counterexamples, he does challenge its claim to exclusive rule at the most fundamental level of morality:

> To perceive that justice tends to the good of mankind, would lay no moral obligation upon us to be just, unless we be conscious of a moral obligation to do what tends to the good of mankind. If such an obligation be admitted, why may we not admit a stronger obligation to do injury to no man? This last obligation is as easily conceived as the first, and there is as clear evidence of its existence in human nature. (1788, p. 662)

H. L. A. Hart uses a powerful analogy to illustrate the shortcomings of having to ground our intuitive level of moral thinking in a more sweeping, impersonal perspective, such as utilitarianism: "The moral monster who thinks there is nothing morally wrong in torturing a child except that God has forbidden it, has a parallel in the moralist who will not treat the fact that the child will suffer agony as in itself a moral reason enough" (Hart 1986, p. 52). If we agree with Hart that the suffering of the child is moral reason enough, we can also agree that even rather young children have access to moral concepts at their most fundamental level.

One might object that young children's understanding of torture and cruelty is less sophisticated than that of adults. For example, when our daughter was six, she protested against "Dr. Murder and his armchair assassin"—the family dentist and his assistant! It might be said that, at her tender years, she did not differentiate the pain induced by necessary dental work from cruelty and torture. Yet, even now, many years later, she harbors some suspicion that "Dr. Murder and his armchair assassin" were perhaps a bit over zealous in trying to suppress her screams and her efforts to squirm out of the dental chair. In any case, we should not hold that one has a solid grasp on first level moral concepts only if one's applications of those concepts are unerring. If we held anything like this for children, the implications for adults would be significant, too. There are no age limits for learning more about what is kind, cruel, fair, unfair, and so on.

It is also no serious objection to point out that as we learn more about the world we may find it difficult to condemn torture or cruelty in absolute terms. If we acknowledge that there might be exceptions, should this shake our confidence that, for example, torturing for fun is wrong? Hare acknowledges that we feel certain that torturing for fun is wrong (1981, p. 11). Oddly, in the same paragraph he insists that we cannot back up such convictions by appealing to moral intuitions, "for they have no probative force, and the two sides in the most important moral arguments will have different intuitions." Yet we may fairly wonder what "intuition" might be pitted against the conviction that torturing *for fun* is wrong?

We expect a moral defense of taking exception to the general prohibition against torture to provide good reasons for taking exception. Thomas Nagel provides a possible case (1986, p. 176). You have a car accident in a remote area. Your passengers are seriously injured. You seek help at a house occupied by a grandmother looking after her grandchild.

There is no phone, but there is a car in the garage. Frightened by the intrusion of a stranger, the grandmother locks herself in the bathroom, leaving you alone with the grandchild. She will not come out and you have not been able to find the car keys. Should you try to persuade her to come out by twisting the child's arm until the cries of pain bring the grandmother out of the bathroom? Even those who find this course of action acceptable are likely to feel uneasy. This uneasiness reflects our general abhorrence of torture. The acceptance of torture in this kind of situation is hardly an endorsement of torture for fun.

Finally we arrive at the question of the extent to which children might have access to morality at its most fundamental level. In his "A Plea for Excuses," J. L. Austin says of ordinary language that, while it may not have the last word, we must remember that "it *is* the *first* word" (1961, p. 133). We certainly should acknowledge that children do not have the last word on morality, but they do have some access to morality at its most fundamental level. Reid might add, if they do not, neither do we. Moral understanding begins in childhood. Experience and reflection can correct, modify, or add to that understanding, Reid might say, but they cannot totally *displace* it.

3
Accountability, Understanding, and Sentiments

It is manifest great part of common language and common behavior over the world, is formed upon supposition of such a moral faculty; whether called conscience, moral reason, moral sense, or Divine reason; whether considered as a sentiment of the understanding, or as a perception of the heart; or which seems the truth, as including both.

— *Joseph Butler*, Of the Nature of Virtue

The psychopath is asocial. His conduct often brings him into conflict with society. . . . The psychopath is highly impulsive. He is a man for whom the moment is a segment of time detached from all others. . . . He can commit the most appalling acts, yet view them without remorse. The psychopath has a warped capacity for love. His emotional relationships, when they exist, are meager, fleeting, and designed to satisfy his own desires. These last two traits, guiltlessness and lovelessness, conspicuously mark the psychopath as different from other men.

— *William and Joan McCord*, Psychopathy and Delinquency

As moral agents, we regard ourselves as generally accountable for our conduct, and even, to some extent, for our attitudes and character. Broadly speaking, the moral appraisals we make of ourselves and others are blame- and praise-related. Jonathan Bennett suggests that we regard someone as accountable for an action "if a blame- or praise-related response to the action would not be inappropriate" (Bennett 1980, p. 15). I will follow this usage of "accountable."

It might be objected that if a moral agent simply meets minimal moral standards, he or she is neither blameworthy nor praiseworthy but is simply acting appropriately. However, the failure to meet those standards would ordinarily elicit blame. Furthermore, small children are often praised for meeting minimal standards as an important part of their moral training. So, blame- and praise-related responses do seem to de-

39

limit the range of appraisals suitable for moral agents reasonably well, even if some appraisals amount to nothing more than acknowledging that one has acted in a morally appropriate manner.

Of course, we are not morally accountable for what we do from the moment of birth. But just when moral accountability begins is difficult to determine. Aside from signs of responsible behavior, what do we look for in children? I will discuss three interrelated matters concerning features that we expect to find in adults, only to a greater degree. First, we look for indications that children have some *understanding* of the moral concepts we want them to take seriously. Second, we look for indications that they experience *moral sentiments*; examples are feelings of guilt, remorse, shame, indignation, and concern for the well-being of others. Third, we look for indications that children's moral understanding and sentiments work together. This third feature I will call *participant* understanding. It is fundamental to regarding oneself as a moral agent and also assists us in understanding the perspectives of those whose moral values may differ significantly from ours.

Philosophical discussions of responsibility tend to concentrate on adults who, it is assumed, do have minimal understanding and concern. But if we focus on children, questions about understanding and concern must be faced. As adults, we hope that very young children will soon begin to accept responsibility for what they do. How this transition is best accomplished poses many practical problems. Are there any related philosophical problems? One might think not. After all, we know what counts as understanding moral concepts and what it is genuinely to care about moral matters—and that understanding them is one thing, caring about them quite another. We know what relevance each has to the question of whether someone is morally accountable for what he or she does. Or do we? Consider the McCords's description at the outset of this chapter of the social psychopath (1965). Intelligent, impulsive, conscienceless—these are the traits commonly ascribed to the social psychopath. Are there really individuals like this? Apparently many psychiatrists think so. But I am less interested in whether their diagnoses are accurate in particular cases than in the question of what we should say about such persons if this characterization were accurate.

What are we to say of such persons, seemingly devoid of moral sentiments? Are they moral agents, albeit irresponsible ones? Or do they, like small children and nonhumans, fall outside the sphere of moral accountability altogether? The issue is complicated by the fact that most psychopaths seem quite capable of making ordinary moral distinctions. Can it be denied that they have the requisite understanding? If we cannot deny this, we are faced with these alternatives. On the one hand, we could hold that since psychopaths understand moral concepts but lack moral concern, they are morally irresponsible. On the other hand, we might hold with Herbert Fingarette that caring about morality is also a necessary condition for moral agency (Fingarette 1967, Ch. 2). Thus psychopaths would be nonresponsible (amoral) rather than irresponsible (immoral).[1]

I agree with Fingarette that psychopaths as characterized here are best viewed as nonresponsible. This does not mean that they are *justified* in behaving as they do; nor does it mean that they are *excused* from behaving in morally responsible ways or from having moral sentiments. Instead, they should be viewed more like nonhuman animals—as simply lacking moral agency. Thus, although not morally accountable for what they do, they need not be allowed to do whatever they please.[2]

However, I believe that Fingarette is mistaken in separating understanding and caring in the way he does. There is a sense of "understanding" vital to moral agency that presupposes caring about moral matters. Psychopaths may have an "intellectual" understanding of morality, but that is not enough—as I will now try to show.

MORAL AGREEMENT AND DISAGREEMENT

Since much of morality is interpersonal it is important to ask, What makes meaningful moral communication between moral agents possible? For some this might suggest the question, What makes it possible for moral agents to come to agreement about moral matters? Paradoxical as it may seem, the answer to this is the same as the answer to the question, What makes moral disagreement possible? Let me explain.

Suppose I believe that there should be laws permitting euthanasia in some circumstances. If I ask my daughter if she agrees and she answers, "No," does this mean that she and I morally disagree? Not if she is only two years old. What is missing here is something essential to all disagreement in belief—moral or otherwise. She and I would lack a common understanding in terms of which our "disagreement" can be articulated. This may be what Wittgenstein has in mind when he refers to the importance of a shared "form of life":

"So you are saying that human agreement decides what is true and what is false?"—It is what human beings *say* that is true and false; and they agree in the *language* they use. That is not agreement in opinions but in form of life.

If language is to be a means of communication there must be agreement not only in definitions but also (queer as this may sound) in judgments. (1953, p. 88e)

Wittgenstein's notion of a shared "form of life" is by no means precise, but it is suggestive. To take a simple example, my wife and I might disagree about the dimensions of our living room. But if our two-year-old offers a third "estimate," she does not add to the disagreement. To disagree with us, she must first share our concepts of measurement, as evidenced by her judgments of measurement being similar to ours on other occasions. Disagreement (in opinion) here presupposes prior agreement (in "form of life").

With something as straightforward as measuring the dimensions of rooms, we expect much more agreement than disagreement. Mistakes are relatively easy to detect and rectify. With morality, it will be objected, matters are quite different—except possibly in very conservative, closed moral communities. Furthermore, it seems quite possible for two people to understand one another's views very well while at the same time disagreeing fundamentally and, perhaps, irrevocably. Disagreements about abortion, for example, seem to have this character.

However, it must be asked how far differences can extend and still be fairly characterizable as disagreements. Even on issues as seemingly intractable as abortion, the disputants share some values. They may disagree about whether abortion is murder; still, they widely agree otherwise about what counts as murder—and that it is morally unacceptable. Suppose there were no such background agreement concerning the moral undesirability of murder, cruelty, harm, injustice, and the like. Would we say that the differences were still matters of disagreement? Or would we say that the differences are so radical that there is no shared "form of life" that makes disagreement intelligible?

Wittgenstein says:

We also say of some people that they are transparent to us. It is, however, important as regards this observation that one human being can be a complete enigma to another. We learn this when we come into a strange country with entirely strange traditions; and, what is more, even given a mastery of the country's language. We do not *understand* the people. "And not because of not knowing what they are saying to themselves." We cannot find our feet with them. (1953, p. 223)

We may have some optimism that, eventually, we will understand such people and that they will understand us. After all, we are talking about a society, a country with traditions that have underlying moral values—values which we may someday come to understand to bear some significant similarities to our own, however different they might otherwise be. We cannot find our feet with them *yet*, we might say.

However, with psychopaths there seems to be little reason for such optimism. We are more inclined to think that we *cannot* find our feet with them. There does not seem to be anything recognizable as underlying moral values. We speak the same language, but everything we understand to be even a possible moral value for anyone is dismissed or not seriously entertained by psychopaths. To find such persons *within* our midst is indeed disconcerting and puzzling.

For children, learning a language is an integral part of coming to share the kind of understanding that makes it possible for them to agree or disagree with others. However, as Wittgenstein insists, learning a language is not merely learning how to use words. It is also learning how to think, perceive, feel, relate to others, and practically engage in the world. Thus Wittgenstein says, "to imagine a language is to imagine a form of life" (1953, p. 8e). What is disconcerting and puzzling about psychopaths is that they share so little of the "form of life" with those whose language they speak. What kind of understanding (or "agreement") is presupposed by agreement and disagreement in moral opinion? It is tempting to say that the only necessity is that each person have a minimal ability to engage in moral conversation. Let us call this "intellectual understanding." Certainly the psychopath has an intellectual understanding of moral concepts, but this is not enough to account for the possibility of agreement and disagreement in moral opinion.

We must bear in mind that morality is inextricably bound up in the practical, rather than the merely theoretical, affairs of human beings. For there to be anything recognizable as morality, there must be persons with certain practical concerns along with moral competence to bring to bear on these concerns. What counts as moral competence? There must be some ability to reflect on moral matters; this is compatible with practical indifference. Yet since morality is more than simply an exercise in thought, it is necessary for there to be practical concern as well. And this the psychopath lacks.

Strawson reminds us of commonplaces about ordinary interpersonal relationships:

> We should think of the many different kinds of relationship which we can have with other people—as sharers of a common interest; as members of the same family; as colleagues; as friends; as lovers; as chance parties to an enormous range of transactions and encounters. Then we should think in each of these connections in turn, and in others, of the kind of importance we attach to the attitudes and intentions towards us of those who stand in these relationships to us, and of the kinds of *reactive* attitudes and feelings to which we ourselves are prone. In general, we demand some degree of goodwill or regard on the part of those who stand in these relationships to us, though the forms we require it to take vary widely in different connections. (1968, p. 76)

There are many ways in which we show such concern for one another. In addition to acting in morally appropriate ways, we have dispositions to react with resentment or indignation at the wrongs done by others and guilt, remorse, and shame at our own recognized shortcomings. Strawson calls these reactive tendencies "participant attitudes." Contrasted with participant attitudes are "objective attitudes," which are primarily concerned with social policies designed to control, treat, or manipulate the behavior and attitudes of others. Someone with an objective attitude might make use of knowledge of the tendencies people have to experience participant attitudes. In such a case the participant attitudes would be regarded from a detached, third-person perspective. In contrast, Strawson's participant attitudes are "essentially natural human reactions to the good or ill will or indifference of others towards us, as displayed in their attitudes and actions" (1968, p. 76).

Fingarette agrees with Strawson's view that participant attitudes play a fundamental role in morality, but he does not see this as providing an essential link between understanding moral concepts and the tendency to experience moral sentiments. Strawson, on the other hand, says: "Only by attending to this range of attitudes can we recover from the facts as we know them a sense of what we mean, i.e., of *all* we mean, when, speaking the language of morals, we speak of desert, responsibility, guilt, condemnation, and justice" (1968, p. 94). After considering Fingarette's views in some detail, I will try to show why Strawson's statement is right.

UNDERSTANDING AND CARING

Fingarette claims that people are not morally accountable for what they do until they show signs of genuine acceptance of responsibility. He notes that we do not begin to hold children morally accountable until we think they are able to accept responsibility. Such acceptance may be shown in inner moral conflict, self-restraint, remorse, guilt feelings, or by behaving responsibly. Yet what if the child shows none of this? Then, says Fingarette, we have chosen the wrong moment for holding the child accountable. We must wait. But what if the child grows into adulthood never displaying such concerns? Fingarette devotes the bulk of his discussion to this question by considering in detail the characteristics of psychopaths.

Unlike very young children, psychopaths can enter into sophisticated moral conversation, and they are capable of very persuasively feigning guilt feelings and the desire to fulfill responsibilities. Yet, they, like very young children, apparently lack genuine moral sentiments. Fingarette does not ask why psychopaths think and act as they do. Finding out, for example, that they suffer from brain damage or lack of parental affection would only add reasons for judging them not morally accountable for what they do; Fingarette thinks there are already sufficient reasons. He is not interested here in any questions related to the free will/determinism controversy, mental disease, or insanity. Instead, Fingarette holds, quite apart from these matters, those who think and act as psychopaths do, for whatever reason, have made it pointless to consider or treat them as morally accountable for what they do.

Why does Fingarette draw this conclusion? His main argument seems, at first glance, to be one of social utility, focusing on the "incorrigibility" of psychopaths. Presumably, someone who is incorrigible is incorrectable, intractable, unmanageable, or unresponsive to the suggestions and proddings of others. Fingarette might be saying that it is pointless to regard psychopaths as morally accountable for what they do because they will never be convinced, in any practical sense, that they have certain responsibilities. At most, they will "intellectually" assent. All of this seems to be true of psychopaths, with their typical pattern of impulsiveness, unreliability, and repeated confrontations with penal and mental institutions (McCord and McCord 1965; Cleckley 1976).

But psychopaths are not the only "incorrigibles." As Vinit Haksar points out, nothing seems to dissuade serious protestors such as Gandhi or Bertrand Russell from violating laws in the name of various causes (1965, p. 94). Yet, such persons are often regarded as paradigm cases of morally responsible individuals—even by virtue of their "incorrigibility." Also, there are always hard-headed individuals we know will never change their minds (about racial, political, or religious matters, for example). Are they, like psychopaths, to be exempted from moral accountability in these areas—on grounds of their intractability? Given its pervasiveness, incorrigibility alone does not seem to be a sufficient ground for exempting persons from moral accountability. In fact, it is often a person's incorrigibility on certain matters that provides a basis for moral criticism.

However, Fingarette suggests that there is something very special—and unsettling—about the incorrigibility of the psychopath: "If an individual will not play a game with us, we can still fall back on the intelligible framework of everyday life outside that game. But what if he will not enter life's fray itself in the spirit in which we enter it? To face such a person, such a reality (and not merely to think it) is to experience a deep anxiety; a queasy helplessness moves in our soul" (1967, p. 37). Here we see that the psychopath is not merely intractable or hard-headed. It is as if we have nothing in common with such a person, even though we use the same words and perhaps even the same gestures. There is nothing familiar and shared that we can fall back upon to ease this anxiety. This is not a Gandhi or a Russell, with different moral ideals from most, or someone with different information or a different moral interpretation of a situation. No, the psychopath is more radically different. How should this difference be characterized?

Fingarette characterizes it in terms of the psychopath's complete indifference to moral responsibility. This, it seems to me, is right. But it cannot clearly be seen to be right unless one makes a move Fingarette resists. He resists linking the concepts of caring and understanding because "it de-emphasizes acceptance and care by placing them in the shadow of that glamorous hero of the philosophic tradition, 'Knowing.'

This, in effect, reinforces the previously mentioned tendency to neglect accepting and caring; it hinders us from seeing them as essential, distinguishable things we must do in order to achieve responsibility" (1967, p. 22). The problem with this view is that, although it does overcome the neglect of the concepts of accepting and caring, it does so at the price of distorting those concepts. It forces one to reject the notion that in many instances the way in which we understand something is inseparable from our caring about it. Accepting this inseparability of understanding and caring neither neglects caring nor falls into the philosophical tradition that Fingarette opposes. It does not neglect caring because to exclude caring from understanding is to view understanding too narrowly. For the same reason, it does not reinforce that philosophical tradition; rather, it breaks new ground in philosophical discussions of human knowledge and understanding.[3]

By emphasizing that psychopaths do lack the kind of understanding (as caring) essential for moral agency, we can see more clearly why it is appropriate to say, as Fingarette wishes to say, that psychopaths do not share with others the relevant "form of life." To develop this thesis it will be helpful to consider Arthur Murphy's concept of practical understanding (1965).

PRACTICAL UNDERSTANDING

Arthur Murphy, like Fingarette, argues that those lacking moral concern are not morally responsible for what they do. He, too, emphasizes the pointlessness of trying to deal with such persons in terms of responsibility or accountability. However, unlike Fingarette, he maintains that what is missing is practical understanding. He explains this by considering how children learn moral concepts.

On Murphy's account, moral reasons are justificatory grounds for action. As such, they are practical reasons, reasons for doing or not doing something. How do children learn to relate competently to such reasons? "Training here is prior to significant argument, logically as well as temporally, since without this working basis of normative concern and competence—the concern and competence to get things right—all our talk of practical reasoning, would, as Wittgenstein has put it, 'hang in the air,' and we should have no common ground on which to stand" (Murphy 1965, p. 10). Children can be encouraged to develop normative concerns either by deliberate prompting or by examples set by those who already have normative concerns. Of course, children also develop normative concerns in ordinary interactions with siblings, playmates, and adults where there is no deliberate attempt to train them. Still, learning takes place through their being expected to share, take turns, have regard for the feelings of others, keep their word, and take proper care of what is entrusted to them. Children are exposed to praise, sympathetic concern, fair play, consideration, respect, trust, and helpfulness, as well as to criticism and the full range of reactive attitudes and feelings.

Children are not merely observers of such social interaction. They are encouraged to share the attitudes and concerns of others. Typically, as targets of these attitudes and concerns, they gradually become participants in the ways of life of those around them. Their responses to these ways of life can vary. There may be various degrees of reciprocation, acceptance, rejection, resistance, and puzzlement. Fundamentally, the original acquisition of moral concepts is not an exclusively (or even primarily) theoretical or intellectual accomplishment, even though rational capacities are developed and exercised in the process. The world of the young child is not primarily a world of intellectual understanding; it is one of practical endeavor.

The development of attitudes and concerns of a participant in a moral community should not be confused with a blanket acceptance of the conventional. One might think that, for the most part, children become morally acculturated by uncritically adopting the moral conventions that prevail in their communities. Some leading developmentalists, such as Lawrence Kohlberg and his followers (1981), claim that the vast majority of *adults* never get beyond this. However, there are two basic responses to this; both are discussed in some detail by Robert Fullinwider (1989). First, learning moral conventions is itself a complex endeavor that calls for critical and discerning judgment. Conventions typically incorporate a wide range of subtle distinctions. For example, children are expected to learn similarities and differences among the deliberate, intentional, unintentional, accidental, negligent, and so on. They must learn to distinguish between bravery and cowardice, loyalty and disloyalty, fairness and unfairness, considerateness and inconsiderateness. Even conventional moral rules are not self-interpreting. Their application calls for discerning judgment. Second, as Fullinwider points out, confusing "conventional" with "uncritical" betrays a "failure to appreciate the abundance in our culture of conventions for appraising and criticizing other conventions" (1989, p. 335). This is particularly so in pluralistic societies. Fullinwider continues: "Criticism and convention go together. The power and force of social criticism generally resides precisely in its imaginative application and extension of well-known precepts or paradigm cases or familiar critical practices" (1989, p. 335).

Since much that children observe is unresolved tension and conflict, some questioning and puzzlement is to be expected. Children cannot sensibly believe everything they hear or that others want them to believe. Admittedly, children resolve some of the confusion they are confronted with by relying on authoritative figures or their peers. But critical judgment in some areas of moral concern can, and often does, begin at a fairly young age.

Of course, children do learn from examples. But, as we have seen in the case of developing an understanding of fairness (Dworkin 1977, p. 133), examples provide them with only a starting point from which they may go on to deal competently with novel instances. We should not think of children's acquisition of moral ideas as analogous to learning a recipe or a mathematical formula. Thus, Murphy should not be seen as neglecting the importance of critical thinking in the growth of practical understanding. His point is only that this understanding must begin somewhere, and that place is in particular communities of persons with normative concerns.

It does not take long for young children to begin to exhibit a sense of justice or fair play. We might be tempted to think that having a sense of justice or fair play requires only some minimal conceptual understanding of justice or fairness. But John Rawls seems to be right when he says, paraphrasing Rousseau, "The sense of justice is no mere moral conception formed by the understanding alone, but a true sentiment of the heart enlightened by reason" (1963, p. 282). Since a sense of justice is a blend of reason and sentiment, it is important that neither aspect be slighted. But what especially should be noted here is that, whatever rational features of a sense of justice we cite, they will not capture what Rawls has in mind unless they are connected with moral sentiments such as fellow-feeling, resentment or indignation at injustices done by others, and feelings of guilt, remorse, or shame at one's own unjust acts.

The connection between having a sense of justice and moral understanding can be seen more clearly by drawing an analogy. Consider what is involved in having a sense of humor: having some ability to identify situations as being humorous. Someone with a sense of humor must also respond emotionally to these situations by finding them laughable, hilarious, or simply amusing. That is, one must genuinely laugh, be in a mood of hilarity, or be amused. This does not mean that someone with a sense of humor will always respond in this way to humorous situations. I may not be in the mood to laugh, but still recognize that something is humorous. But if I am never in the mood to laugh or be amused, I lack a sense of humor. So, we can speak only of tendencies to respond.

We could imagine a very observant person who lacks a sense of humor, but who closely studies others in humorous situations. Conceivably he or she could acquire a knack of determining what is regarded as humorous by others. This might even provide the basis for writing humorous books. (Imagine such a person as a straight-faced comedian.) Furthermore, the laughter of others could be simulated. Despite this, such a person would not have a sense of humor. Everything is completely parasitic on the responses of others. A full understanding of humor is lacking. Although there is no lack of "information" or "data" that others have, such a person does not see what they do.

Both a sense of humor and a sense of justice require certain kinds of cognitive abilities and dispositions to respond emotionally. We could also imagine someone who lacks a sense of justice studying the behavior of those with a sense of justice. If such a person were sufficiently observant and cautious in behavior, he or she might acquire a reputation as a reasonably good judge of issues of justice. He or she might pay close attention to what others count as relevant in dealing with issues of justice, feign guilt feelings or act apologetic when criticized for acting unjustly, appear indignant at injustices, and put on a show of other-regard and positive concern to be just. However, since all of this is only simulating the behavior of others, this person would lack a sense of justice. One mark of this would be the inability to depart significantly from views already expressed by others. This might go unnoticed, since we seldom closely study the attitudes and behavior of those who seem to support the prevailing, conventional standards of justice. Thus, even though lacking a sense of justice, a "benign" psychopath might escape our notice.

Still, Anthony Duff's diagnosis of the psychopath's lack of understanding seems basically right:

> A psychopath's incapacity, his lack of understanding, is revealed by the fact that he is capable of no more than a stereotyped and rigid

application of moral formulae he has learned. His relation to moral concepts is like that to aesthetic concepts of a person lacking in aesthetic sensitivity (which is distinct from an actual concern for the artistic objects he is discussing): he can parrot certain stereotyped judgments, and apply them to new cases which fall under such descriptive criteria as he has learned; but he can neither understand, nor intelligently discuss, criticise, or extend the rules he has picked up. (1977, p. 196)

In a sense, the psychopath has particular moral conceptions—those picked up from others. But the psychopath has no sense of being guided by moral concepts, of which these conceptions are only rough, and correctable, approximations.

Duff is not saying that we can understand only those moral values we ourselves accept. However, a participant understanding of *some* moral values is necessary for fully understanding any moral values—whether one's own or another's (Duff 1977, p. 196). Intellectual understanding is not enough. There must also be the sensitivity and imagination found only in those who take some moral values seriously. Thus, our moral values may differ significantly from others; but since we do take moral values seriously, we can understand what different moral values mean to others.

Consider what it means to understand the wrongness of hurting someone. As Duff says, we must be able to understand what it *is* to hurt someone. To understand this, we must appreciate the significance of interests, emotions, and relationships in human life generally. Thus, Duff concludes: "An understanding of the moral aspects of my actions, and of the moral values of others, requires an understanding of that dimension of human life which includes both moral values and those interests and emotions which make our actions morally significant: it is this which a psychopath lacks" (1977, p. 198). We can, then, have a practical understanding of the moral values of others even if we do not share those values. But those who have no participant understanding of moral values are barred from this practical understanding. At best, they have only an intellectual understanding.

What is it that intellectual understanding leaves out? Arthur Murphy's view is that it leaves out both moral concern and competence. Someone lacking moral sentiments, says Murphy: "could 'regard an action as a duty' in the sense of recognizing, perhaps with complete practical indifference, that it had the traits by which an action is socially identified as 'right.' . . . What he could never in this way 'see' is how such rightness bound him as a moral agent to the performance of the action in question, . . . He could not understand why he ought to do it" (1965, p. 126). No matter what such persons might say about their "responsibilities," they do not take them seriously because they do not see (i.e., understand) why they should take them seriously. Nor do they see why others should take their "responsibilities" seriously—regardless of how similar or different others' moral values might be to those they "accept."

It cannot be denied that psychopaths have some kind of understanding of moral concepts. However, for people with moral sentiments, experiencing particular sentiments often *is* how having responsibilities is understood. In these instances, there is no gap between understanding and caring. Still, one might want to say that, since there is a sense in which one can understand without caring, caring must be different from understanding. But what must be kept in mind is that caring is always about something; it has an object. Furthermore, caring about something is in many instances the most fundamental way of regarding it. In such cases it is not that one has a certain understanding of something and then, superadded as it were, one also cares about it in a certain way. One may not regard it in a detached, observing way at all. For example, I do not first "observe" my son's wound, registering the "information," and then as a result of this perception have some sort of concern for his plight. Rather, I perceive what has happened to him as a *wound*. My recognition of it as a wound is seen in the immediate concern I have to help him. If I were to react at first in a detached, observing way to his wound, it would indicate some sort of failure of recognition. "Don't you see that he is *hurt*?" I would need a jarring back into reality—the reality that I share with my son, who needs my help.

When care or concern is an essential feature of how we perceive a situation we have a participant, rather than merely intellectual, understanding. This enables us to appreciate the participant understanding others may have, even though there may be significant differences between their values and ours. Psychopaths, however, seem to be more radically different, so much so that, as Fingarette says, we experience a "queasy helplessness." The source of this sense of helplessness is that, despite appearances, there can be no genuine meeting of minds between psychopaths and others on moral matters.

Among those who take morality seriously there is a common concern to be justified in what we do. Although there might be serious disagreement about what specific responsibilities we have, at least the idea of responsibility is taken seriously. But there seems to be no shared ground to fall back upon when confronted with psychopaths. It is as though they are from another world, another "form of life." The queasiness comes, not from feeling that they will never be convinced of our point of view (an everyday matter), but from the realization that they do not even share normative concern. It is as though there is at best mimicry or mockery, not mutual understanding. Quite apart from the question of whether one can get psychopaths to change their ways, there is the prior question of what one should even say to those who "will not enter life's fray itself in the spirit in which we enter it." It is not merely that they do not understand our "form of life"; we do not understand theirs.

Wittgenstein says, "If a lion could talk, we could not understand him" (1953, p. 223). Psychopaths do talk. They use familiar gestures and even the same moral language, but this is not enough for mutual understanding. As Murphy insists, moral reasons are not addressed to everyone but only to those who are somewhat disposed to take moral reasons seriously: "It is *for* such an agent that they are practical reasons, i.e., reasons for doing something, not merely for thinking or believing that something is the case, and as in this way practical that they have a normative function in our conduct" (1965, p. 123). Moral reasons can be practical only for those who are to some extent morally concerned. If justificatory reasons are to be practical reasons, they must be capable of being motivating reasons as well.

This does not mean that justifying reasons must always motivate. Moral agents have other concerns as well, concerns that encourage ignoring, suppressing, or rationalizing away moral considerations. Self-deception, too, is an ever present possibility. Still, as Murphy points out, the very presence of self-deception about morality indicates a concern to be justified (1965, Ch. 6). Both Murphy and Fingarette connect self-deception with a concern to maintain some kind of integrity or wholeness. Since psychopaths have no moral integrity to protect, if they are capable of any kind of self-deception, it is related to some other kind of integrity.

MORAL AGENCY

Even if psychopaths lack moral integrity, it could be argued that they can lead reasonably well-integrated lives. Haksar (1965) points out that psychopaths have some concern about the future, they may have jobs, and, however careless they may be, they typically avoid getting killed. Noting this, Robert Smith (1984) explores the possibility that psychopaths may be more like the rest of us than we might otherwise suspect. Psychopaths seem to act "in character," not from inner compulsion or external coercion. Following the suggestions of Robert Arrington (1979), Smith tries to show similarities between the values of psychopaths and values widely shared in our society.

Smith agrees with Arrington's suggestion that psychopaths could operate from *principled egoism*. Even though they are typically very particularistic in their aims, psychopaths might embrace a form of egoism that "could be raised to a maxim if it were voiced for everyone, i.e., became universal egoism" (Smith 1984, p. 182). Also, typical characteristics of psychopaths bear some similarity to values widely accepted in our society, albeit in less extreme forms. We even have clichés for these values. Smith compares psychopaths' impulsive giving in to the temptation of the moment to "fly now—pay later"; their limited concern or affection for others to "look out for number one"; their aggressiveness to "sell yourself"; their lack of shame, sense of guilt, or regret to "do your own thing"; and their inability to learn from experience to "live for today for tomorrow we may die."

These comparisons call for several comments. Of course, these clichés do have some currency in our society—no doubt much more than most of us like. Even if they reflect widely recognized values, they do not represent *moral* values—at least not insofar as they are associated with the corresponding psychopathic traits. It will not do to suggest, as Smith does, that these comparisons bring psychopaths closer to moral agency. If anything, they point out tendencies that threaten to undermine *our* moral agency. Showing that we share some values with psychopaths does not show that we share moral values with them—or even that their values resemble moral values.

It might be objected that psychopaths' values are like moral values if psychopaths are principled egoists. Here we must look carefully at what "principled" can mean. If all we mean is that psychopaths do not object to others acting as they do, this is an odd use of "principled." This would not imply that they think anyone *ought* to act in any particular way and is still compatible with the rejection of all normative concern—moral, prudential, or otherwise. Could psychopaths be principled egoists in the sense that they take seriously the idea that they and everyone else ought to behave egoistically? Even if there are such principled ego-ists, it does not seem plausible to characterize psychopaths in this way. Evidence that they accept such a norm as applying to themselves and others would be their reactive attitudes to failures to satisfy the norm. Sincere regret, self-reproach, or even self-criticism are notably absent even when psychopaths seem to fail miserably in serving their own in-terests. How well others fare is similarly of little concern to them.

There is a philosophical view of principled egoism that does take re-sponsibility seriously—enlightened self-interest, which embraces a prin-ciple that takes seriously both short- and long-term self-interest. It also serves as a basis for self-criticism, since we frequently fall short of satis-fying its demands. If universalized to others, it also serves as a basis for criticizing their behavior. Whether this view is ultimately coherent is a matter of considerable controversy. In any case, it is much too serious and restrictive to be embraced by psychopaths. We might say, then, that psychopaths pose a challenge for prudential as well as for moral points of view. Thus it is implausible to think of psychopaths as accepting a *principled* anything.

If this response to Smith is appropriate, what should we say about psychopaths as moral agents? In arguing that they are more like ordinary moral agents than we might otherwise think, Smith seems to be urging us to regard psychopaths as moral agents—albeit, extreme and irrespon-sible ones. I have countered that we may be more like psychopaths than we realize, but that does not bring them closer to morality. Instead, it takes us further from morality. Even so, Smith might reply, since psycho-paths have an intellectual grasp of the difference between right and wrong, they are moral agents; and since they regularly flout moral prin-ciples without any qualms, they act immorally.

Certainly we can say that psychopaths engage in moral wrongdoing, if by this we mean that they fail to conform to principles that moral agents support. The question remains whether we should think of them as moral agents. I am still inclined to hold that we should not. Like Mur-phy, I see moral discourse as addressed "to whom it may concern." Psy-chopaths do not enter into such discourse except perhaps in what Straw-son would call an objective rather than participant manner. Although they, like others, can use moral language in manipulative ways to try to get what they want, their success depends on others having a partici-pant understanding of morality. Because others *do* take morality seriously, psychopaths, as well as others, are able to affect people through the use of moral language.

It is important to distinguish the view that psychopaths are not moral agents from other views with which it can be confused easily. For example, viewing psychopaths in this way does not require us to say that one's only moral responsibilities are those one has explicitly acknowledged. As Fingarette insists, much of the substance of our moral lives is coming to discover the responsibilities one has implicitly accepted by virtue of accepting our moral agency. It is because one is a certain kind of person (a moral agent), and not simply because of acts one has performed, that one has moral responsibilities. Particular acts can alter one's responsibilities (promising, for example), but one cannot divest oneself of a responsibility simply by becoming indifferent to it or by failing to acknowledge it. It must be borne in mind that the psychopath's indifference is pervasive. The psychopath is incorrigible in a way unlike ordinary moral agents—even very stubborn or highly egocentric ones.

One might object, "This makes things much too easy. All we have to do to relieve ourselves of the burdens of moral responsibility is to rid ourselves of moral concerns—to become amoralists." The short reply to this is, "Easier said than done." First, relieving oneself of moral responsibility does not leave one free to do whatever one pleases. This surely is not our attitude toward small children, those with serious mental deficiencies, and nonhuman animals. (And the more dangerous the animal, the more protection is provided.) Second, to divest oneself of all moral concern would be an enormous undertaking for most.[4] One would have to rid oneself of fellow-feeling, hardening oneself to the joys and sufferings of others. One would have to cease to be aroused by injustices done to others and no longer resent injustices to oneself. One would have to eliminate all feelings of guilt, shame, remorse, regret, or apology when treating others in objectionable ways. None of this would be easy for those who have moral sentiments, nor is it clear that we could reflectively consider it desirable even to try. Finally, serious consideration of such an attempt would be resisted by those with moral integrity.

Still, some might think it important to renounce the psychopath's amorality in the strongest possible way—by regarding such a person as a paradigm case of an irresponsible moral agent. It is not clear what moral advantage this would provide. It will not bring us closer to understanding the psychopath, or vice-versa. Nor will it reduce our perplexity about how, in practical terms, the psychopath should be dealt with. The psychopath remains an anomaly, even if viewed as a moral agent.

Whichever way this issue is resolved, there is one matter upon which agreement is important. The psychopath, as clinically described, should not be taken seriously as providing us with an alternative *moral* point of view that must be weighed alongside others in deciding how morally we should live our lives. Insofar as we engage in moral reflection in deciding how we should live, there is no need to consider how a psychopath might handle the question. That is, questions of moral justification are questions for those who have genuine moral concerns, even if the answers are about how those who do not have such concerns should be treated.

What this suggests, however, is that questions of moral justification belong inside morality. We may want morality to be rationally irresistible, but trying to convince even psychopaths that rationality requires them to take morality seriously is a futile and unnecessary task. Whatever rationality morality has can be made transparent only from within a moral point of view. As Strawson puts it:

> Inside the general structure or web of human attitudes and feelings of which I have been speaking, there is endless room for modification, redirection, criticism, and justification. But questions of justification are internal to the structure or relate to modifications internal to it. The existence of the general framework of attitudes itself is something we are given with the fact of human society. As a whole, it neither calls for, nor permits, an external 'rational' justification. (1968, p. 94)

Strawson compares this to inductive reasoning, which he says is "original, natural, nonrational (not *ir*rational), in no way something we choose or could give up."

The psychopath can be thought of as a limiting case. If all of us were psychopaths, morality would gain no foothold in our lives. Whether we would nevertheless survive is extremely doubtful. The similarities Smith and Arrington see between the values of psychopaths and nonmoral values that are pervasive in our society are cause for concern. These shared values point to the fragility of morality. Still, this should not be regarded as cause for moral skepticism or for doubts about the importance of reason within morality.

4
Reason and Resentment

The indignation raised by cruelty and injustice, and the desire of having it punished, which persons unconcerned would feel, is by no means malice. No, it is resentment against vice and wickedness: it is one of the common bonds, by which society is held together; a fellow-feeling, which each individual has in behalf of the whole species, as well as himself.
—*Joseph Butler*, Sermon 8

Resentment is not inconsistent with good will; for we often see both together in very high degree; not only in parents towards their children, but in cases of friendship and dependence, where there is no natural relation. These contrary passions, though they may lessen, do not necessarily destroy each other. We may therefore love our enemy, and yet have resentment against him for his injurious behaviour towards us. But when this resentment entirely destroys our natural benevolence towards him, it is excessive, and becomes malice or revenge.
—*Joseph Butler*, Sermon 9

In "Freedom and Resentment" (168), P. F. Strawson maintains that there is a general framework of moral attitudes that we must simply accept as a fundamental feature of human society. This framework, he says, neither has nor needs an external, rational justification. Yet, within this framework there is, as he puts it, "endless room for modification, redirection, criticism, and justification" (1968, p. 94). This chapter explores the last claim and focuses primarily on the reactive attitude of resentment.

REACTIVE ATTITUDES

Strawson says that our reactive attitudes are responses to the attitudes and feelings others have toward us: their good will, ill will, respect, disrespect, contempt, and indifference. Morally reactive attitudes express "the demand for the manifestation of a reasonable degree of good will or regard, on the part of others, not simply towards oneself, but toward all those on whose behalf moral indignation may be felt" (1968, p. 85). It is important to realize that, for Strawson, reactive attitudes are constitutive features of ordinary interpersonal relations. Among adults, accountability is normally assumed. However, various forms of incapacity for ordinary interpersonal relations rule out or at least seriously modify accountability—for example, mental illness, insanity, and, as I have argued, psychopathy.[1] With children, incapacity of varying degrees may be due to inexperience or not yet having fully developed rational and moral powers. Also, since reactive attitudes express our concern for the attitudes of others, our attitudes will need modification when we discover that we have misunderstood the attitudes of other persons.

These modifications all occur within a larger framework of accountability. For Strawson, there is no question of the possible eradication of such attitudes entirely, at least not without eradicating our humanity.[2] Jonathan Bennett offers the following helpful picture: "There is a large 'accountability' circle within which reactive feelings are confined: it roughly coincides with the circle within which moral-pressure therapies have some chance of success. Inside that, there are smaller circles marking areas from which it is prudent to exclude reactive feelings because they are so counter-productive there" (1980, p. 23). Of course, to say that reactive feelings should be excluded from some areas because of their bad consequences is not to say that their inclusion elsewhere is grounded in consequentialist considerations.

In ordinary interpersonal relations, for example, we do not feel resentment *in order to* bring about certain desired changes. No doubt we sometimes feign resentment, or even try to cause ourselves to feel resentment, so that we can affect others in this way, but this is not the ordinary case. This view seems to be what Bennett has in mind when he denies that reactive attitudes are *teleological* (Bennett 1980, p. 37). Our resentment may bring about desired changes, but the resentment itself is our protest against behavior or attitudes we find objectionable.

Bennett argues that reactive attitudes are best understood in terms of relations toward which they point, rather than in terms of already existing relations between persons: "If I resent someone's treatment of me, there may have been antecedently no special kind of relation between us; but my very resentment creates one, or sets the stage for one" (1980, p. 44). He adds, "If reactive attitudes essentially embody or point towards or prepare for interpersonal relations, then it is clear how someone's incapacity for the latter makes it inappropriate to have reactive attitudes toward him" (1980, p. 44). Again, the psychopath seems to be a limiting case. This suggests that, as Gary Watson puts it, reactive attitudes are "incipiently forms of communication, which make sense only on the assumption that the other can comprehend the message" (1988, p. 264). That is, through these attitudes we address one another, at least potentially.

Watson characterizes Strawson's view of accountability as an *expressive theory of responsibility* (1988, p. 261). Regarding people as responsible for what they do is not to be understood as a propositional belief that can be shown to be true or false independently of our reactive attitudes. Watson says, "It is not that we hold people responsible because they *are* responsible; rather, the idea (*our* idea) that we are responsible is to be understood by the practice, which itself is not a matter of holding some propositions to be true, but of expressing our concerns and demands about our treatment of one another" (1988, p. 258). Thus, our attribution of responsibility to others is grounded in our reactive attitudes: "To regard another as morally responsible is to react to him or her as a moral self" (1988, p. 286).

However, does reacting to another as a moral self require *retributive* sentiments such as resentment? Watson raises serious doubts about this. Often linked with envy, malice, spite, and vindictiveness, resentment might be seen as something we would be better off without. It would be ironic if, in our more reflective moments, we excised from Strawson's general framework of attitudes presupposed by human society the very reactive attitude featured in the title of his essay. Of course, Strawson could reply that we cannot sustain this more reflective posture. Like the philosophic skeptic who abandons skepticism when engaged in practical affairs, we lapse into resentment when offended by others. Yet this would be small consolation for Strawson. The inevitability of a reactive attitude does not, in itself, give it a constructive role in moral life. If, for example, we have some ineradicable sadistic tendencies, it would not follow that these tendencies should be accorded any moral respect. We could regret having such tendencies, do our best to reduce them, try to redirect them in constructive ways, and try to make amends to their victims.[3]

Should resentment then go the way of sadism, or can it be embraced within the general framework of morally acceptable attitudes? Strawson does not really develop an answer to this question; but two prominent eighteenth-century philosophers, Joseph Butler (1730) and Thomas Reid

(1788), discuss resentment in great detail. Their conclusion is that, suitably modified by reason, resentment does have an appropriate and important place within morality. Reid uses his account of resentment as a reply to David Hume's doubts about the role of reason in morality. A close examination of Butler's and Reid's views will, I think, both clarify and vindicate Strawson's basic thesis about the general framework of moral attitudes and will also reserve a secure place for resentment within that framework.

PASSION, SENTIMENT, AND REASON

David Hume's claims about the relationship between reason and morality are, to understate the case, provocative. In one of the most famous passages of his *Treatise of Human Nature*, Hume says: " 'Tis not contrary to reason to prefer the destruction of the whole world to the scratching of my finger. . . . 'Tis as little contrary to reason to prefer even my own acknowledg'd lesser good to my greater, and have a more ardent affection for the former than the latter" (1740, p. 416). It is difficult to resist replying that only someone gone mad could prefer the destruction of the world to the scratching of his or her finger; and we might wonder what could be more unreasonable than having greater affection for our *acknowledged* lesser than greater good. So it is natural to ask what might have prompted Hume to make such an unusual set of claims.

Thomas Reid's explanation is that Hume was led astray by a fundamentally confused view of the passions: "Mr. Hume gives the name of *Passion* to every principle of action in the human mind; and, in consequence of this, maintains that every man is and ought to be led by his passions, and that the use of reason is to be subservient to the passions" (1788, p. 571). This response might seem to be merely a quibble over words. But when we notice that, for Hume, judgment is entirely distinct and separate from passion, it is evident that something more substantial is at stake. For if Hume's view is correct, judgment (and, therefore, reason) is entirely distinct and separate from principles of action. As Hume himself puts it, "In short, a passion must be accompany'd with some false judgement, in order its being unreasonable; and even then 'tis not the passion, properly speaking, which is unreasonable, but the judgement" (1740, p. 416).

This separation of judgment and passion has important implications for the role of reason in morality. Hume concludes, "Since a passion can never, in any sense, be call'd unreasonable, but when founded on a false supposition, or when it chuses means insufficient for the design'd end, 'tis impossible, that reason and passion can ever oppose each other, or dispute for the government of the will and actions" (1740, p. 416). This seems to reduce passions to mere sensations or feeling-states of some sort, but whatever sort they are must be recognizable independently of whatever judgments might "accompany" them. As we shall see, however, there is a serious problem in distinguishing sensations from one another in ways that allow us to make all the distinctions we want to make among the various human emotions and sentiments.

In contrast to Hume, Reid insists that it is an "abuse of words" to use the word "passion" in such a broad way. He says, "passion" refers properly not just to any principle of action, but to those that cause a "perturbation." For example, resentment may or may not be a passion: "Thus, a man may be sensible of an injury without being inflamed. He judges coolly of the injury, and the proper means of redress. This is resentment without passion. It leaves to the man the entire command of himself" (1788, p. 571). But, Reid continues, "On another occasion, the same principle of resentment rises into a flame. His blood boils within him; his looks, his voice, and his gesture are changed; he can think of nothing but immediate revenge, and feels a strong impulse, without regard to consequences, to say and do things which his cool reason cannot justify. This is the passion of resentment" (1788, p. 572).

On Reid's view, the passions are *animal* principles of action which, to some extent, we have in common with "brute animals." In contrast, there are *rational* principles of action, which presuppose the use of reason and judgment. Whereas Hume contrasts violent and calm passions, Reid holds that all passions are violent and contrasts them with sentiments. For both, sentiments involve feeling, but for Reid they must include judgment as well:

> Authors who place moral approbation in feeling only, very often use the word *Sentiment*, to express feeling without judgment. This I take likewise to be an abuse of a word. Our moral determinations may, with propriety, be called *moral sentiments*. For the word *sentiment*, in the English language, never, as I conceive, signifies mere feeling, but *judgement accompanied with feeling*. . . . So we speak of sentiments of respect, of esteem, of gratitude; but I never heard of the

pain of the gout, or any other mere feeling, called a sentiment. (1788, pp. 674-75)

Once again this may sound like a verbal quibble, but it is not. Reid discusses particular sentiments at some length to support his view that reason and judgment are essential ingredients of the sentiments rather than simply "accompaniments." His discussion of resentment nicely illustrates this.

Before turning to that discussion, however, it is important to be clear about what is and what is not at stake. Reid is not really challenging Hume's view that sentiments are essential to morality. They provide principles of action without which morality would be nothing. Reid accepts the idea that principles of action, not merely of belief, are needed.[4] What he is challenging is Hume's analysis of the sentiments. Reid wants to establish that there are rational principles of action that apply to morality.

BUTLER AND REID ON RESENTMENT

Reid's view of resentment is drawn largely from the earlier account of Joseph Butler (Sermons 8 and 9, 1730). Resentment is a natural reaction to being hurt or caused pain. There is a resistance to the hurt and a desire to retaliate; this response is common to humans and many animals. However, like Butler, Reid makes a distinction between *sudden* and *deliberate* resentment. The first is a "blind impulse arising from our constitution" and "may be raised by hurt of any kind." The second "can only be raised by injury real or conceived." Deliberate resentment, then, is a rational principle of action. This does not mean that it is always reasonable. Rather, Reid says, it means that "it is proper to man as a reasonable being, capable, by his rational faculties, of distinguishing between hurt and injury; a distinction which no brute-animal can make" (1788, p. 568).

According to Reid and Butler, the natural end of resentment is defense, especially when there is no time for deliberation. This response can be compared with efforts to regain one's balance. There may not be enough time for reason to help one prevent a dangerous fall, but one might react immediately with more muscular strength and control than would result from deliberation about the danger. Still, there is an important difference between the functions of sudden resentment and sudden muscular exertions to regain one's balance, or blinking one's eyes when they are exposed to danger. Sudden resentment "operates both upon the defender and assailant, inspiring the former with courage and animosity, and striking terror into the latter" (Reid 1788, p. 569). The muscular reaction or eye blink serves the defender, but there is no aggression against an offender.

Resentment, Reid says, "supposes an object on whom we may retaliate" (1788, p. 569). Yet if this is so, he asks, why do we often see animals, and sometimes even humans, react with resentment against inanimate objects? Reid answers, "There must . . . be some momentary notion or conception that the object of our resentment is capable of punishment; and if it be natural, before reflection, to be angry with things inanimate, it seems to be a necessary consequence, that it is natural to think that they have life and feeling" (1788, p. 569). Thus, Reid concludes, we should not think that reflection and experience enable us to consider things as animate that we first thought were inanimate. Rather, we learn that things we formerly regarded as animate are really inanimate and, therefore, not proper objects of resentment.

Even those who are capable of reflection might have sudden resentment against an inanimate object, but reflection can overcome this reaction. Still, Reid says, "I confess it seems to me impossible that there should be resentment against a thing which at that very moment is considered as inanimate, and consequently incapable either of intending hurt, or of being punished" (1788, p. 569). This is a conceptual point, and it is difficult to imagine that Hume could appreciate it without admitting that judgment enters into the sentiment of resentment itself.

As children's capacities for reflection and reason develop, they learn that in order for resentment to have a proper object, and in order for it to be reasonable, certain conditions must be satisfied. Understanding this, and being able to determine when these conditions have or have not been met, requires somewhat developed rational capacities. What are some of the things that reflection teaches us about resentment? "A small degree of reason and reflection teaches a man that injury only, and not mere hurt, is a just object of resentment to a rational creature. A man may suffer grievously by the hand of another, not only without injury, but with the most friendly intention; as in the case of a painful chirurgical operation. Every man of common sense sees, that to resent such suffering, is not the part of man, but of a brute" (1788, p. 570).

Like Butler, Reid holds that *injury* is an essentially moral concept, presupposing the concept of being wronged or done an injustice. Anyone capable of deliberate resentment must be capable of making certain discriminations concerning the causes of hurt and pain. Furthermore, for the resentment to be reasonable, it must be reasonable to ascribe moral responsibility to the cause of the hurt or pain. This, in turn, requires one to be able to make distinctions between intentional and unintentional behavior, voluntary and involuntary action, negligence and excuse, and the like. In short, since only certain sorts of causal agents, in certain sorts of circumstances, can reasonably be held responsible for the hurt, only rational agents can make the relevant kinds of discriminations for their resentment to be reasonable.

Reid's discussion weaves together a number of moral concepts. Injury is connected with justice, as is the idea of favor. Justice is the standard one appeals to in determining whether what has occurred is either a favor, making gratitude appropriate, or an injury, making resentment appropriate. Reid says, "Their very nature and definition consist in their exceeding or falling short of this standard. No man, therefore, can have the idea either of a favour or of an injury, who has not the idea of justice" (1788, p. 570).[5] This same idea of justice can be used to check excessive resentment, "for, as there is injustice in doing an injury, so there is injustice in punishing beyond measure" (1788, p. 570).

However, even though resentment's association with justice may be looked on favorably, its ties to punishment raise worries. Could it be that resentment's desire for punishment is so negative, vengeful, and vindictive—and so full of malice and envy—that it does more harm than good? Butler and Reid realize that resentment can nourish vice as well as virtue. It is precisely because of this danger that they emphasize the role of reason in harnessing sudden resentment in behalf of morality. Butler replies: "The indignation raised by cruelty and injustice, and the desire of having it punished, which persons unconcerned would feel, is by no means malice. No, it is resentment against vice and wickedness: it is one of the common bonds, by which society is held together; a fellow-feeling, which each individual has in behalf of the whole species, as well as of himself" (1730, p. 129). Vice, Butler says, "in general consists in having an unreasonable and too great regard to ourselves, in comparison of others" (1730, p. 130).

Suitably refined resentment can serve as a check against unreasonable self-regard as well as excessive partiality toward those for whom we have special attachments. Both Butler and Reid note our tendency to be more aroused by alleged injury and injustice to ourselves and those we are immediately concerned about, which invites distorted judgment. So, Butler urges that we restrict resentment, even in our own behalf, to that "which persons unconcerned would feel." But this more impartial perspective does not imply indifference. Impartial resentment should be viewed as a reasonable complaint against unreasonable self-regard or partiality by others.

Reid insists that resentment should conform to first principles of morality, such as the requirement that moral judgments be generalizable: "It is a first principle in morals, That we ought not to do to another what we should think wrong to be done to us in like circumstances" (1788, p. 590). If we cannot see the appropriateness of this principle, at least in moments of serious reflection, Reid says, we are not moral agents—nor can we be convinced of the principle by reasoning. When we apply this principle to judgments about the wrongdoing of others, we see that we should resent what others do to us only if we would fault ourselves for doing the same to them.

Both Butler and Reid point out our tendency to evade acknowledgment of our own wrongdoing through self-deception and our tendency to exaggerate the extent to which others wrong us. Because of these tendencies, they counsel tempering resentment with forgiveness. Reid adds:

> To a man of candour and reflection, consciousness of the frailty of human nature, and that he has often stood in need of forgiveness himself, the pleasure of renewing good understanding after it has been interrupted, the inward approbation of a generous and forgiving disposition, and even the irksomeness and uneasiness of a mind ruffled by resentment, plead strongly against its excesses. . . .
> Every malevolent affection, not only in its faulty excesses, but in its moderate degrees, is vexation and disquiet to the mind, and even gives deformity to the countenance. . . . [It should be considered as] a nauseous medicine, which is never to be taken without necessity; and even then in no greater quantity than the necessity requires. (1788, p. 570)

This is the "man of candour and reflection." Neither Butler nor Reid suggest that we are always capable of such a disposition. We all have moments in which resentment will not loosen its grip, even in the face of considerations that, if we were in a more reasonable frame of mind, should remove or reduce our resentment. Of this Butler says: "In this there is doubtless a great mixture of pride; but there is somewhat more, which I cannot otherwise express than that resentment has taken possession of the temper and of the mind, and will not quit its hold. It would be too minute to inquire whether this be anything more than bare obstinacy: it is sufficient to observe, that it, in a very particular manner and degree, belongs to the abuses of this passion" (1730, p. 132).

We could say that Butler and Reid are recommending that we try to bring sudden resentment more under the control of reason. Deliberate resentment moves us in this direction, but even deliberate resentment needs to be stripped of its distortions and excesses. Moral resentment, however, directs a protest against wrongdoing, a protest registered in behalf of all moral agents, including oneself. This is why Butler and Reid say that, properly regulated by reason, resentment is an expression of good will toward humanity. However, resentment of this sort is possible only for those who have rational capacities employed in the discerning manner described by Butler and Reid.[6]

JUSTIFYING RESENTMENT

Despite their concern to reconcile resentment with good will toward humanity and to disavow any necessary relation to maliciousness, Butler and Reid retain a retributivist perspective. They do not sever resentment's essential connection with the desire for punishment.[7] Nor does Strawson:

> Indignation, disapprobation, like resentment, tend to inhibit or at least to limit our goodwill towards the object of these attitudes, . . . The partial withdrawal of goodwill which these attitudes entail, the modification they entail of the general demand that another should if possible be spared suffering, is . . . the consequence of *continuing* to view him as a member of the moral community: only as one who has offended against its demands. So the preparedness to acquiesce in that infliction of suffering on the offender which is an essential part of punishment is of a piece with this whole range of attitudes. (Strawson 1968, pp. 92-93)

Does this go too far? Recall that Strawson says that not only are these attitudes irremovable, they are also an essential part of our moral response to failures to satisfy reasonable demands.

For Strawson, there is no difference between making moral demands and our disposition to have such attitudes. He says, "The making of the demand *is* the proneness to such attitudes" (1968, p. 93). Our disposition to have these attitudes toward others is essential to regarding them as members of the moral community. However, not everyone accepts this view. Some espouse ideals that refuse to limit good will and that object to the punishment associated with resentment. As Gary Watson puts it, they do this "out of a certain ideal of human relationships, which they see as poisoned by the retributive sentiments" (1988, p. 498). This does not mean that they wholly succeed in dissociating themselves from such sentiments, but the failure to do so is regarded as a moral failure.

With what do they replace retributive sentiments such as resentment? According to Watson, they need not withdraw from contact with others in order to avoid having to confront the wrongdoing of others: "They *stand up* for themselves and others against their oppressors; they *confront* their oppressors with the fact of their misconduct, *urging* and even *demanding* consideration for themselves and others; but they manage, or come much closer than others to managing, to do such things without vindictiveness or malice" (1988, p. 498). Do they do this without *anger*? Anger at wrongdoing need not be associated with either vindictiveness or malice. It need not even be associated with a desire to inflict suffering, at least not suffering beyond that which is essentially involved in the full acknowledgment of wrongdoing. This calls for some explanation.

Strawson links indignation, resentment, and disapproval with the desire to inflict suffering on the wrongdoer. Now it is certainly true that if I express resentment toward someone I want that person to share my judgment. That is, I want that person to agree that his or her attitude or behavior warrants disapproval. This supports Watson's point that reactive attitudes are "incipiently forms of communication, which make sense only on the assumption that the other can comprehend the message" (1988, p. 264). Machines cannot comprehend the message. So, on reflection, our resentment at malfunctioning cars, electric door openers, and refrigerators quickly dissipates—or is redirected at mechanics or at those we think have misused these machines. Very small children may not be able to comprehend the message either, at least not fully. Nor, as I have argued in Chapter 3, can psychopaths comprehend the message *as we intend it*.

How do we intend it? Resentment, as a moral sentiment, expresses serious moral disapproval, criticism, or even condemnation of another's attitude or behavior. What we want, minimally, is for those toward whom our resentment is directed to accept the appropriateness of our attitude. In full measure, this acceptance is expressed through feelings of regret, guilt, remorse, contrition, or shame—perhaps combined with sincere apology or efforts to make amends. This full measure is never forthcoming from psychopaths, despite frequent appearances to the contrary.

However, those from whom the full measure is forthcoming do suffer. Acceptance of the appropriateness of another's resentment can, in this sense, be regarded as a form of (self-imposed) punishment. In this respect, resentment does involve the desire for suffering, but the form of suffering desired is directed toward reconciliation or restoration (Morris 1976). Although such reactive attitudes involve, as Strawson says, a curtailment or withdrawal of good will, this need not be more than temporary. The burden of restoration falls on the wrongdoer—although this may eventually be tempered through forgiveness or mercy by those who have been wronged. None of this need involve malice or vindictiveness. But, of course, it can; and when it does, matters may become much worse. Perhaps some people can stand up for themselves and others, demanding that wrongdoing cease, but not wishing wrongdoers to feel bad for what they have done. Even if they can, it is not clear why this is preferable to moral anger that stops short of sheer malice or vindictiveness.[8]

REID'S REPLY TO HUME

Even if resentment can be defended against its critics in the way I have suggested, there remain some unresolved issues about the relationship between rationality and moral sentiments, so we need to return to Butler, Hume, and Reid. As an admirer of Butler's thought, Hume was likely aware of his views on resentment. Yet he says little about resentment, and what he says about the passions seems contrary to Butler's main thesis about the role of reason in regard to resentment. Why would Butler's views not have led Hume to modify his apparently radical views about reason and morality?

The answer seems to be this. Hume was quite aware that we are tempted to distinguish calm passions from violent passions in terms of the former being "determinations of reason." Of these calm passions (which Reid would call moral sentiments) Hume says:

> Now 'tis certain, there are certain calm desires and tendencies, which, tho' they be real passions, produce little emotion in the mind, and are more known by their effects than by the immediate feeling or sensation. These desires are of two kinds; either certain instincts originally implanted in our natures, such as benevolence and resentment, the love of life, and kindness to children; or the general appetite to good, and aversion to evil, consider'd merely as such. When any of these passions are calm, and cause no disorder in the soul, they are very readily taken for the determinations of reason, and are suppos'd to proceed from the same faculty, with that, which judges of truth and falsehood. Their nature and principles have been suppos'd the same, because their sensations are not evidently different. (1740, p. 416)

Hume thinks that calm passions are confused with determinations of reason because "their sensations are not evidently different." But if the sensations are not evidently different, just how are the passions themselves different, either from one another or from determinations of reason? After all, for Hume, a passion is a kind of sensation, independently of whatever judgments causally associated with it. How do we know, independently of whatever cognitive content we might ascribe to our state of mind, whether the sensation, or feeling-state, is one of resentment, mere anger, gratitude, embarrassment, guilt, or shame?

This problem does not arise for Reid. For example, he can distinguish mere anger or irritation from moral indignation in terms of the attribution of moral fault, blame, or affront present in the latter, but absent from the former. Since Hume excludes judgment from sentiment, and the attribution of fault presupposes judgment, he must differentiate moral indignation from mere anger in terms of some introspectional differences in their respective sensations. But Hume himself admits the difficulty, if not impossibility, of doing this. Attempts by psychologists have been no more successful.[9]

For example, consider shame and guilt. Assuming that there are sensations, or feeling-states, experienced when one feels shame or guilt, how do they differ? One is at a loss to say. Yet the judgments included in each do enable us to distinguish shame from guilt. In general, both are forms of self-appraisal, but the appraisals differ significantly. Shame is more closely associated with the belief that one has failed to be the sort of *person* one aspires to be. Guilt is more closely associated with the failure to *do* what is believed to be right (Lynd 1958; Morris 1976). Thus Reid's criticism of Hume's view of the passions is well placed. The "calm passions" are what Reid calls *sentiments*, and they do include judgment as an essential component.

Now we must ask what implications Reid's correction of Hume has in regard to the relationship between reason and morality. Reid thinks he has established that there are rational principles of action, both of a self- and other-regarding nature. These principles are called rational "because they can have no existence in beings not endowed with reason, and, in all their exertions, require not only intention and will, but judgment and reason" (1788, p. 579). Reid's critique of Hume's account of the passions does establish that there are rational principles of action in this sense. Still, we must ask whether this is all Hume has in mind when he questions the role of reason in practical affairs. As we shall see, the answer is no.

Reid and Hume agree that reason can determine the appropriate means to any end that is desired. But Reid says that Hume's view is that reason cannot determine the ends we should seek: "This, he thinks, is not the office of reason, but of taste or feeling" (1788, p. 580). For Reid, this would mean that reason cannot really be a principle of action. Reid replies that he will try to show that "among the various ends of human actions, there are some, of which, without reason, we could not even form a conception; and that, as soon as they are conceived, a regard to them is, by our constitution, not only a principle of action, but a leading and governing principle, to which all our animal principles are subordinate, and to which they ought to be subject" (1788, p. 580). Reid then argues that only those capable of reason can form a conception of what is good for one on the whole. Therefore, a principle of action in regard to self-interest must be a rational principle. Also, Reid's discussion of the interconnections of moral concepts such as duty, favor, justice, injustice, gratitude, and resentment shows that the idea of duty is possible only for someone with rational capacities (1788, p. 580).

Still, forming the conception of a possible end of action and actually desiring it as an end are, in principle, two different things. Reid does say of the conception of what is good for one on the whole and the conception of our duty that "as soon as they are conceived, a regard to them is, by our constitution, not only a principle of action, but a leading and governing principle." How is this *constitutional* determination to be explained? Is Reid saying that any rational being must be so constituted? So far, he has established just that only a rational being could be so constituted.

Suppose we ask, with Hume, what presuppositions we are making when we claim that it is contrary to reason to prefer the destruction of the world to the scratching of our finger, or to prefer our acknowledged lesser good to our greater good. Among other things, we might cite the value we attach to our health and happiness, not to speak of our continued existence, and at least a modest concern for the well-being of others. Hume regards all of these as ends we value. Although he refuses to say that these ends are commended by reason, he is as firmly and deeply committed to them as anyone. While attempting to dethrone reason, Hume does not think he is in any way undermining values in general, or morality in particular. Instead, he seeks to identify their proper grounding, a grounding deeply rooted in human nature. Rather than commend these ends to us in the name of reason, Hume appeals to "certain instincts originally implanted in our natures, such as benevolence and resentment, the love of life, and kindness to children; or the general appetite to good, and aversion to evil, consider'd merely as such" (1740, p. 417).

However, for Hume, these "natural instincts" and our "general appetite to good and aversion to evil" are not sufficient to generate morality. They are much too particular and partial to qualify as moral sentiments themselves. Hume observes, "Now it appears, that in the original frame of our mind, our strongest attention is confin'd to ourselves; our next is extended to our relations and acquaintance; and 'tis only the weakest which reaches to strangers and indifferent persons" (1740, p. 488). Even our efforts to inject moral considerations often fall short of the mark. Our natural partialities influence our moral ideas in distorting ways, which leads Hume to conclude "that our natural uncultivated ideas of morality, instead of providing a remedy for the partiality of our affections, do rather conform themselves to that partiality, and give it an additional force and influence" (1740, p. 489).

Thus Hume concludes that the full remedy "is not deriv'd from nature, but from *artifice*." He goes on to argue that "from their early education in society" people recognize the advantages of justice. Justice is a convention designed to serve the interests of each of us. As a moral ideal, justice is impartial. Hume insists that it is "only when a character is considered in general, without reference to our particular interest, that it causes such a feeling or sentiment, as denominates it morally good or evil" (1740, p. 472). Finally, since our duties are so vast and varied, our natural instincts need assistance from more general principles. Hume concludes that it is "necessary, therefore, to abridge these primary impulses, and find some more general principles, upon which all our notions of morals are founded" (1740, p. 473).

Reid might ask, how is all of this to be accomplished without the use of reason? Here Hume no doubt would say that reason is required, but as a means to an end. Reid's reply to this is that the ends in question are rational in the sense that only rational agents can understand them and be moved by them. Still, this shows only that morality presupposes rationality, not that rationality requires morality. If an agent is rational, must he or she accept the ends of morality as principles of action? What has Reid to say about this?

Like Hume, Reid agrees that giving reasons for something has to stop somewhere. Reid stops with first principles of action. Examining the status Reid ascribes to them can best be done by considering his response to what he takes to be Hume's argument about the role of reason in practical affairs. Reid summarizes: "(1) There must be ultimate ends of action, beyond which it is absurd to ask a reason of acting; (2) the ultimate ends of human actions can never be accounted for by reason; (3) but recommend themselves entirely to the sentiments and affections of mankind, without any dependence on the intellectual faculties" (1788, p. 678). Reid has no difficulty accepting (1). He accepts (2), however, only after providing some clarification of Hume's meaning.

Hume uses the example of exercise. We can answer the question "Why exercise?" with "To be healthy." Health is desired, in part at least, to avoid the pain and suffering of illness. But Reid quotes Hume, "If you push your inquiries further, and desire a reason why he hates pain, it is impossible he can ever give any. This is an ultimate end, and is never referred to any other object" (1788, p. 678). Reid agrees with Hume on this point. He says, "To account by reason for an end, therefore, is to shew another end, for the sake of which that end is desired and pursued. And that, in this sense, an ultimate end can never be accounted for by reason, is certain, because that cannot be an ultimate end which is pursued only for the sake of another end" (1788, p. 678). Since Reid has already argued that the conception of these ultimate ends presupposes reason, he rejects (3) as not following from (1) and (2).

The rejection of (3) does not by itself challenge Hume's deeper point. Suppose Hume were to concede that the ultimate ends of human action require the use of intellectual faculties. To satisfy Hume on his deeper point it must be shown that there is something about these ends that makes it impossible for a rational being to conceive them but not be moved to desire them.[10] Reid never entertains the possibility that there could be a rational being that can conceive these ends but not desire them. Hume does, in a letter he wrote to Hutcheson:

> I wish from my heart, I could avoid concluding, that since morality, according to your opinion as well as mine, is determined merely by sentiment, it regards only human nature and human life. This has been often urged against you, and the consequences are very momentous. . . . If morality were determined by reason, that is the same to all rational beings: but nothing but experience can assure us, that the sentiments are the same. What experience have we with regard to superior beings? How can we ascribe to them any sentiments at all? They have implanted those sentiments in us for the conduct of life like our bodily sensations, which they possess not themselves.[11]

How much is changed if we substitute Reid's view of the sentiments for Hume's in the above passage? This would mean that, for Hume, morality would be determined by judgments and feelings (Reid's sentiments), not just feelings. Would Reid challenge this? He never questions the view that sentiment is essential to morality. As we have already seen, Reid says that, when properly understood, "Our moral determinations may, with propriety, be called *moral sentiments*. For the word *sentiment*, in the English language, never, as I conceive, signifies mere feeling, but judgment *accompanied with feeling*" (1788, p. 674). Furthermore, Reid acknowledges that rational principles of action require more than simply the forming of judgments. As he puts it, they "can have no existence in beings not endowed with reason, and, in all their exertions, require not only intention and will, but judgment and reason" (1788, p. 579). Finally,

Reid says, "Our moral judgments are not like those we form in specula-tive matters, dry and unaffecting, but, from their nature, are necessarily accompanied with affections and feelings" (1788, p. 592).

Reid assumes we are so constituted that we cannot be indifferent to certain ends once we are able to conceive them. It seems never to have occurred to him that there might be rational beings who are indifferent to them. Hume entertains this possibility and concludes that morality as we understand it is for humans only. Our morality is grounded in our *humanity*, not simply in *reason*.[12]

Although Hume raises the possibility that moral sentiments may mean nothing to rationally "superior beings," he does not see this as loosening the foundation of morality. The moral sentiments are secure "since there never was any nation of the world, nor any single person in any nation, who was utterly depriv'd of them, and who never, in any instance, shew'd the least approbation or dislike of manners. These sentiments are so rooted in our constitution and temper, that without entirely con-founding the human mind by disease or madness, 'tis impossible to ex-tirpate and destroy them" (1740, p. 474). Evidently Hume did not seri-ously entertain the idea that there might be psychopaths of the sort described in the last chapter. Nor did Reid.

How disturbing to their views should the prospect of psychopaths be? Not very, I would say, because both Hume and Reid accept the general framework of moral attitudes on which Strawson relies. Both agree that the viability of society, and tolerable social existence generally, depends on the sorts of participant attitudes to which Strawson refers. However, the extent to which actual societies are viable, and social life is tolerable, is an entirely contingent matter. Hume and Reid optimistically hold that none of us is a through-and-through psychopath. Strawson (1985) does not share this optimism. Still, all three would regard the psychopath as an aberration, as falling outside the general framework. And none seems in the least inclined to modify his views about the content of morality in light of the possibility that some (whether "superior beings" or psycho-paths) lack moral sentiments.

Strawson notes that Reid

> draws an explicit parallel between our natural commitment to belief in external things and our natural proneness to moral or quasi-moral response. He is careful not to suggest that the child in the womb or newly born has such a belief or proneness; at that stage he may

be, as Reid puts it, "merely a sentient being"; but the belief and proneness in question are, he says, *natural* principles, implanted in his constitution, and *activated* when, as he agreeably puts it, the growing child "has occasion for them." Here we see Reid aligning himself with Hume the naturalist against Hume the skeptic. (1985, p. 33)

This passage nicely sums up Reid's views on the natural moral development of children. For whatever reasons, psychopaths are "exceptions to the rule," but this does not make it any less natural that others are attracted to morality.

Strawson's direct comparison of Reid and Hume is worth pursuing. It suggests that they are less far apart than Reid himself thought. Hume and Reid agree on the importance of sentiments for morality. They differ in their analysis of what a sentiment is. This is no small difference, as it does reflect important differences about the role of reason in morality. However, it seems clear that both assume that morality is applicable only to those who are not indifferent to its claims. There is no need for further evidence in Hume's case, but one more passage should remove any doubt about Reid:

> A being endowed with the animal principles of action only, may be capable of being trained to certain purposes by discipline, as we see many brute animals are, but would be altogether incapable of being governed by law.
>
> The subject of law must have the conception of a general rule of conduct, which, without some degree of reason, he cannot have. He must likewise have a sufficient inducement to obey the law, even when his strongest animal desires draw him the contrary way.
>
> This inducement may be a sense of *interest*, or a sense of *duty*, or both concurring.
>
> These are the only principles I am able to conceive, which can reasonably induce a man to regulate all his actions according to a certain general rule or law. They may therefore be justly called the *rational* principles of action, since they can have no place but in a being endowed with reason, and since it is by them only that man is capable of either political or of moral government. (1788, p. 586)

This passage suggests that Reid's and Hume's views are closer than Reid realizes. Furthermore, there are passages in Hume that suggest the differences between Reid and Hume on the role of reason in morality may be less severe than Reid supposes. Consider this one, for example: "Human nature being compos'd of two principal parts, which are requisite in all its actions, the affections and understanding; 'tis certain, that the blind motions of the former, without the direction of the latter, incapacitate men for society: And it may be allow'd us to consider separately the effects, that result from the separate operations of these two component parts of the mind" (1740, p. 496). This sounds very much like something Reid would say, except that he resists the bifurcation of reason and sentiment generally postulated by Hume. Still, Hume's view here does not sound like one that regards reason as "the slave of the passions." Reason here is not portrayed as having blindly to obey its master's every call. Rather, it is passion that is blind and in need of reason's guidance.

Is this simply a glaring inconsistency on Hume's part? Perhaps. A more charitable interpretation is that Hume chose an unfortunate metaphor in referring to reason as the slave of the passions. Hume's main point is that reason without passion (calm or violent) is, practically speaking, inert. Hume's concept of "superior beings" supports this point, as do psychopaths. Nothing that Reid says undermines this.

An advantage of Reid's position is that, in the case of both moral and self-regarding sentiments, reason and feeling are inseparable. One of the virtues of considering Hume and Reid together is that this enables us to see what kinds of presuppositions need to be made about human nature in order for reason to gain a foothold in our practical affairs. It is interesting to note that, despite apparent disagreements, neither Reid nor Hume attempts to demonstrate the rationality of morality independently of these presuppositions.

5

Integrity, Dignity, and Justice

For those who believe in the absolute preciousness of life, there is no proof that the feelings and images involved in such a belief are correct or even plausible. They can only *show* their belief, the way a mother can show how precious her child is to her by rushing without hesitation into a fire to save it. Trocme and the Chambonnais showed the value they put upon human life by four years of deeds.

. . . .

Such a realization, such an imaginative perception of the connection between the preciousness of my life and the preciousness of other lives, is the vital center of life-and-death ethics. If we do not discern that connection, the "laws" of ethics are empty patterns of sounds and shapes, without meaning or force.

—*Philip Hallie*, Lest Innocent Blood Be Shed

I have argued that resentment has a place within a reasonable moral point of view. Although resentment can be disguised as envy, petty vindictiveness, or sheer malice, it need not be. It belongs among those participant attitudes that, for Strawson, are part of the indispensable general framework of moral attitudes. In this chapter I will connect resentment, as well as other attitudes typically associated with one's sense of justice, with one's sense of dignity and regard for the dignity of others. Linking all of these elements together is one's *integrity*, both moral and personal.

As noted earlier, John Rawls holds that a sense of justice is "no mere moral conception formed by the understanding alone, but a true sentiment of the heart enlightened by reason" (1963, p. 281). His point is that a reasonably well-developed sense of justice involves more than an ability to discuss matters of justice in an intelligent manner. There must also be some degree of genuine concern to do what one thinks is just or fair. In cases of acknowledged failure, one has a tendency to feel guilt, re-

morse, or shame. One also has a tendency to feel resentment or indignation at being treated unjustly. And, to at least some extent, one has a tendency to feel indignation or dismay at injustices done by others to
others. Having a sense of dignity involves self-respect, self-esteem,
pride, shame, resentment, and indignation. Neither a sense of justice or
a sense of dignity requires well-worked-out, comprehensive principles
of justice or dignity. Although most people have a sense of justice and a
sense of dignity, few have well-worked-out, comprehensive principles.
Still, our ideas of justice and dignity are clear and substantial enough to
deserve a secure place in any acceptable moral theory.

INTEGRITY AND DIGNITY

Since we seldom think explicitly in terms of human dignity, it may seem
odd to give it much moral weight. Moreover, those most self-consciously
concerned with dignity often seem excessively prideful, self-righteous,
or simply pompous. Insofar as it is associated with deference to those oc-
cupying "dignified" social roles, the notion of human dignity may have
an aura of unattractive stuffiness, and it may be associated with class
consciousness. However, I am not concerned with these senses of "dignity" but with dignity that does not distinguish some people from others. It is something shared by all, regardless of their offices or social
standing.[1] There need be nothing egotistical or stuffy about having a
sense of dignity qualified in this way. No doubt the self-regard of some is
wildly exaggerated, but all that a sense of dignity requires is a minimal
degree of self-respect. This self-respect can be seen in such common-
place attitudes as resentment at being manipulated by others or at having one's rights ignored. It is shown in reluctance to act in ways regarded
as "beneath one's dignity" or in ways that will make one feel shame, as
well as in the pride naturally taken in one's accomplishments. While
these attitudes are common, they are not necessarily experienced self-
consciously. We can feel resentment, shame, or pride without explicitly
spelling out to ourselves how we feel, or why we feel that way. We might
even be surprised to learn that we do resent something, or that we feel
shame or pride about something. The difficulty of articulating what having a sense of dignity amounts to is understandable.

I wish to show that our sense of dignity has a special relationship to
personal integrity. Abraham Edel (1969) suggests that bearing pain with

dignity can be contrasted to reacting with panic. In bearing pain with dignity, one exhibits strength of will, maintaining self-control despite the suffering. In contrast, one who panics has lost self-control; having "fallen apart," one is temporarily not oneself. Panic-stricken, one is rendered vulnerable to external control. Torturing for manipulative purposes exploits such vulnerability.

Since the question of whether one can "hold oneself together" is at stake, the notion of *integrity*, or wholeness, comes into play. Mark Halfron (1989) suggests some difficulties with understanding integrity in terms of wholeness and identifies two. First, the idea of wholeness is not sufficient to clarify the varied uses of "integrity" (Halfron 1989, p. 8). Honesty, sincerity, authenticity, "soundness of principle," and autonomy all lay claim to being forms of integrity. Halfron says it is unlikely that "they all share the common characteristics of wholeness" (1989, p. 8). What this view overlooks, however, is that the honest, sincere, principled, or autonomous *person* has integrity. Honesty is an important element of the wholeness of a person of integrity.[2] Autonomy is also linked to one's wholeness, or integrity. This does not mean that honesty and autonomy themselves "share the common characteristics of wholeness." Rather, they jointly contribute to the integrity, or wholeness, of those who have these attributes.

Of course, what constitutes integrity, or wholeness, varies widely depending on the nature of whatever has integrity. Butler (1730) argues that what is crucial is how the parts or features are related to one another: "Let us instance in a watch—Suppose the several parts of it taken to pieces, and placed apart from each other: let a man have ever so exact a notion of these several parts, unless he considers the respects and relations which they have to each other, he will not have anything like the idea of a watch" (1730, pp. 6-7). What is necessary, Butler says, is that we

form a notion of the relations which those several parts have to each other, shewing the time of day. . . . Thus it is with regard to the inward frame of man. Appetites, passions, affections, and the principle of reflection, considered merely as the several parts of our inward nature, do not at all give us an idea of the system or constitution of this nature; because the constitution is formed by somewhat not yet taken into consideration, namely, by the relations which these several parts have to each other. (1730, pp. 7–8)

For Butler, it is conscience that serves the integrating function, making persons whole. Despite his theologically grounded view of nature as teleological, Butler is well aware that there are serious obstacles in the way of achieving this integrity. Narrow pursuit of self-interest is not the only obstacle. Butler points out that our passions often tempt us to act contrary to self-interest. In fact, he bemoans our neglect of genuine self-love as much as that of conscience. However, it is the function of conscience to bring everything (including self-love) together in due proportion. Whether we realize it or not, "in reality the very constitution of our nature requires, that we bring our whole conduct before this superior faculty; wait its determination; enforce upon ourselves its authority, and make it the business of our lives, as it is absolutely the whole business of a moral agent, to conform ourselves to it. This is the true meaning of that ancient precept, *Reverence thyself*" (1730, p. 9).

This is indeed a tall order. To many modern ears it may seem excessive. This leads to Halfron's second difficulty with thinking of integrity in terms of wholeness. There seem to be several different kinds of personal integrity—for example, intellectual integrity, religious integrity, professional integrity, and moral integrity. To this list we can add Bernard Williams's (1973) notion of personal projects and commitments that give our lives meaning and purpose. How do these different kinds of integrity relate to one another? Insofar as they constitute deep divisions within a given individual, they seem clearly to disrupt the overall integrity of the person. Such division is a serious problem for those who find their role-responsibilities as professionals conflicting with their conceptions of themselves as morally responsible individuals in their nonprofessional roles (Postema 1983). Trying to fit the various kinds of integrity together in a single individual is a formidable challenge. The extent to which this attempt fails is a good measure of the difficulties in living a fully integrated life—and of the difficulties in achieving wholeness.

Many may reject Butler's demand that conscience reign supreme, and they may be willing to settle for integrity *with respect to* this or that: honesty in private life, steady adherence to professional standards, unyielding religious commitment, or whatever. Whether this results in serious internal conflict is another matter. If it does, there is a problem of integrity, or wholeness, in need of resolution. If it does not, such persons will lead what, from their perspectives at least, are reasonably well-integrated lives.

These are complex issues which will surface in various forms in later chapters. At this point, however, it is important to focus on connections between integrity and dignity at a level that seems to cut across distinctions among persons. We need to return to Edel's example of how we respond to torture. Just how are integrity and dignity related here? This can be seen by considering shame. Those who panic or give in to torture often feel shame at their failure to retain composure because, rightly or wrongly, they feel they have behaved in an unworthy, or undignified, manner. As Helen Merrell Lynd (1958) points out, typically we feel shame because we think we have failed to be the kind of person we thought we were or should be. If we feel we should be able to remain composed under stress, it is understandable that panic could make us feel shame. If deeply felt, this shame may result in lowered self-esteem, a feeling that we have lowered or even lost our dignity.

When we speak of breaking down or losing self-control in ways that threaten our sense of dignity, what seems to be at stake is our ability to maintain integrity. Edel's example of "falling apart" under threat of severe pain or torture suggests that the idea of violence may be importantly related to integrity, or wholeness. This suggestion is usefully explored in Newton Garver's provocative essay, "What Violence Is" (1970). Garver's aim is to broaden and deepen our understanding of violence. He argues that, in addition to overt, physical violence, there is also psychological violence; and violence can be done to us by physical, psychological, and even institutional means.[3]

Garver begins his analysis with the etymological observation that "violence" and "violation" both come from the Latin root "*violens*," which has the sense, "to carry force at or toward." This, Garver says, "suggests to us the interesting idea that violence is somehow a violation of something: that carrying force against something constitutes in one way or another a violation of it" (1970, p. 353). But it seems that he cannot fully accept this suggestion, since he goes on to say: "The idea of violence in human affairs is much more closely connected with the idea of violation than it is with the idea of force" (1970, p. 355). Garver does not explain just how he might distinguish the ideas of violation and force. Instead, he simply contrasts violence in nature (as force) to violence in human affairs (as violation of persons).

Outside of human affairs, Garver says, "violence" often is synonymous with "force." For example, a violent storm is simply a storm with very great force. Garver offers several examples to show that this equation will not work in human affairs: "It is clear that force is often used on another person's body and there is no violence done. For example, if a man is drowning—thrashing around and is apparently unable to save himself—and you use the standard Red Cross life-saving techniques, you will use force against his body although certainly you won't be doing any violence to him. . . . Similarly, surgeons and dentists use force on our bodies without doing violence to us" (1970, p. 355). These are legitimate exceptions to the equation of "violence" and "force," but Garver fails to note that there are exceptions outside of human affairs as well. For example, a bird uses force on a dead twig when removing it from one location to build a nest, but there is no violence done to the twig. We do unhesitatingly characterize storms as violent because of their great force on the grounds of the *destructive* potential of that great force.

Comparing the bird's forceful removal of the twig with Garver's examples, we find a common element. The bird does no violence to the twig because the bird has not caused damage, harm, or destruction. In Garver's examples, no violence is done to persons because they have suffered no damage, harm, or destruction.[4] So neither in nature nor human affairs is a simple equation of violence and force plausible. Since Garver wants to distinguish violence done to persons from violence in nature by invoking the notion of violating persons, he must talk about more than the damage, harm, or destruction common to both. He does this, but only sketchily, and I will try to fill in some of the gaps.

If violence done to something implies that damage, harm, or destruction has occurred, then that to which violence is done must initially have some kind of integrity, or wholeness, rendering it vulnerable.[5] This seems reasonably clear and unproblematic in the realm of inanimate objects. For example, if someone smashes a stone, violence is done to it; its integrity is forcibly destroyed. But if someone vigorously polishes off its rough surface, its integrity is left intact. Thus the integrity, or wholeness, of an object is not simply the sum of whatever qualities it happens to have at a given moment; some of its qualities are more essential to its integrity than others.

Living matter poses a greater challenge. The identity of inanimate objects remains relatively fixed, but living matter is understood partly in terms of its growth and development. Forceful intervention in the potential for growth and development of a living organism could constitute violence done to it. A storm might do violence to a building by shattering its windows, but it can do violence to a plant simply by exposing its roots.

Still, as long as we concentrate on the potential for physical growth alone, matters remain relatively unproblematic, even when considering nonhuman animals. Yet if we consider their sentient qualities, the identification of violence done can be more difficult, and not solely because the violence done might be less visible or harder to detect. There may also be considerable disagreement about what is harmful to animals. For example, is conditioning rats by means of electric shocks harmful to them? What about prefrontal lobotomies? In the case of lobotomies, there is a concern not only for the physical health of an animal, but also for the kind of life it will have after a portion of its brain is removed. At some point in animal experimentation questions like these are bound to become controversial.

The problems are even more difficult when we turn to human beings and see the many ways in which integrity comes into play. In each instance the kind of integrity in question is constituted by an integration of otherwise diverse elements into a somewhat coherent whole. At the level of human behavior, there is the coordination of muscles, bones, and the organs of touch, sound, and sight enabling us to move about, communicate, play, and work. The complexity of behavior can range from relatively simple activities such as walking and talking to such sophisticated activities as making and executing intricate plans. As we move from childhood to adulthood, we typically acquire greater ability and desire to assume control over the course of our lives. This movement toward greater autonomy requires increasing ability to adapt to our natural and social environment. Essential to this is self-consciousness, a source of a form of rationality that, as Errol Harris puts it, provides us with "the power of self-objectification and self-organization, which does not simply abstract from feeling but which informs, refines and resolves the conflicts within feeling, which transforms man from a mere appetitive animal to a person" (1966, p. 123).

Self-consciousness is a special attribute of human beings. It enables us to ask questions about our humanity. The question of what it is to be human is as much about what is worthy of human aspiration as it is about biological identity. Any attempt to characterize the nature of human beings beyond a merely biological description invites normative disagreement. Yet there is evidence that the question of what is worthy of human aspiration is a fundamental human concern; consider our liability to experience shame when we feel we have fallen woefully short of such ideals. Of course, our liability to shame is also linked to aspirations and ideals that may be more particularly one's own, or which may be shared only with more specific groups or communities of persons. In either case, what suffers is one's self-respect or self-esteem.[6]

It might seem odd to focus on something as negative as shame in considering what is distinctive of our humanity. Some may wish to bury shame alongside original sin so that we can get on to better things. However, it seems that John Rawls is right in saying, "since being moved by ends and ideals of excellence implies a liability to humiliation and shame, and an absence of liability to humiliation and shame implies a lack of such ideals, one can say of shame and humiliation also that they are part of the notion of humanity" (1971, p. 489).

It is important to note that being self-conscious is not merely witnessing, or observing, what one is or does. Rather, it is, to an important degree, determining what one is and can be. We not only have desires and aims; we also reflect on them. Further, we can assess how well we are living up to our expectations. As Karl Marx says, "The animal is immediately one with its life activity. It does not distinguish itself from it. *It is its life activity.* Man makes his life activity itself the object of his will and his consciousness" (1844, pp. 274–75). For Marx, it is this ability that makes it possible for us, unlike nonhuman animals, to become alienated—from our labor, from ourselves, and from our fellow humans. Nevertheless, we are not necessarily fully and explicitly aware of our self-assessments. For example, it is quite possible to experience shame without fully recognizing it as such. Shame, involving lowered self-esteem, can be so painful that we often go through a variety of self-deceptive maneuvers to avoid fully facing it (Lynd 1958; Fingarette 1969). Pride, too, is often not an object of full and explicit awareness. When it is, it frequently is exaggerated self-respect or self-esteem.

We need to distinguish self-regard as a form of self-consciousness from self-consciousness about our self-regard. This distinction is analogous to what can be said about self-confidence. If a self-confident athlete begins to focus attention on her self-confidence, attention is deflected from its original object (the game), resulting in diminished performance and lessened self-confidence. Self-confidence returns only after she redirects her attention to the game. Analogously, self-regard can become vanity, arrogance, pomposity, or excessive self-righteousness. It is important that in our concern to maintain self-respect or self-esteem we not confuse either with self-congratulatory distortions of them.

Despite these possible distortions, the value of self-respect and self-esteem must be stressed. Rawls characterizes self-respect as including our sense of our own value and confidence in our ability to fulfill our intentions.[7] He concludes, "It is clear then why self-respect is a primary good. Without it nothing may seem worth doing, or if some things have value for us, we lack the will to strive for them. All desire and activity becomes empty and vain, and we sink into apathy and cynicism" (1971, p. 490). This perception seems to be shared by oppressed minorities attempting to encourage pride in their children. The effort is not merely an attempt to eliminate the shame a child might experience for seeming to lack what others have. The experience of shame is a diminishment of self-respect or self-esteem, implying their prior existence. But children are not born with self-respect or self-esteem; these traits must be encouraged and developed. Thus a critical task is to encourage enough self-respect and self-esteem in children that they will not actually regard themselves as inferior to others.

Given this view of the importance of self-respect and self-esteem, Garver can be seen to be right in emphasizing the importance of autonomy as well as bodily integrity when talking about violating persons. He emphasizes the capacity to make and carry out decisions, which initially requires encouraging the development of this capacity in children. It also requires opportunities to exercise this capacity once it is developed. If we regard autonomy, in this sense, as an essential aspect of the integrity, or wholeness, of persons, it is easy to see why Garver would say that attacks on autonomy can violate persons. However, Garver's exclusive concern with bodily integrity and autonomy as making and carrying out decisions may mislead. His account may seem too individualistic, viewing persons "atomistically," as isolable, independent units.[8] This view is neither explicitly held nor rejected by Garver, but it is important to consider whether his account nevertheless commits him to such a view of persons because it does not seem plausible to restrict the notion of violating persons to the kinds of examples he offers.

To see this, consider again the central role Rawls attaches to self-respect and self-esteem. If self-respect and self-esteem are essential to the maintenance of the integrity of persons, then autonomy is only one aspect of that integrity. Rawls also emphasizes the importance of having positive relationships with others: being accepted and encouraged by others; being loved by others (such as parents); and developing bonds of friendship. In fact, each of these relationships is seen by Rawls to play an essential role in encouraging the development of that degree of self-confidence necessary for effective autonomous functioning. Thus, instead of viewing autonomy in highly individualistic terms, we could view it as fitting within a framework of social interdependence.[9]

This social interdependence is as much a feature of the identity (or integrity) of persons as their bodies and their autonomy. Thus, a radical alteration of one's social relationships can profoundly affect a person, even to the point of leaving the person feeling "shattered" or "broken." A betrayal of trust could be as damaging as a physical beating in some instances. Beyond attacks on a person's body or autonomy, his or her integrity can be attacked by deliberately undermining trust and friendship. Destroying a friendship is not only, if at all, attacking autonomy; for the relationship of friendship is more than mutual respect for autonomy. Broadening our understanding of the integrity, or wholeness, of persons beyond Garver's examples should also broaden our understanding of how persons can be violated. But, so far, no explanation of what it means for a person to be violated has been given. This will now be considered.

VIOLATING PERSONS

Although Garver notes that "violence" and "violate" have the same etymological root, he restricts "violate" to human affairs. He offers no reason for this restriction, but the most plausible basis seems to be the social implications of "violate." Consider a sampling of the kinds of things we say can be violated: laws, religious practices, places of worship, flags, language, rules of etiquette, rights. In each instance there is a normative element, suggesting that to violate something is to go against some norm or rule. Further, a lack of respect is shown for that which is violated. Nothing like this is suggested by the violence of a storm, and for good reason. Although a storm can be an agent of destruction, it cannot be an agent of impropriety.

The notion of violation, then, presupposes a context in which there are agents capable of appreciating the nature of their acts. Neither nonhuman animals nor very small children can violate the law, even though either might do something which, if done by an adult, would be a violation of the law. Thus, although a storm, an animal, or a very small child is capable of doing violence to a person, it does not follow that a person is violated. (There must be at least this much qualification of Garver's claim that violence in human affairs is the violation of persons.) In contrast to talk about violence in general, then, to say that someone or something has been violated is to say as much about the agent of the violation as its victim, or the prevalent social norms.

Garver might well accept such an analysis of "violation," but he remains silent on this point. Instead, he talks about presuppositions of the idea that persons can be violated, invoking the idea of natural rights:

> If it makes sense to talk about violating a person, that just is because a person has certain rights which are undeniably, indissolubly, connected with his being a person. . . . One of the most fundamental rights a person has is a right to his body—to determine what his body does and what is done to his body—because without his body he wouldn't be a person anymore. . . . Apart from a body what is essential to one's being a person is dignity in something like the existentialist sense. The dignity of a person does not consist in his remaining prim and proper or dignified and unruffled, but rather in his making his own decisions. (1970, p. 355)

These rights Garver refers to as "the right to one's body and the right to autonomy" (1970, p. 356). Thus, Garver's view is that to violate a person is to violate one or more of these fundamental rights.

It should be emphasized that Garver is not saying that the violation of just any rights constitutes a violation of persons. The rights he is talking about are only those that are "undeniably, indissolubly, connected with his being a person," which leaves us with a question. If some of a person's rights can be violated without the person being violated, evidently there must be something special about persons themselves that makes the violation of certain rights a violation of persons. What Garver needs to explain, but only hints at, is why we should not say simply that a person's rights are violated, rather than that a person is violated as well. His reference to existential dignity is the hint. If that which is violated is thought of as demanding respect, then a lack of respect for the dignity of persons can be thought of as a violation of persons.

This means that, rather than directly appeal to natural rights to explain how persons can be violated, Garver should first explain what it is about persons that warrants the kind of respect demanded by those rights. The argument for those rights could then go like this: Since persons have dignity, they are worthy of respect. One way of according them this respect is to acknowledge (in word and deed) that they have certain fundamental rights. So, rather than explain the violation of persons in terms of natural rights, Garver should show that the latter notion would be derivative from the former.[10]

The question still remains of how these notions of dignity and violation of persons are related to integrity. Consider the various images suggested by the notion of the violation of the human body, as in physical torture or assault—images of the body being broken down, divided, torn apart, left asunder, dismembered, shattered, made un-whole, or disintegrated. In short, we think of a variety of possible ways in which the integrity of the body is attacked. Again, consider what it is to bear pain with dignity. One remains relatively composed, not "breaking up" or "falling apart." Torture exploits our vulnerabilities here. Even the threat of physical torture can attack the integrity, or wholeness, of a person. The prospect of such torture can be so terrifying that one will "break down" and be willing to do whatever one's tormentors demand. There is a loss of autonomy in that one no longer has self-control. One is likely to feel degraded. In turn, this may evoke both shame at giving in and resentment at the tormentors for causing one to be shamed or humiliated. These attitudes, related as they are to one's self-respect and self-esteem, are manifestations of one's sense of dignity.

Since self-respect and self-esteem are central to one's sense of dignity, it is evident why it is appropriate to connect the notions of dignity and violation when talking about persons. Both are related to the integrity of persons, dignity supporting it, violation attacking it, which helps explain why we *resent* as well as fear being violated by others. The most obvious forms of violation are instances of physical violence, but Garver is right in suggesting that the violation of persons is not confined to such violence. He offers examples of psychological and institutional means of violating the autonomy of persons as well. Furthermore, as Rawls points out, to maintain a sense of dignity (self-respect and self-esteem), it is important to develop positive social relationships (such as mutual trust and acceptance, friendship, and love). This adds more dimensions to Garver's notion of dignity, as well as more possible ways of violating persons.

PERSONAL AND MORAL INTEGRITY

So far the emphasis has been mainly on possible violations of our integrity; Here we see persons as potential victims. If we focus more positively on how integrity is related to us as agents, other considerations arise. Lynne McFall (1987, p. 9) suggests that personal integrity requires us to have a consistent set of principles or commitments that we uphold in the face of temptation or challenge, and for what we take to be the right reasons. Acknowledging that someone has personal integrity does not require us to approve of that person's principles or commitments. McFall emphasizes that not just any principles or commitments will do. We recognize them to be "ones that a reasonable person might take to be of great importance and ones that a reasonable person might be tempted to sacrifice to some lesser yet still recognizable goods" (1987, p. 11). This rules out, she says, the shallowness of those obsessed with pleasure seeking, the artificiality of mere approval seekers, and the expediency of those dominated by profit-seeking motives.

We can see from this that the concept of personal integrity is not value-neutral. It reflects our own views of what might reasonably be regarded as important. Furthermore, ideas about personal integrity are typically related to moral integrity. Moral integrity requires a somewhat unified moral stance (without implying a well-worked-out, comprehensive moral theory). Those with moral integrity can be expected to refuse to compromise their moral standards for the sake of personal expediency. This does not mean that one refuses *for the sake of* one's moral integrity. However, one's refusal *expresses* this integrity if one is acting *from* the principles or commitments that constitute one's integrity.[11]

As Bernard Williams (1981) points out, self-consciously focusing on one's integrity can be corrupting. Gabrielle Taylor (1985) maintains that integrity is a higher-order virtue, requiring that we care about something other than our own integrity. As McFall puts it: "If integrity is a moral virtue, then it is a special sort of virtue. One cannot be solely concerned with one's own integrity, or there would be no object for one's concern. Thus, integrity seems to be a higher-order virtue. To have moral integrity, then, it is natural to suppose that one must have some lower-order moral commitments; that moral integrity adds a moral requirement to personal integrity" (1987, p. 14).

There are many ways in which we can to some extent fall short of moral integrity.[12] There is conscious hypocrisy, the knowing maintenance of double standards. There is also self-deception, a refusal to acknowledge to ourselves that we have certain concerns in basic conflict with one another. According to Herbert Fingarette (1969), this refusal is a device to protect what we take to be our integrity, even though such a refusal actually results in what is in some sense a "divided self."[13]

A third and less common way of falling short of moral integrity is seen in psychopaths, who lack moral integrity because they lack moral concern entirely, having no guilt feelings, remorse, or concern for doing anything other than what they have an impulse to do. Having no enduring moral aims or ideals, psychopaths seem unable to feel shame. It is not clear what it would mean for them to act in ways they regard as "beneath their dignity," not because they have a particularly low regard for their own worth (perhaps thinking themselves inferior to others), but because they seem simply not to regard themselves in terms of any kind of dignity at all. The notion of self-respect seems totally out of place. In addition to having no sense of their own dignity, they seem to have no regard for the dignity of others, as is shown in their lack of enduring concern for others and the failure to have any genuine feelings of guilt or remorse for the ways in which they treat others.

It should also be noted that clinical descriptions of psychopaths suggest that they experience time quite differently from most people. They frequently describe their own past as if it were someone else's, using third person references to themselves as "he" or "she." The future also seems to be viewed in a similarly detached manner. Thus, psychopaths seem to lack what John Kekes (1983) calls *identity conferring* commitments—commitments that project one into the future and that take one's past seriously.

From these remarks about integrity we can go on to make two claims of importance about connections between the notions of integrity and dignity. First, the various forms of personal integrity are to a large extent human achievements rather than things that merely happen to us. This is clear in the case of being able to coordinate one's goals and activities in leading a relatively satisfying life; but it is no less true of learning to walk and talk, activities we normally take for granted. This claim does not negate the factor of luck. Williams (1981) and Nagel (1979) are right to point out how much in our lives is a matter of (good or bad) luck, which does not deny the importance of achievement but simply denies that achievement is the whole story.

Our achievements often give us a sense of accomplishment, enhancing self-esteem, but equally if not more important, failure can result in loss of self-esteem. Thus slow readers may feel inferior to classmates not just in reading but as human beings. This feeling of inferiority may be intensified by criticism or ridicule. Essential to a well-developed sense of dignity is learning to accept one's shortcomings without feeling that they render one less than fully human. Unfortunately, this is sometimes difficult in a society that seems often to measure human worth in terms of competitive success and physical appearance.

The second claim about the connections between integrity and dignity is that these forms of integrity all involve some degree of autonomy, or self-regulation. The connection between autonomy and dignity is shown in the resentment often felt when we believe our autonomy is being unjustifiably interfered with. It is also shown in the shame one feels when failing to maintain autonomy under pressure, as in the case of torture.

A passage from Bernard Malamud's *The Fixer* (1966) graphically illustrates the connections between dignity, integrity, autonomy, shame, and resentment, or indignation. Yakov Bok, the fixer, is imprisoned on the pretext that he has killed a boy. Knowing that the government simply wants a Jew as a political scapegoat, the fixer steadfastly refuses to give in to his tormentors. He is regularly required to submit to searches of his entire body while stripped to only his undershirt. There is a seemingly insignificant alteration in the final search:

"Take off that stinking undershirt," ordered the Deputy Warden.
I must calm my anger, thought the fixer, seeing the world black. Instead his anger grew.
"Why should I?" he shouted. "I have never taken it off before. Why should I take it off now? Why do you insult me?" (1966, p. 325)

Despite the humiliating nature of the preceding searches, the fixer had been able to retain his sense of dignity. Why should removal of his undershirt be connected with his sense of dignity? One possible explanation is that the undershirt had been something he could count on, a partial protection or covering. Not all of him had been exposed. The sudden change threatened his physical covering and the psychological protection it provided. As Lynd points out, nakedness as total exposure to others, when sudden or unexpected, can make one feel weak or vulnerable (1958, Ch. 2). Those so affected by exposure often feel shame. Fearing shame and realizing that this is just what his tormentors wanted, the fixer indignantly resists. As an expression of his sense of dignity, this indignation was his refusal to accept degradation. With respect to what his tormentor most wanted from him, total submission, the fixer remained autonomous; having "held himself together," the fixer retained his psychological integrity.

As Butler and Reid point out, resentment, as a *morally* reactive attitude, must be distinguished from such reactive attitudes as mere anger, frustration, or annoyance.[14] They emphasize that only beings with a fair degree of rationality are capable of feeling such resentment, whereas even lower-order animals can be angry, frustrated, or annoyed. "Deliberate" resentment is directed against only what are believed to be moral wrongs or injuries, but the other attitudes are not similarly restricted.

It is clear that we can be angry either with ourselves or with others. However, although we can resent how we are treated by others, we cannot resent our own behavior. It might seem that Butler's and Reid's account of resentment explains this. If we hold that we cannot morally wrong ourselves, then their account of resentment in terms of moral wrongs or injuries would explain why we cannot resent our own behavior. But since anger need not be a morally reactive attitude, there is no reason why we cannot be angry with ourselves. But this explanation will not do. Fortunately, it is not necessary to resolve the issue of whether we can morally wrong ourselves to see that this is so.[15] Even if it can be shown that we can morally wrong ourselves, this does not in the least show that we can resent wrongs done to ourselves. We might feel regret, remorse, guilt, or shame, but not resentment.

How, then, is the difference between anger and resentment to be explained? My suggestion is that the resentment a person feels reflects some degree of self-esteem or self-respect. This is shown in the resentment we feel when we think we are merely being used by others, or when we feel we are being treated with disrespect. Threats to the various forms of integrity often arouse resentment because we feel that we have a right to have them respected. Thus, as a morally reactive attitude, resentment is an expression of one's sense of dignity. So we can see why this kind of resentment is thought of as *indignation*. This account of the difference between anger and resentment also sheds light on why the fixer might have felt shame if he had given in to his tormentors. His resentment is a reaction to their attempt to undermine his sense of dignity. Had he given in, the fixer might have felt at least partially responsible for his own degradation in that he could have resisted longer. Harsh as this self-reproach seems, it clearly could elicit a feeling of shame. What this means is that our sense of dignity is central to both resentment and shame. Both are reactions to what we take to be attacks upon or affronts to one's dignity, the former coming from without, the latter from within.

Human dignity is typically characterized as a kind of worthiness of respect. What can this mean? Herbert Spiegelberg suggests that respecting something requires standing back from it with an attitude of noninterference (1971, p. 58). He refers to respect for human dignity as "personal respect." Persons have intrinsic worth, but some of this (natural beauty, for example) has nothing to do with human dignity. He adds, "Only certain kinds of intrinsic values qualify for the kind of dignity which is answered by personal respect. . . . I submit that respect in this sense depends on the fact that the value is to some extent under control of the worthy person. . . . Human dignity is the kind of intrinsic worth which attaches to a human being in his capacity of being a responsible person" (1971, p. 59).

Spiegelberg's appeal to responsible agency and "value [that] is to some extent under control of the worthy person" parallels the view that various forms of integrity are to some extent human achievements rather than things that merely happen to us. This suggests that, for Spiegelberg, responsibility, dignity, and integrity are interrelated. Further evidence of this is that, after providing a list of possible indignities a person might suffer, he concludes that "the revolting thing about it is not only the physical happenings but the attempt to break down the personalities of the victims and deprive them not only of the respect of others but of self-respect" (1971, p. 60).

DIGNITY AND JUSTICE

At this point, the notions of dignity and justice can be brought into relationship with each other. There are some people, unlike the fixer, who in varying degrees have had their spirits broken and consequently have been unable to maintain a robust sense of dignity. To take an extreme example, enslavement has often resulted in slaves regarding themselves as inferior to their masters and to free persons. Being owned and forced to work by another, even when tempered with kindness from the master, can make it difficult to maintain a steady regard for oneself as the equal of one's master and free persons. This is especially evident in the case of those born into slavery. The difficulty can only be compounded for those forced to perform menial tasks, eat in back rooms, or not enter front doors.

Such feelings of inferiority can have a serious effect on one's sense of justice. Consider, first, those slaves who do retain a sense of themselves as the moral equals of masters and free persons. We would expect them to be especially sensitive to the injustice of enslavement and to feel the appropriate resentment. In contrast, slaves who actually regard themselves as inferior to their masters might well be less sensitive to these injustices. We can imagine them resenting excessive whipping, but accepting their lack of freedom as just. Rather than feeling resentment for having to enter the back door, they might well regard this as fitting for those of their "standing." On being criticized for entering the front door, slaves who resent their enslavement and those who do not might react very differently. Those in the first group might feel shame at their impotence to escape the humiliation and degradation to which their masters continually subject them. Such shame might be accompanied by resentment against their masters for making them feel this way. The second group might feel shame at having initially regarded themselves as worthy of entering the front door. We would not expect any accompanying resentment.

Slavery is one of the more blatant forms of oppression that seriously threatens self-respect and self-esteem. Of course, racist and sexist practices, however subtle, pose a similar threat. The need to make special efforts to instill pride in children in oppressed minority groups is ample evidence of the debilitating effects of that oppression. Insofar as having self-respect and self-esteem is necessary for being able to recognize that one is a victim of injustice, it is clear why leaders of the oppressed stress the importance of having a sense of dignity.

When we shift our focus from the reactions of victims of injustice to agents of injustice, the notion of dignity is no less relevant. Given opportunities to gain at the expense of injustice to others, those with a sense of justice may regard resorting to such means as beneath their dignity. Those who realize they have already acted in this way may feel shame, or unworthiness. Socrates's refusal to escape his death sentence seems to have been based on a concern not to act beneath his dignity. He refused on the ground that he would be committing an injustice against the state that had nurtured him; to escape, he thought, would be a violation of all that he had stood for. This is not merely a concern to be consistent—although it is that. It is Socrates's concern not to violate his integrity.

The question of one's dignity can arise even when one is not responsible for injustices done to others. Again this is illustrated by the fixer: "Overnight a madman is born who thinks Jewish blood is water. Overnight life becomes worthless. . . . So what can Yakov Bok do about it? All he can do is not make things worse. He's half a Jew himself, yet enough of one to protect them. . . . He will protect them to the extent that he can. This is his covenant with himself. If God's not a man he has to be. Therefore he must endure to the trial and let them confirm his innocence by their lies" (1966, p. 274). Here the fixer's moral integrity is at stake. In his eyes, not to resist amounts to moral complicity with his oppressors. The fixer's sense of his own dignity is intimately related to his respect for the dignity of others. His sense of his own worth, as reflected in his moral integrity, demands that he stand up for the dignity of others.

There are many other ways those with a sense of justice can show regard for the dignity of others. The genuine conviction that others are entitled to fair treatment in itself shows regard for their dignity, or worthiness of respect. Taking positive steps to promote justice for others, or to prevent injustice, can indicate respect for their dignity. Also, regard for the dignity of others is shown in the tendencies to make amends, feel apologetic, guilty, or remorseful when we think we have treated others unjustly. Finally, indignation at others' injustices to those other than ourselves shows regard for the dignity of the victims.

The kind of respect referred to here should not be confused with such attitudes as respect for another's beliefs or social standing. It is not necessary that those whose dignity we respect be thought of as having especially worthwhile opinions, or as people to whom we might turn for inspiration or guidance. Edmund Cahn provides an example showing that even contempt for another is compatible with having respect for his dignity: "The defendant is convicted of treasonable utterances by which he successfully sought to impair the morale and obedience of combat soldiers in time of war. The sentence of the court is that he be compelled to submit to a surgical operation on his vocal cords, so that thereafter he may only bark like a dog. This affronts the sense of injustice" (1962, p. 17). No doubt there are some to whom this sentence seems just. However, there are many who, while regarding the defendant's behavior contemptible, agree with Cahn. Their objection is not merely that the punishment is too *cruel*, a notion applicable to dogs as well as humans; it is too *degrading*.

The connection between justice and dignity can be further illuminated by considering the familiar and seemingly unchallengeable maxim of justice, "Treat equals equally." What is so special about persons that such a maxim applies to them? After all, if we have two identical machines, we may treat them as unequally as we like. An obvious reply is that the maxim applies only to persons, not things, but this is question-begging unless there are some relevant differences between persons and things. Though there are innumerable differences between persons and machines, there is one important similarity: both can be treated merely as means to some end. Why, a skeptic might ask, should we take seriously the idea of fair wages for a day's work? Machines, too, work very hard, but the notion of fair wages obviously does not apply to them.

Is it that persons, unlike machines, complain of being underpaid? Employers who pay "fair wages" only to keep employees from complaining do not show a direct concern for justice. Besides, workers might not complain when they should, or they might complain when they should not. What must be acknowledged is the justice or injustice of the complaints, not merely that they must be taken into account if there is to be "business as usual." Why should such an acknowledgment be made?

Is it that persons, unlike machines, have certain basic rights? This may be so, but what makes it so? As long as employers regard their employees only as rather complicated means to their ends, it will seem perfectly arbitrary to insist that persons, but not machines, have such rights. Employers can acknowledge and satisfy the needs of machines for lubrication, electricity, and general upkeep without invoking any notion of justice. Persons may sometimes exhibit a peculiar kind of resistance, but employers can acknowledge and satisfy their needs for food, clothing, shelter, and work incentives without invoking any notion of justice. The demand for equality can be regarded as simply a species of envy, and employers can try to calculate how close they need to come to equal treatment in order to keep the envy compatible with efficient operation. Employers might even think that envy can provide incentives for greater productivity. Those who are envied may strive to sustain their advantage; the envious may strive to catch up. How just, or fair, a reward scheme would have to be for employers to exploit these possibilities is entirely contingent. It is not at all obvious that only a just, or fair, scheme will work.

That recognition of human dignity is what is missing is evidenced by the indignation typically felt by those who believe they are being regarded in unjust ways. If we think of ourselves as having only instrumental value, we will not feel such indignation, although we might feel anger, frustration, or irritation. Thus, it is our sense of dignity, or intrinsic worth, that is the basis of our moral demand for just treatment. Of course, if there are legal provisions for just treatment, we may simply make legal demands (for example, in regard to affirmative action or equal employment opportunities). But if these legal demands have a moral basis as well, acknowledgment of human dignity must be made. If it is not, although we could still avail ourselves of the law, it is not clear how we could argue for either the justice or injustice of any actual or possible legal provisions.

GROUNDING DIGNITY

Even if it is conceded that having a sense of justice involves having a sense of dignity, we might still wish to know what relevance, if any, having a sense of dignity has to actually having dignity. John Rawls makes a very strong claim in this regard: "One may hold that the sense of justice is a necessary part of the dignity of the person, and that it is this dignity which puts a value upon the person distinct from and logically prior to his capacity for enjoyment and his ability to contribute to the enjoyment of others through the development of his talents" (1963, p. 303). Rawls does not explain why having a sense of justice is a necessary part of having dignity, but he may have something like this in mind. Those with a sense of justice are to some extent willing to view their practical problems from a standpoint that can be shared by others, in that they take into consideration the interests of others as well as their own. Insofar as they are willing to show others the respect they want others to reciprocate, they have moral worth, or dignity. Their stance, we might say, is a mark of their moral integrity and thereby entitles them to respect from others.

The problem with this view is that it requires persons actually to have a sense of justice in order to be viewed as having dignity. The most it seems reasonable to require is a capacity for developing a sense of justice. One reason for saying this is that those who are treated as if they do not have dignity prior to their having a sense of justice are perfectly warranted in complaining later that they were treated unjustly. It hardly seems reasonable to hold that one is justified in treating children as if they have no dignity simply because they have not yet developed a sense of justice. Further, given the potentialities of very young children, they certainly are capable of suffering degradation even though lacking a sense of justice. Finally, treating very young children as if they have dignity prior to their actually having a sense of justice may be essential to developing that sense. Not being so treated can block the development of self-respect, which in turn can interfere with coming to have respect for others. I am not claiming that full-blown self-respect develops before one has a sense of justice at all. In fact, self-respect and one's sense of justice are mutually reinforcing. Furthermore, elements of a sense of justice show up very early in childhood. Still, it seems important to treat children with respect before their sense of justice has had time to take much shape.

Rawls's view could be revised to meet these objections by saying simply that having the capacity for a sense of justice is a necessary part of the dignity of the person. This is a reasonable modification. However, I prefer a broader ground for attributing dignity to persons: the capacity for a sense of dignity. Even though such a capacity may not apply to more persons than the capacity for a sense of justice, it does provide a different basis for saying that persons have dignity. It also focuses attention on more than justice, which embraces only a part of our concern for the dignity of persons.

What implications does acknowledging the capacity for a sense of dignity have for treating persons with dignity? Consider, first, those who already have a sense of dignity. Treating them as if they had no dignity would betray a callous attitude toward the sensitivities their sense of dignity includes. That persons are capable of suffering feelings of degradation or humiliation, for example, is surely as morally relevant as any other kind of suffering we can inflict on one another. Also, treating those with a sense of dignity as if they have no dignity shows a remarkable indifference to, if not maliciousness toward, those aspects of human personality related to their sense of dignity (such as, for example, personal integrity).

Second, consider those, such as very young children, who have not yet developed a sense of dignity. If they are not treated as if they have dignity, how are they to be treated? On developing a sense of dignity, are persons not warranted in objecting to those who previously treated them as if they had no dignity? Leaders of oppressed and discriminated-against minority groups recognize the importance of their children developing a strong sense of dignity. They also realize that this sense of dignity will not flourish unless children are encouraged from a very early age to feel that they have dignity.

At this point it might seem tempting to say that it is one thing to treat persons as if they have dignity and quite another to be committed to the view that they actually have dignity. However, aside from the air of perversity such a stance has, it seems to overintellectualize what it is to treat persons as if they have dignity. Is it genuine or only feigned indignation that we are to feel in behalf of injustices to others? Is it that we only say, but do not feel, that certain ways of treating others are degrading? Do we only say, but not really believe, that others should not be treated as mere means to another's ends? And what of ourselves? How is our own resentment, indignation, shame, self-esteem, and self-respect to be understood? If, as I have maintained, these attitudes show that we do genuinely feel we have dignity, consistency and sensitivity should lead us to feel similarly about others.

Still, one might object, this only attests to our feelings and commitments. How *reasonable* is it to have such feelings and commitments? If my claims about the connections between justice and dignity are right, to challenge the reasonableness of our concern for dignity is to challenge the reasonableness of our concern for justice. Having a sense of dignity is not merely contingently connected with those attitudes and feelings that express our sense of justice. Rather, resentment, indignation, remorse, feelings of guilt and shame are themselves expressions of our concern for human dignity.

Is this way of regarding persons ultimately defensible? One might think that the appeal to the capacity for a sense of dignity shows that we believe we have dignity, but it hardly shows that we do have dignity. This is right. Demonstrative arguments are not available. Attempts to demonstrate, or prove, that we have dignity seem either to fall short of the desired conclusion or to contain premises antecedently committed to it. This might seem like a weakness, but I suspect it is not. It may be essential to the integrity of this perspective, as well as to the integrity of those committed to it, that one not attempt to detach oneself from commitment to human dignity when speaking in its behalf. The dangers of doing so are pointed out by Peter Winch in a related context: "I think the situation is something like this. If one looks at a certain style of life and asks what there is in it which makes it worthwhile, one will find nothing there. One may indeed describe it in terms which bring out 'what one sees in it', but the use of these terms already presupposes that one does see it from a perspective from which it matters. The words will fall flat on the ears of someone who does not occupy such a perspective even though he is struggling to attain it" (1972, p. 190).

The case of the psychopath illustrates this. If we temporarily divest ourselves of our concern for dignity in order to see what, from an "objective" point of view, can be said on its behalf, we are likely to be disappointed. The disappointment will dissipate only when, in our struggle to see what is there, we remind ourselves of what matters to ourselves and to others. But to appreciate this reminder is to lose one's detachment ("objectivity") and resume our role as participants in a world of shared moral concern. That is, we must drop our attempt intellectually to simulate the psychopath and allow our moral sentiments a role in our judgments.

Bearing this in mind, consider a hypothetical individual, David. Why should David be regarded as having dignity? How others answer this question might differ importantly from how David himself would answer it. Others might say, for example, that David's well-being is dependent on his self-respect and self-esteem. If he is not regarded by others as having dignity, his self-respect and self-esteem may suffer. Thus, he will suffer. David might well acknowledge that these claims are true, but this does not mean that he would agree that he should be treated with dignity because of its personal utility to him. Instead, he might insist that being treated with regard for his dignity is appropriate because he is worthy of being so treated. (More likely, his attitudes of self-regard will *express* this, rather than David actually *asserting* it.) If David values being treated with dignity primarily because of its personal utility, there is a danger that he will value this way of being treated merely as a means to some other end—for example, his happiness. Dignity, for David, will be viewed only from an 'external' standpoint. As Winch says, "So one will see oneself perhaps as a prospective object of such admiration. And then what one is aiming at is to be such an object of admiration. 'What was internal becomes external'" (1972, p. 190). Assuming that such an attitude does not adequately reflect David's sense of dignity, it also does not reflect the kind of recognition he wants from others—namely, as someone who *has* dignity, rather than simply as someone whose well-being or happiness will be affected by being treated *as if* he does.

All of this is bound to disappoint those who seek an external, rational ground for human dignity. But the demand for such a ground is misplaced to the extent that it suggests having the attitudes which express our concern for dignity is a matter of *choice* or *decision*. Although decision making may contribute to the development of dispositions to have these attitudes, we no more choose to have these dispositions than we choose to be human.

Again, I advert to Strawson's rejection of the demand for an external, rational justification of the general framework of attitudes which, I have tried to show, include those associated with our concern for dignity: "Compare the question of the justification of induction. The human commitment to inductive belief-formation is original, natural, non-rational (not *irrational*), in no way something we choose or could give up. Yet rational criticism and reflection can refine standards and their application, supply 'rules for judging of cause and effect.' Ever since the facts were made clear by Hume, people have been resisting acceptance of them" (1968, p. 94). The unnerving possibility of psychopathy suggests that the parallel with induction is overstated—not so much so, however, that it should be viewed as just one possibility among the many from which we must choose or decide. To view psychopathy as an object of choice, were this possible, would in itself threaten to place oneself outside that "form of life" which takes human dignity seriously. I have not tried to determine precisely where it should fit in this form of life, only that it is not excludable without radically changing both the form of life and the fundamental character of its participants.

6
Moral Psychology and
Respect for Persons

The sense of justice is no mere moral conception but a true sentiment of the heart enlightened by reason.
—*John Rawls, "The Sense of Justice"*

Although respect for the dignity of persons has a central place in my account of morality, I have made no attempt to prove that we actually have dignity. Still, we can ask to what extent principles of moral psychology explain how we might come to take respect for the dignity of persons seriously. John Rawls is well aware of the importance of asking this question. He devotes a considerable portion of Part 3 of his landmark work, *The Theory of Justice*, to psychologically grounding his concept of justice as fairness. The voluminous response to his work concentrates on his principles of justice and their philosophical justification. Rawls's attempt to interrelate moral and psychological theory has received relatively little attention. However, he regards this attempt as essential to his theory of justice because "however attractive a conception of justice might be on other grounds, it is seriously defective if the principles of moral psychology are such that it fails to engender in human beings the requisite desire to act upon it" (1971, p. 455).

PSYCHOLOGICAL PRINCIPLES

Fundamental to Rawls's theory of justice is the view that "each person possesses an inviolability that even the welfare of society as a whole cannot override" (1971, p. 3). This may seem extreme. Nonutilitarians need not go this far in insisting that respect for dignity is not simply a derivation from the principle of utility. Even if there are conceivable circumstances in which nonutilitarians might agree that one person may be violated for the sake of the greater number, this does not mean that a principle of equal respect for all must be grounded in utility. Overriding nonutilitarian concerns do not eliminate them. In any case, it will prove useful to see to what extent Rawls's reflections on moral psychology explain how we might come to take a principle of equal respect seriously.

It should be noted at the outset that Rawls's discussion of principles of moral psychology is severely limited in that he confines his attention to how persons in a well-ordered society might come to have a sense of justice. A well-ordered society is one in which "(1) everyone accepts and knows that the others accept the same principles of justice, and (2) the basic social institutions generally satisfy and are generally known to satisfy these principles" (1971, p. 5). Further, the particular type of well-ordered society Rawls concentrates on is one in which his concept of justice as fairness is operative (as distinct from, say, a utilitarian concept of justice).

Nevertheless, the principles of moral psychology that Rawls relies on are applicable to other types of society, including less than well-ordered ones.[1] Thus it is possible to consider the relationship between principles of moral psychology and a sense of justice in other types of society, even though, for the most part, Rawls chooses not to.[2] However, there are reasons for thinking that his failure to do so is unfortunate. First, the concept of justice as fairness must be related to less than well-ordered societies if it is to be of any relevance to actual problems of justice, for it is in such societies that we all live and are likely to continue to live in the foreseeable future. If, as Rawls says, the acceptability of a concept of justice is dependent on the extent to which it can be supported by the principles of moral psychology, we need to consider how these principles might operate in less well-ordered societies as well. Second, there is a methodological objection to Rawls's confining his attention to a well-ordered society that is based on justice as fairness. Because justice is well-established in such a society, it seems that the adults in that society would already have the requisite sense of justice. Rawls is concerned only with how children might acquire a sense of justice in these benign circumstances. However, by assuming the existence of such a society as a premise, Rawls is assuming, without argument, that the principles of moral psychology are supportive of a sense of justice. That is, by beginning his argument with a well-ordered, just society, Rawls must assume that his concept of justice does "engender in human beings the requisite desire to act upon it." The only question left to consider is precisely how this desire is passed on to children.

But suppose we ask how the adults in the well-ordered society acquired *their* sense of justice. The answer depends on how long we suppose the society to have existed in its present form. Presumably, there must have been a time when the well-ordered society was evolving into its present state from a less well-ordered one. What we need to know is whether the principles of moral psychology can also explain how members of that less well-ordered society could have acquired a sense of justice adequate to support Rawls's ideal society. If these principles cannot, we have no reason to believe that Rawls's ideal society is a possible society. And if that is the case, we should have little interest in the question of how the principles of moral psychology would operate in such a society. It would be clear that Rawls's concept of justice so far exceeds what we are psychologically capable of taking seriously that it needs to be modified. Unfortunately, Rawls's unargued assumption—that the original establishment of a well-ordered society based on justice as fairness is compatible with the principles of moral psychology—masks this potential difficulty.

To illustrate how psychological principles might interfere with the establishment of Rawls's well-ordered society, we might consider psychological egoism. Interestingly, if Rawls were convinced of the truth of psychological egoism, he would not think that a well-ordered society based on justice is even possible. No one would have a sense of justice (as fairness), and there would be no direct concern to adopt the principle of equal respect. Since Rawls would hold that egoists could never establish a well-ordered society based on justice as fairness, he would consider it pointless to ask how psychological principles would operate in such a society. Of course, Rawls does not believe that psychological egoism is true, and his principles of moral psychology offer an alternative perspective. However, it cannot be assumed that psychological egoism is the only psychological theory that could render pointless the consideration of how psychological principles might operate in Rawls's ideally just society.[3] It is necessary, then, to ask whether Rawls's principles of moral psychology have the potential to support the kind of sense of justice required for the original establishment of a well-ordered society based on justice as fairness.

Following Jean Piaget's *The Moral Judgment of the Child* (1932), Rawls advances a theory of moral development consisting of three stages. First, there is the morality of authority, based on reciprocal love between child and parent, with the parent laying down precepts accepted as authoritative by the child. Next, there is the morality of association, based on mutual trust and friendship. Finally, there is the morality of principles, wherein one has a sense of justice, and concern is shown even for those with whom one has no acquaintance. At each level a psychological principle of *reciprocity* applies: "The active sentiments of love and friendship, and even the sense of justice, arise from the manifest intentions of other persons to act for our good. Because we recognize that they wish us well, we care for their well-being in return. Thus we acquire attachments to persons and institutions according to how we perceive our good to be affected by them. The basic idea is one of reciprocity, a tendency to answer in kind" (1971, p. 494). It is important to notice that this tendency to reciprocate is not merely a self-interested response. One does not reciprocate only in order to receive benefits. One reciprocates because of receiving benefits from others, but the response is one of genuine other-regard.

However, it must be emphasized that this sentiment toward others is precipitated only by having received benefits, and, at each stage of moral development we have a *return in kind*. This seems to bring the notions of gratitude and indebtedness into preeminence. Whether this is sufficient to generate respect for all is another matter. Even if psychological principles of reciprocity are sufficient to generate respect for those from whom one has received respect, this falls short of what Rawls seems to require of the sentiment of justice as fairness. Rawls says, "for one who understands and accepts the contract doctrine, the sentiment of justice is not a different desire from that to act on principles that rational individuals would consent to in an initial situation which gives everyone equal representation as a moral person" (1971, p. 478). The principles adopted by contractors in Rawls's hypothetical original position extend to those who have only the potential to reciprocate, and even to unborn generations, which is in line with the principle of equal respect. Yet it seems to transcend the psychological principles of reciprocity, which are concerned only with returning in kind.

At times Rawls seems to acknowledge that one's sense of justice extends beyond simply returning in kind: "We desire to act on the natural duty to advance just arrangements. And this arrangement goes beyond the support of those particular schemes that have affirmed our good. It seeks to extend the conception they embody to further situations for the good of the larger community" (1971, p. 474). But if persons are confined to principles of reciprocity, it is not clear what could account for their adopting this wider concern. Also, it should be noted that this passage might not take us as close to the principle of equal respect as it first appears. Supporting the good of the larger community does not necessarily mean supporting respect for each member of that community. This would be so only if the good of the larger community never threatens respect for some of its individual members. As Rawls's worries about utilitarianism indicate, this is at best a contingent matter, hardly enough to warrant saying, "Each person possesses an inviolability founded on justice that even the welfare of society as a whole cannot override."

The difficulties Rawls's psychological account presents for the adoption of the principle of equal respect are most evident in his description of the morality of association: "It would seem that while the individual understands the principles of justice, his motive for complying with them, for some time at least, springs largely from his ties of friendship and fellow-feeling for others, and his concern for the approbation of the wider society" (1971, p. 473). Thus described, individuals at this stage would seem to lack a sense of justice. Yet, since they understand principles of justice, they cannot be very young children or have serious intellectual disabilities. If they nevertheless lack sentiments of justice toward those from whom they have not benefited, it seems plausible to conclude that they lack the capacity for such sentiments.

Even if Rawls were to modify his psychological account in light of this problem, another problem would remain. In a well-ordered society there will be some who have not yet done their part, such as small children and unborn generations. How can the notion of reciprocity include them? It could be argued that, once we have progressed to Rawls's third stage, the morality of principles, we will recognize that our future well-being is dependent on the continued strength of the institutions from which we benefit. So, there will be some concern for the well-being of those with the potential for reciprocity, the hope being that, when their time comes, they will return in kind.

However, such self-interested regard for those with the potential to reciprocate seems to fall far short of the attitude of respect for the dignity of others. Nor is it clear that, from this self-interested standpoint, we need extend this concern very far into the future. For many, only some unborn generations (say, those within two generations) need be considered. Furthermore, we naturally will support most strongly those institutions that have been most beneficial to us. If this is so, is it clear that we will acknowledge the inviolability of each person? We need not be completely self-interested, nor lack the tendency to reciprocate, not to acknowledge this. For example, we might hold that some individuals are not needed to support society. As long as they make no contribution, their needs can be ignored, as no basis for reciprocity would be established. This view should be especially worrisome to those outside, but nevertheless affected by, a well-ordered society, but it also could have profound effects on those within a well-ordered society who have not yet done their part.

Because Rawls assumes a well-ordered society based on justice as fairness, it might seem that the problem of those who have not yet done their part is exaggerated. After all, part of this assumption is that members of the society are committed to institutions that are recognized to satisfy the principles of justice as fairness. Yet the psychological principles of reciprocity say only that "we acquire attachments to persons and institutions according to how we perceive our good to be affected by them" (1971, p. 494). To ensure the stability of his well-ordered society, Rawls would have to show that, in the future, support for the principle of equal respect is necessary to sustain the institutions of that society "insofar as we perceive our good to be affected by them." But commitment to institutions on this basis need not imply unwillingness to introduce changes in those institutions. What makes the principle of equal respect more precarious than seems desirable for a theory of justice is that its continued acceptance is made contingent on the members of the society agreeing that its acceptance is necessary for the continuation of reciprocal benefits.

For example, suppose that reliable methods were developed for determining which among newborns would create the greatest problems for society—such as those with serious intellectual or physical disabilities, those who will contract crippling or disabling diseases relatively early in life, or those who will end up being dissenters in society and try to bring down its institutions. If a society adopted the practice of removing such newborns (either by infanticide or by sending them to less well-ordered societies), it would seem to be consistent with principles of reciprocity, assuming the newborns had made no significant contribution to society. As far as reciprocity is concerned, there is no reason why such a practice could not be accepted by everyone, and the basic social institutions could be known to satisfy principles of justice acceptable to all. By the time a person is old enough to understand and accept the principles of justice, he or she will already have survived possible removal. The rights and responsibilities of full membership can then gratefully be accepted.

However fanciful these suggestions may seem, the problems become real enough when we turn to less well-ordered societies, and it is these problems that Rawls's principles of moral psychology must face in order to show that there is any reason at all to consider how these principles might operate in an ideally just society. Do Rawls's principles of reciprocity have the potential to support the evolution of his ideally just society? Or, like psychological egoism, does Rawls's psychological theory seem to defeat the very possibility of such a society?

Unfortunately for Rawls, the latter seems to be the case. Once we turn to less well-ordered societies we find that there are many people on the fringes who, for one reason or another, are not visibly supporting institutions that are benefiting others. In fact, they might be contributing to the instability of those institutions (for example, by violent protest, crime, or adding to welfare expenses). That their circumstances may have been thrust on them by others, rather than deliberately chosen, is irrelevant from the standpoint of reciprocity. Given only the tendency to reciprocity, it is difficult to see how Rawls's principle of equal respect would ever be extended to them by those in more advantageous positions. To urge that this is unjust is to beg the question, at least as long as it is maintained that we are moved only by considerations of self-interest or reciprocity. From this perspective, justice *is* reciprocity.

Rawls might reply that the principle of equal respect is also a principle of reciprocity. He says that "by giving justice to those who can give justice in return, the principle of reciprocity is fulfilled at the highest level" (1971, p. 511). But giving justice to those who *can* give justice is not the fulfillment of a principle of reciprocity. Rather, it is respecting those who have the *potential* for reciprocity, implying that the recipients may have done nothing to elicit a return in kind. Thus the gap between the principle of equal respect and the psychological principles of reciprocity remains.

If Rawls were to replace his principle of equal respect with a principle of reciprocity, his concept of justice would be much less attractive as a moral ideal. For surely one of its most attractive features is its demand that the dignity of each person be respected. To withhold this respect from those who, through no fault of their own, have not supported just institutions is quite arbitrary and should strike us as unjust. It is to be hoped that some plausible modifications of Rawls's psychological theory can be made that will account for how someone might adopt the principle of respect, even in a less than well-ordered society.

To this end, we might begin with a remark made by Rawls about some moral concerns other than justice. He says we have "duties of compassion and humanity" toward animals (1971, p. 512). Since these are not duties of justice, he regards them as beyond the scope of his inquiry. Were he to consider them further, he undoubtedly would agree that these duties, as well as his principles of justice, need psychological support. Presumably, one of the duties we have toward animals is not to treat them cruelly. But the psychological basis for our taking this seriously surely is not that we know we have received benefits from them (even if, in fact, we do know it). Therefore we must call on something other than Rawls's reciprocity principles.

Consider an example. A six-year-old boy rescues a bird from an attack by a cat. The boy is extremely upset by the attack. He has never seen the bird before; he has no reason to believe the bird has ever benefited him or that it ever will. Reciprocity, then, is out of the question. The most plausible explanation for his response seems to be that this is a sympathetic reaction to the suffering of the bird at the hands of an attacker. There is no reason to suppose that the boy's capacity for sympathy does not extend to other sentient creatures, including humans.[4]

We can agree with Rawls that a child will not care for others unless first cared for by someone else, but this could be understood in the following way. As Rawls points out, being cared for by others plays an essential role in developing self-esteem and self-confidence. That is, it enables one to care for oneself. If caring for oneself makes caring for others possible, Rawls's first principle is supported. However, rather than say simply that the child shows reciprocity toward those who have cared for him or her, one could regard Rawls's first principle as giving an account of how one's capacity for sympathy for others (even in the absence of benefits received) is aroused. Thus, Rawls's first principle of moral psychology could make use of the notion of reciprocity (in that love is returned for love in the case of parent-child relationships), but it would not be confined to it.

Supplemented with the notion of a capacity for sympathy, Rawls's account of associative morality could be very different. It could now be said that because the capacity for sympathy is not restricted to associates from whom one benefits, once those at the associative stage understand the principles of justice, they are moved by sentiments of justice as well as friendship and loyalty. It could still be true that one's sense of justice is manifested primarily in relationship to one's associates, but this would be due mainly to a lack of awareness of wider considerations rather than to acting on something other than principles of justice. Also, it should be noted that Rawls himself points out that even those who have reached the stage of the morality of principles are more readily and intensely moved by injustices to themselves and their associates (1971, p. 475).

The introduction of a capacity for sympathy helps Rawls's psychological account in several ways. It removes the gap between the tendency to reciprocate and acceptance of his principle of equal respect by supplementing rather than replacing the psychological principles of reciprocity. There is no need to deny that the tendency to reciprocate is a fundamental feature of interpersonal relationships. In fact, we should acknowledge that it can enhance our sympathetic tendencies. Bringing a capacity for sympathy into the account of the development of a sense of justice also supports Rawls's claim that the sense of justice is continuous with the love of humanity. The reciprocity principles can go no further than an exchange theory of morality, but it is difficult to extend a morality of exchange to all members of a single society, let alone the rest of the world. The capacity for sympathy can include the tendency to reciprocate but extend beyond it as well.

Finally, introducing a capacity for sympathy allows for a more gradual development of a full sense of justice than Rawls's account suggests. On his view, those at the associative level do not have a sense of justice, even though they understand the principles of justice and their application in society. However, even prior to this level, there seems to be a semblance of a sense of justice in children who display willingness to take turns in games (faulting others for not doing so), do their part in joint endeavors, share with others, and protest punishing the innocent. What prevents Rawls from acknowledging this semblance is his belief that such attitudes are strictly confined to associates. Yet the implicit generality of the capacity for sympathy is incompatible with his belief. The limited context in which children operate explains the nearly exclusive concern for associates. There is no reason to suppose that a child would not extend considerations of fairness to unknown others, should the occasion ever arise. Given the capacity for sympathy, such an extension need not be based on children's belief that those unknown others have promoted their good, or that they can be expected to in the future. By supplementing reciprocity with sympathy, we see one's sense of justice as developing gradually with increasing understanding of issues of justice, rather than as making its first appearance at Rawls's third stage of development.

Despite the essential role given to moral sentiments, Rawls's account of the development of a sense of justice suffers from being overly intellectualistic. Perhaps this is a consequence of building his account too much around principles of justice that are the endpoint of his theory of justice. For Rawls, a sense of justice is a highly articulate concern for justice, presupposing a rather sophisticated understanding of the content and application of principles of justice. A more plausible account would emphasize the varying degrees of articulateness and comprehensiveness of a sense of justice, beginning with relatively prereflective, or pretheoretical, manifestations in very young children and ranging to something like the theory-laden sense of justice found at Rawls's third stage of moral development. The capacity for sympathy would ease the transition from one stage to another in Rawls's account because of its unrestricted generality.

Since principles of reciprocity are restricted to those from whom benefits are received, such principles seem inadequate to explain how we could ever come to adopt a principle of equal respect for those from whom benefits are not received. The principle of equal respect is supposed to apply to all who are capable of moral personality and, thereby, of giving justice to others. Even in a well-ordered society the former class of persons might well be larger than the latter class of persons from whom one receives benefits. In less well-ordered societies, which is where our actual problems of justice lie, this seems clearly to be the case.

A UTILITARIAN RESPONSE

Although introducing the capacity for sympathy can help overcome many of the problems in Rawls's account, it also undermines one of his objections against utilitarianism. Rawls believes his account of the sense of justice has the advantage over utilitarianism of not having to appeal to the capacity for sympathy. Of utilitarianism Rawls says, "It is evident why the utilitarian stresses the capacity for sympathy. Those who do not benefit from the better situation of others must identify with the greater sum (or average) of satisfaction else they will not desire to follow the utility criterion" (1971, p. 500). This claim assumes that the application of utilitarian principles will actually result in some not benefiting when the greater good is served, and that this will not happen in the case of justice as fairness. However, at best, it is only in a well-ordered society based on justice as fairness that one can have any assurance that everyone will benefit from increased justice to others. In less well-ordered societies increased justice to those less well off might well result in a loss of benefits to the more advantaged.

In fairness to utilitarians, Rawls must allow them to consider whether there really are individuals who do not benefit from the greater sum (or average) of satisfaction in a well-ordered society that is based on utilitarian principles. (And, if the answer is affirmative, we must ask whether the frequency is greater than in a well-ordered society based on justice as fairness.) This is a contingent claim, and one that might well be contested by utilitarians. That utilitarians can have no principled objection to such a consequence, should it occur, is irrelevant, as here the only issue is whether, in fact, it would happen, and how this might affect the stability of society.

But this exclusive concentration on well-ordered societies is really beside the point. If the original establishment of a well-ordered society based on justice as fairness requires more from us psychologically than the principles of reciprocity provide, then it seems that Rawls's concept of justice is as much in need of the capacity for sympathy as utilitarianism is. This need is especially evident when we consider the problems that principles of reciprocity pose for making a transition from less than well-ordered societies like those in which we live to those that are a closer approximation to Rawls's ideally just society. It is not at all clear that considerations of reciprocity alone can inspire those who are better off to make the sacrifices needed to improve the lot of those entitled to more than they have.

Interestingly, the psychological theories Rawls uses as a basis for formulating his own do not shy away from appealing to our capacity for sympathy. For example, Lawrence Kohlberg's theory of moral development, a theory inspired by Piaget's earlier studies, quite explicitly cites the importance of sympathy in developing a sense of justice. (However, as will be seen in Chapter 7, Kohlberg's account of the role of sympathy is seriously deficient.) Emphasis on the importance of sympathy is no less evident in Piaget, as Rawls himself points out (1971, p. 459). Yet for

Rawls, appealing to our capacity for sympathy is a disadvantage because, although we do have such a capacity, our altruistic inclinations "are likely to be less strong than those brought about by the three psychological laws formulated as reciprocity principles; and a marked capacity for sympathetic identification seems relatively rare" (1971, p. 500). Rawls is very likely right about the relative strengths of our tendencies to reciprocity and sympathy, but this is a disadvantage that justice as fairness must share with utilitarianism. Whatever advantages Rawls's concept of justice might have over utilitarianism, being able to ignore our capacity for sympathy is not among them.

OPTIMISM VERSUS PESSIMISM

My suggestion that Rawls needs to supplement his account of the development of a sense of justice with our capacity for sympathy can be regarded as friendly criticism. However, John Deigh's criticisms (1982) are more severe, and they challenge my emendations as well. Deigh distinguishes between optimistic and pessimistic accounts of moral development. Rawls's claim that the sense of justice is "continuous with a love for mankind" is on the optimists' side. Those who emphasize the punitive side of morality, such as Freud and Hobbes, hold a more pessimistic view. Deigh sides with the pessimists against the optimists. Despite departures from Rawls, my own views fall on the optimists' side—perhaps even more than Rawls's.[5]

As we have seen, Rawls's account of the development of a sense of justice identifies three levels of moral development: those of authority, association, and principle. Each level is marked by feelings of guilt on the part of those who knowingly fall short of moral expectations. However, Deigh contends that Rawls fails to distinguish two very different conceptions of guilt. One links guilt with rules, indebtedness, and punishment. The other links guilt with caring for the well-being of others. Deigh suggests that the second conception be referred to as *remorse*. The problem, Deigh argues, is that only the first conception is directly linked to the sense of justice, but it is derived from the fear of punishment rather than from love. Justice is concerned with moral requirements. For Deigh, a sense of justice "denotes the moral sense that concerns matters of right and wrong, duty and obligation, which is to say, justice in that general sense covering whatever we owe others and ourselves as human beings" (1982, p. 391).

Acceptance of moral requirements, however, "generates respect for the authority of the moral rules or moral rights from which these requirements derive" (Deigh 1982, p. 403). Deigh accepts Rawls's notion that our sense of justice begins with respect for authority; his point of departure is that he does not believe Rawls successfully links love and authority. Here the pessimists fare much better. Children not only love their parents, they also fear their power:

> As external authorities, they appear to the child as powerful figures who can use their power to secure its obedience, and the prospect of their doing so inspires fear. At this stage, fear is the emotion that they in their role as authorities evoke in the child. Then, as their authority becomes internal, as the child comes to see itself as part of a moral order over which its parents preside, its fear of their power is transformed into respect for their authority. Correspondingly, its fear of punishment—or of whatever evil the child senses will be the consequence of disobedience—becomes a liability to guilt. (Deigh 1982, p. 413)

In contrast to this account, Rawls apparently links children's love for their parents with respect for rules laid down by the parents. Deigh's objection is that this overlooks other, more plausible, explanations of why children obey their parents. First, children have self-interested reasons for obedience—namely, the promise of punishment and reward, but this is basically the pessimistic line. Second, if children love their parents, they will want to please them and avoid displeasing them. If they take obedience as a way of expressing their love, they will be inclined to obey; but this is not a recognition of parental *authority*. Love-based guilt at disappointing their parents will be remorse rather than the kind of guilt associated with the violation of authoritative moral rules. Similar problems arise at the level of associative morality.

There is no reason to deny that the pessimistic account is at least partially correct. Fear of punishment does play an important role in childhood (and adulthood, for that matter). And it is plausible to link such fear to acceptance of authority. Whether those who accept authority through fear regard this as *moral* authority is another matter; certainly many seem to. A fundamental question remains: Is it true that acceptance of the moral requirements of justice presupposes respect for authority—whether in the form of parental injunctions, institutions, moral rules, or moral rights? Deigh seems to think so.

The answer to this question depends on what we take respect for authority to be. If, as Deigh suggests, it must be derived from fear of power and punishment, I answer in the negative. Justice can be linked with direct concern for others, without respect for punitive or powerful authority. Of course, the pessimist is right in saying that one can feel guilty for having violated the rights of another without really caring about that person at all. That is, guilt does not presuppose love, friendship, or direct concern for others, but this does not mean that justice *typically* is not linked directly to concern for others.

Deigh says that remorse "is felt over violence one does to things one treasures or persons for whom one cares and for whose welfare one is concerned" (1982, p. 400). He then says that, for the sake of simplicity, he will restrict his understanding of remorse to that which is "felt over evil one does to someone one loves." Unfortunately, this approach allows him to overlook the remorse one might feel at unjustly harming a total stranger. Of course, the sense in which such remorse expresses care and concern for a stranger is different from that for a loved one. Still, in either case there is a sense in which one identifies with the other. As Deigh himself puts it, "One's identifying with others generates care and concern for them. These attitudes indicate appreciation for pleasures and pains that those with whom one identifies feel and for benefits and harms that come their way" (1982, p. 402).

There is a more active concern for loved ones and friends than for strangers. However, we do have a capacity to be moved by the plight of strangers, what I have called a capacity for sympathy. It may show itself in remorse at our being agents of harm and injustice to others, indignation at harms and injustices to others by others, and unwillingness to inflict harm and injustice on others in order to achieve our ends. Even though those with a capacity for sympathy may fall short of actively seeking out opportunities to promote justice or prevent injustice for strangers, they nevertheless show some concern for the well-being of others.

A capacity for sympathy has as much claim to contributing to the development of a sense of justice as respect for rules and rights that originate in fear of power and punishment has. Rawls's emphasis on authority in parent/child relations and his reluctance to acknowledge the role of a capacity for sympathy invite Deigh's objections. Authority at this level does suggest links with fear of power and punishment. However, if the love of parents for children is seen as instrumental to the development of their capacity for sympathy, groundwork is laid for a kind of respect that focuses directly on the worth of persons, rather than on moral rules and rights that presuppose that worth.[6]

There is a curious contrast between Rawls and Lawrence Kohlberg's use of Piaget's pioneering work on moral development. On the one hand, Rawls accepts Piaget's notion that authority is predominant at the first stage of development. Kohlberg rejects that aspect of Piaget's account, insisting that respect for authority arises only much later (Kohlberg's fourth stage, in his second of three levels of development). On the other hand, Kohlberg's account places much less emphasis on the affective aspects of moral development than Rawls's. Reciprocity is a fundamental feature of both accounts, but Kohlberg's emphasis is on cognitive changes related to reciprocity, whereas Rawls's is equally on affective changes. I believe Rawls is right to place greater emphasis on affective aspects of moral development. If he were to agree with Kohlberg's reservations about Piaget's account of respect for authority in parent/child relations, he would be in a better position to avoid Deigh's objections. But, ultimately, as I have argued, he needs to acknowledge the importance of our capacity for sympathy.

The notion of respect for persons looms as large for Kohlberg's account of moral development as for Rawls's. Kohlberg does acknowledge the importance of our capacity for sympathy in his account. However, despite his protestations to the contrary, he seriously misrepresents its role. Ironically, although Kohlberg regards justice as the central concept in his theory of moral development, he seriously misrepresents it also. These misrepresentations will be discussed in the following chapter.

7
Cognition and Affect
in Moral Development

Can a convincing account be given of the genesis of the 'moral' emotion of respect without postulating a 'natural' basis of it in compassion?
—*R. S. Peters*, Psychology and Ethical Development

It is . . . conceivable that a person could understand the social order and see its functional rationality quite well, discuss moral dilemmas of others intelligently and take the role of most anyone—and still act immorally himself and experience little or no guilt over doing so. Indeed, these social insights might just as readily serve Machiavellian as moral purposes.
—*M. L. Hoffman*, "Moral Development"

The most influential and widely discussed theory of moral development during the last quarter century is Lawrence Kohlberg's cognitive-developmental theory (1981; 1984). This theory is distinguished by its insistence that there is an invariant and irreversible order of stages of moral development. It is called a *cognitive-developmental* theory because, following Piaget, it maintains that each stage of moral development parallels a stage of cognitive development. For Kohlberg, there are six stages of moral development, and one cannot advance to a higher stage until one has gone through each of the preceding stages.[1] The six stages are divided into three levels: preconventional, conventional, and postconventional (or autonomous).

One of the most persistent criticisms of Kohlberg's theory is that it does not do justice to the affective aspects of moral development (Peters 1974; Hoffman 1970, 1976). Despite Kohlberg's numerous attempts to respond to this criticism, his critics are essentially right—and they are right in ways that threaten Kohlberg's core notion that moral development proceeds in the manner he describes. Since Kohlberg, like Rawls, intends his account to explain how a universal principle of respect for persons can be grounded psychologically, it should prove instructive to examine his theory in some detail.

THE PROBLEM OF EGOISM

Kohlberg's theory of moral development culminates in stage 6, which affirms a universal principle of the right of persons to be respected as having dignity, or intrinsic worth. This is the essentially Kantian view that persons are not to be regarded merely as means to the ends of others, but are to be regarded as ends-in-themselves. It is clear that Kohlberg intends to contrast stage 6 reasoning with exclusively self-interested, or egoistic, reasoning. Although egoistic reasoning might advocate serving the interests of others, it would be only insofar as such service is required from the standpoint of self-interest. At least in principle, an egoist is prepared to treat others merely as a means to his or her ends. Regardless of the actual outcome of the reasoning, there is a sharp contrast between the reasons behind prescriptions for conduct accepted by egoists and those in Kohlberg's stage 6.

Since we are not born with this attitude of respect for the dignity of persons, any theory of moral development that incorporates it must explain how it can arise. According to R. S. Peters (1974), neither Piaget (whose highest stage also incorporates respect for persons), nor Kohlberg provide such an explanation. Piaget, Peters says, seems simply to assume that rationally to take into account another's perspective is tantamount to having a reasonable, sympathetic concern for that other. But, Peters says we cannot assume that rationality and reasonableness are the same; and he asks, "Can a convincing account be given of the genesis of the 'moral' emotion of respect without postulating a 'natural' basis for it in compassion?" (1974, p. 139) Peters's own view is that reasonable respect for persons involves more than simply being rational. What is needed, he believes, is an account of how one becomes "sensitive and sympathetic to their sufferings and to their attempts to make something of their lives" (1974, p. 139).

As Peters notes, this is the same criticism M. L. Hoffman makes of Piaget and Kohlberg. Hoffman notes that it is "conceivable that a person could understand the social order and see its functional rationality quite well, discuss moral dilemmas of others intelligently and take the role of most anyone—and still act immorally himself and experience little or no guilt over doing so. Indeed, these social insights might just as readily serve Machiavellian as moral purposes" (1970, p. 281). If the accounts of psychiatrists are to be believed, it is more than conceivable. Hoffman's description fits the psychopath discussed in Chapter 3. Thus the question is, How is reasonable respect for persons to be accounted for, given that it is not entailed by rationality alone?

This question might seem odd since it is clear that both Piaget and Kohlberg acknowledge the importance of sympathy and concern for others in moral development. But Hoffman is quite aware of this: "It is true that Piaget occasionally suggests that affective concepts play an important role. In particular he states that sympathy . . . becomes an important contributing factor later in the development of moral autonomy. But the process by which sympathy operates is not specified. Motivational concepts are also considered by Kohlberg. . . , but no attempt is made to account for their origin" (1970, p. 280). A close examination of Kohlberg's writings shows that it is not really fair to say that he has made no attempt to account for the origins of motivational concepts, but there is reason to worry about whether his account is adequate. In fact, as we shall see, there are aspects of Kohlberg's theory that seem to invite precisely the kind of criticism raised by Peters and Hoffman concerning how the attitude of respect for persons can be accounted for.

Hoffman remarks: "Western psychology has evolved along lines seemingly antithetical to giving consideration for others a central place in the overall view of personality. The doctrinaire view, present in both psychoanalysis and behaviorism, has been that altruistic behavior can always be explained ultimately in terms of instrumental self-serving motives in the actor" (1976, p. 124). It is clear that Kohlberg is as concerned as Hoffman to make a break from this egoistic perspective. However, there are features of Kohlberg's theory that play into the hands of egoism and, consequently, make this break more difficult, and less plausible, than is necessary.

Consider Kohlberg's first two stages of development. Both are characterized by essentially egoistic reasoning and motivation. The following, for example, is found in a table on motivation:

Stage 1. Action is motivated by avoidance of punishment and "conscience" is irrational fear of punishment. . . .
Stage 2. Action is motivated by desire for reward or benefit. Possible guilt reactions are ignored and punishment viewed in a pragmatic manner. (Kohlberg 1984, p. 52)

Elsewhere Kohlberg says of these same first level, preconventional stages: "At this level the child is responsive to cultural rules and labels of good and bad, right or wrong, but interprets these labels in terms of either the physical or the hedonistic consequences of action (punishment, reward, exchange of favors), or in terms of the physical power of those who enunciate the rules and labels" (1981, p. 17). Of stage 2 in particular, Kohlberg says: "Right action consists of that which instrumentally satisfies one's own needs and occasionally the needs of others. Human relations are viewed in terms like those of the market place. . . . Reciprocity is a matter of 'you scratch my back and I'll scratch yours,' not of loyalty, gratitude, or justice" (1981, p. 17). Later he refers to stage 2 reasoners as "instrumentally egoistic people" (1981, p. 182).

However, at stage 3 there is a seemingly abrupt change. Children now have cognitive abilities that enable them to recognize simultaneous or mutually reciprocal orientations. They can, for example, not only anticipate what others are likely to do; children can anticipate what others anticipate they are likely to do. In the moral domain, children can imagine themselves simultaneously in two different roles that are oriented to each other.

Kohlberg provides a pair of examples to contrast stages 2 and 3. Two children are asked why one should go along with the Golden Rule. The first child gives a stage 2 answer: "If you follow the Golden Rule, other people will be nice back to you." The second, a ten-year-old boy, gives a stage 3 answer: "Well the Golden Rule is the best rule, because like if you were rich, you might dream like that you were poor and how it felt, and then the dream would go back in your own head and you would remember and you would help make the laws that way" (1981, p. 149). Stage 2, Kohlberg says, is based on actual exchanges. Stage 3 allows for ideal, or imaginative, reciprocity—reciprocity based on what one imagines the other's perspective is and what it would be like to be that other. At this stage we find "mutual affection, gratitude, and concern for one another's approval" (1981, p. 149).

It seems evident that Kohlberg intends stage 3 to be understood as transcending egoistic reasoning and motivation. Here there is genuine concern for the well-being of others, and for their sake, not simply for one's own sake. But the question that naturally arises is, If up to this point children have been wholly egoistic, what accounts for the emergence of genuine other-regard? If we focus on previous motivational patterns, nothing suggests even the potential for such a change. If we focus on the new cognitive abilities, it is still not clear why egoism would be transcended.

In fact, one might attempt to interpret stage 3 egoistically. Those in stage 3 are concerned with the approval of others. Instead of emphasizing mutual trust, affection, loyalty, and gratitude, one might try to construe the concern for approval egoistically. Approval can be sought for self-interested reasons of varying sorts—for the sake of having a good reputation, in order to be entrusted with positions of prestige and power, in order to get through cooperation what one cannot get alone, and so on.

Similar comments could be made about stage 4, which is rooted in concern for "law and order." Here it could be said that the children see the need for some form of law and order and uncritically accept the system of law that is prevailing at that time. The perception of this necessity could be based on the belief that without law and order one's life and property would be insecure. Thus the new cognitive abilities of stages 3 and 4 would provide, not nonegoistic forms of reasoning and motivation, but greater insight into what is required to maintain self-interest in a society of very complex social interaction and interdependency.

Operating from within such an egoistic framework would enable one to explain why, as Kohlberg so often claims, most members of our society fail to advance beyond stage 4. Since stages 5 and 6 hold that others have rights that must be respected even if considerations of self-interest commend their violation, one would expect people to draw up short of those stages. As for those who apparently do go on to stages 5 and 6, they could be said to be either opportunists (out to win the admiration and trust of others) or victims of self-deception. Those who are really clearheaded about human nature can, on this view, see that stages 5 and 6 are, at best, rationalizations.

For example, the egalitarian tone of these stages could be construed as a rationalization for one's failure to "make it," or as an expression of envy of those who have been more successful. Here there could be an attempt to raise one's self-esteem by bringing others down to one's social or economic level, or by preventing them from rising above it. Those who have "made it," who espouse the principles of stage 5 or 6, could be construed as wanting to appear as if they are "on the right side," a posture that can gain them admiration and approval, and which they can afford as long as their social and economic positions remain unthreatened. Of course, not all who espouse the principles of stage 5 or 6 could be plausibly analyzed in just these ways, but there does not seem to be any insuperable difficulty in imagining other ways of interpreting their attitudes along egoistic lines.

Contrary to Kohlberg's view that the postconventional, critical thought that enables one to engage in meta-ethical thinking (e.g., asking "Why be moral?") will lead to the sincere adoption of universal principles of human rights and dignity, the egoistic perspective would instead cast its critical eye in such a way that the first four stages would all be transformed into *enlightened* egoism. Thus, law and order (stage 4) would be recognized as important, but only insofar as it serves self-interest. There would not be blind acceptance of whatever is lawful. It would also be acknowledged that approval and acceptance by others is important, but not at the expense of self-interest. This amounts to a more sophisticated stage 1 and stage 2.[2]

On this interpretation, we would have a ready explanation of the phenomenon noted by Kohlberg concerning many college students. He observes that many of them temporarily "regress" to stage 2 reasoning when they first engage in critical reflection about the principles they previously simply accepted in stages 3 and 4. However, contrary to Kohlberg's view that this is a temporary "regression" to be followed by advancement to stage 5, from the egoistic perspective this "regression" would actually be a permanent advancement to enlightened egoism.

SYMPATHY

So far, only those aspects of Kohlberg's theory that lend themselves to an egoistic interpretation have been considered, but much that he says is intended to reject a strictly egoistic account. Theories of socialization, Kohlberg says, usually ask how the "selfish" infant develops into a social being. His theory rejects the appropriateness of saying that the infant is "selfish": "the answer of developmental theory is that self is itself born out of the social or sharing process, and therefore, motives for self-realization or self-enhancement are not basically 'selfish' in the pejorative sense, but require sharing" (1984, p. 97). Thus it is quite misleading for Kohlberg to characterize stages 1 and 2 as egoistic, and this passage suggests that some revision in their descriptions is in order. Egoistic motivation presupposes that there already is an ego, or self, but Kohlberg's point is that there is no presocial self. By the time a self emerges from the interaction of the infant with its social environment, it already cares about others in ways that cannot be fairly said to be completely egoistic.

We must now examine how Kohlberg reaches his conclusion. Both Kohlberg and Piaget characterize the child's earliest phases of development as egocentric rather than egoistic. An egocentric child is, in the most extreme form, ego-less. There are varying degrees of egocentricity. Initially the infant presumably makes no distinction between self and others. Then, according to Kohlberg, the infant differentiates itself from certain other subjects, in particular, those persons with whom it has the most intimate contact. Next there is a gradual awareness of the permanence of others, whether persons or physical objects. However, even as awareness of others as permanent subjects (persons) increases, egocentricity persists because the child is still unable to adopt the perspective of others. As far as the child can tell, all perspectives are like his or hers. The ability to imagine what things seem like to others requires, according to Kohlberg and Piaget, the development of cognitive abilities that typically are not in evidence until roughly ages six or seven, when children are first able to reason morally at Kohlberg's stage 3.

It is important to notice that it is only at stage 3 that egocentricity is clearly transcended. A consequence of not noticing this is that behavior of those not yet at stage 3 that is done out of genuine other-regard might be construed as self-seeking. For example, the young brother who, when asked to choose a gift for his older sister, chooses something he would like might be viewed as thinking only of himself and not being concerned at all to please his sister. (After all, he is likely to inherit the present if she has no interest in it.) Although this certainly can be the case, it need not be. It is quite possible that the young brother is assuming that, at least in regard to toys, his sister has the same likes and dislikes he does. That is, this could be an instance of egocentric rather than egoistic thinking. If so, a reinterpretation of much apparently egoistic stage 2 behavior may be in order.

If there is genuine other-regard (however misdirected) prior to stage 3, what is its origin? This is the question Hoffman claims Kohlberg never answers, but Kohlberg certainly tries to answer it. He says that developmental theories offer a very different account from other theories of the birth of social motives: "Other theories have assumed that social motives are either instinctive or result from the association of socializing agents and their behavior with gratification and anxiety to the child. In contrast, developmental theories assume a primary motive for competence and self-actualization which is organized through an ego or self whose structure is social or shared" (1984, p. 97). Kohlberg is drawing from Robert White's theory of effectance, or competence, motivation (White 1963). Competence motivation is called primary because it is not derived from any more basic motivation. For example, the child does not strive for competence in order to win the approval of others (at least not initially). In fact, Kohlberg says, the approval of others is sought as an assurance of competence.

The specific motivation for social attachment, Kohlberg says, should be defined primarily in terms of effectance, or competence, motivation. Social attachment is understood as "a relationship of sharing, communication, and cooperation (or reciprocity) between selves recognizing each other as selves" (1984, p. 153). The primary motive for social attachment is a desire for a social bond with another social self. This desire, Kohlberg says, has the same motivational roots as children's strivings for stimulation, activity, mastery and self-esteem. Social motivation "is motivation for shared stimulation, for shared activity, mastery, and self-esteem" (1984, p. 153). Kohlberg says this view can be contrasted with most other psychological theories in that they deny that the experience of and desire for these shared relationships are primary components of human social bonds. These theories, in contrast to Kohlberg's, are based on the model of attachment to a physical object, rather than to a social object. In fact, says Kohlberg, infants find social objects much more interesting than physical objects, and thus they initially respond more to social objects.

Although the concept of a primary motivation for social bonds with other social selves is relevant to making a break from the egoistic framework Kohlberg is resisting, it is not sufficient to warrant it. We need to know more about the nature of these social bonds. Again, as Hoffman points out, it is conceivable that social relationships can be Machiavellian; and it must be shown why social relationships, even if desired as social, cannot be understood in exclusively manipulative and instrumental terms. Social objects may also be more interesting than physical objects for Machiavellians.

It is likely that Kohlberg's response would involve an appeal to the importance of empathy in socialization. Unfortunately, he does not specify what he means by "empathy." One must rely on contextual interpretation. For present purposes, it is sufficient to sketch out in very rough fashion two possible meanings: (1) empathy as experiencing, and to that extent being able to understand, what others are experiencing; and (2) empathy as having a sympathetic concern for the well being of others, based on one's understanding of others' perspectives. (1) comes closest to the ordinary understanding of "empathy." Hoffman's Machiavellian type could certainly to some extent experience empathy in that sense, but Kohlberg seems to take "empathy" in sense (2). A Machiavellian would not experience empathy in that sense.

Kohlberg's theory relies heavily on the concept of role-taking, imaginatively taking the role of others in order to see things as they see them. This, he says, requires empathy. But empathy in which sense? It cannot be assumed without argument that when one imaginatively "puts oneself in the other's shoes" that the result will be some sort of sympathetic concern for the other. The result might be relief that one is not really in the other's situation; or it might be resentment or envy; or one might be pleased, through better understanding of the other, at having new insights into how to deal with the other (e.g., in manipulative or exploitative ways).

Despite these and other possibilities, Kohlberg most often seems to assume that empathy does involve a sympathetic concern for the well-being of others. The following statements are typical: "Concern for the welfare of other beings, 'empathy,' or 'roletaking,' is the precondition for experiencing a moral conflict rather than a mechanism for its resolution. . . . Psychologically, both welfare concerns (role-taking, empathy) and justice concerns are present at the birth of morality" (1981, p. 175). To avoid confusion, Kohlberg's view of empathy in sense (2) will be referred to as *sympathy*, and *empathy* will be reserved for notions resembling sense (1).

Sympathy in the child, according to Kohlberg, is not the result of either teaching or conditioning: "Empathy does not have to be taught to the child or conditioned; it is a primary phenomenon. What development and socialization achieve is the organization of empathic phenomena into consistent sympathetic and moral concerns, not the creation of empathy as such" (1984, p. 68). If this view of sympathy as a primary phenomenon is accepted, we should not attempt to explain how the egoistic child acquires nonegoistic concerns. Nonegoistic concerns are as primary as egoistic ones (which is not to assess their respective strengths). They may compete with each other, but neither is derivative from the other. What does require explanation is how sympathy takes on the various forms that it does, and Kohlberg's cognitive-developmental theory purports to provide it.

However, it is very important to ask at what point in moral development sympathy begins to play a role. When one looks at Kohlberg's typical descriptions of his stages, it looks as though it would not be present until stage 3. It is this that invites the reinterpretation of his stages along egoistic lines. Yet in a passage already cited, it can be seen that Kohlberg is inclined to say that sympathy is present in one form or another in each stage: "Psychologically, both welfare concerns (role-taking, empathy) and justice concerns are present at the birth of morality and at every succeeding stage, and take on more differentiated, integrated and universalized forms at each step of the development" (1981, p. 175). Unless Kohlberg wishes to exclude stages 1 and 2 from his theory of moral development, they should be redescribed in less egoistic terms.

Furthermore, M. L. Hoffman (1976) presents evidence that sympathetic concern for others can be present in children under two years of age.[3] Although children of this age would fail the cognitive tests that those at Kohlberg's stage 3 pass, they apparently do have some ability to accurately assess the needs of others. They would fail because of limited verbal ability and the complexity of the tests. Hoffman says that "certain forms of role taking in familiar and highly motivating natural settings may precede the more complex forms investigated in the laboratory by several years. The child who can take the role of a familiar person at home may behave egocentrically in the complex role-taking task in the laboratory because he cannot utilize the available cues regarding the inner states of others and must therefore rely on his own perspective" (1976, p. 130).[4] If this view is correct, then sympathy should be given a prominent place prior to stage 3 in Kohlberg's theory. Admittedly, since egocentricity is present in the first two stages, we should not expect sympathy to be as evident as in the subsequent stages; but it seems that children are capable of more types of reasoning than are included in Kohlberg's descriptions of the first two stages.

This can be illustrated by considering stage 2. Kohlberg typically refers to this as a "back-scratching" stage of instrumental hedonism, but consider the following two perspectives: (i) I should return the favor (take my turn) if I expect another's continued cooperation; and (ii) I should return the favor (take my turn) because it's fair (I owe the other that in return). These perspectives (although perhaps not the language in which they are expressed) do not seem beyond the grasp of children who might well fail the cognitive tests those at Kohlberg's stage 3 can pass. But (ii), unlike (i), is not egoistic reasoning. Still, it is restricted to an instance of actual exchange (stage 2), and a child who can grasp its point might well be unable to handle the concepts involved in what Kohlberg calls imaginative, or ideal, reciprocity (stage 3). In addition, although it might be argued that a stage 2 child who accepts (ii) does not understand its full implications, the child's receptivity to it can be based on sympathetic concern for others. It seems unnecessary to suppose that it must somehow be tied down to hedonistic motivation.

Interestingly, there are some occasions in which Kohlberg himself suggests that both (i) and (ii) may be present in stage 2. For example, in the same article in which he says that at stage 2, "reciprocity is a matter of 'you scratch my back and I'll scratch yours,'" not loyalty, gratitude or justice" (1973, p. 631), he also attributes the following reasoning to a child at stage 2: "if you contribute to my needs and interests, it's fair for me to contribute to yours" (1973, p. 642). The second statement suggests that Kohlberg's theory should be receptive to qualifying the egoistic tone of stage 2.

An advantage of reformulating stages 1 and 2 along less egoistic lines is that the abruptness of transition from stage 2 to stage 3 would be removed. Nonegoistic motivation would not make a sudden and inexplicable appearance at stage 3, when the child is already six or seven years old. At the same time, however, some of the sharpness of the distinctions among stages would be lost. With more continuity and overlapping among the stages, there is less reason to insist that there are precisely six qualitatively distinct stages of moral development. Different types of judgment and reasoning could still be identified, along with the degree and kind of cognitive complexity presupposed; and there could still be rough groupings. But whatever stages, if any, we identify would no longer have the appearance of rigidity suggested by Kohlberg's descriptions.

The suggestion that the role of sympathy should be incorporated in the descriptions of stages 1 and 2 is not a minor one and is quite important for those concerned with the moral development of children who try to draw lessons for moral education from Kohlberg's theory. If they focus only on Kohlberg's typical characterizations of moral stages and the typical ages of children in those stages, they might conclude that it is pointless to encourage nonegocentric thinking until children are in the first grade. If children have the capacity to sympathize with others much earlier, there is some possibility of slowing down moral development by not taking that into account. Also, there is the risk that ignoring this capacity in small children might actually diminish their capacity to sympathize. In any case, it seems that careful attention should be given to what is and is not conducive to the development of the capacity to sympathize with others at the very onset of that capacity.

COGNITION AND AFFECT

Unfortunately, there is reason to doubt that Hoffman's evidence that very small children have the capacity to sympathize with others would incline Kohlberg to devote much attention to sympathy in his theory of moral development because, even when Kohlberg does acknowledge that sympathy is an integral aspect of moral stages (from stage 3 on), he shows relatively little interest in attending specifically to it. His main concern still is to consider the factors influencing the cognitive aspects of moral development.

Kohlberg claims that there is not a large gap between cognitive development and moral development. He is sensitive to the criticism that there may be greater motivation for developing cognitive abilities than for attaining the higher stages of moral development. It might be thought, he says, that "cognitive potential is not actualized in moral judgment because of a will, or desire factor. It is obviously to one's self interest to reason at one's highest level in the cognitive realm, less clearly so in the moral realm. Stage 6 may be the cognitively most advanced morality, but perhaps those *capable* of reasoning that way do not wish to be martyrs like Socrates, Lincoln, or King, and *prefer* to reason at a lower level" (1981, p. 139). Kohlberg allows that someone "might conceivably possess the concepts of stage 4, 5 or 6, even though he does not habitually employ them in his moral thinking" (1981, p. 139). But he says, "the slip between logical and moral development is not particularly large in the area involving concepts of sentiments. Thus, a child's stage on the aspect 'concepts of moral sentiments' correlates well with his stage on nonaffective concepts, and correlates about as well with IQ as do the nonaffective concepts" (1981, p. 140).

It should be noted, however, that although this might plausibly be claimed of children who are still developing cognitively, it is most implausible to say the same of cognitively well-developed adults. It should be recalled that Kohlberg believes that the vast majority of adult Americans never go beyond stage 4 in moral development. To continue to maintain that, even among adults, there is not a large gap between cognitive and moral development implies that the vast majority of adult Americans are incapable of formal operational thinking (the level of cognitive development required for the postconventional, critical morality of stages 5 and 6). This seems clearly false, and Kohlberg offers no evidence to the contrary. It appears that some reason other than lack of conceptual understanding is required to explain why more thinking does not occur at stage 5.

Kohlberg's reply seems to be that we are, nevertheless, entitled to focus primarily on the cognitive aspects because stages are differentiated from one another by cognitive rather than affective criteria. Such a reply is misleading, for to make this point Kohlberg must consider affective states independently of their cognitive features. This would contradict his claim that cognition and affect in moral judgment are two sides of the same coin. It also brings into question Kohlberg's acknowledgment that the moral sentiments themselves undergo developmental changes. For example, he says, "The emergence of self-condemnation as a distinctive sentiment in moral judgment is the final step in a series of differentiations" (1981, p. 140).

Nevertheless, Kohlberg maintains:

> In general, then, the quality (as opposed to the quantity) of affects involved in moral judgment is determined by its cognitive-structural development, and is part and parcel of the general development of the child's conceptions of a moral order. Two adolescents, thinking of stealing, may have the same feeling of anxiety in the pit of their stomachs. One adolescent (stage 2) interprets the feeling as "being chicken" and ignores it. The other (stage 4) interprets the feeling as "the warning of my conscience" and decides accordingly. The difference in reaction is one in cognitive-structural aspects of moral judgment, not in emotional "dynamics" as such. (1981, pp. 140-41)

Several things should be said about this passage. First, when Kohlberg refers to "the same feeling of anxiety in the pit of their stomachs," he cannot be identifying this with affective states as such. As his first sentence implies, affective states have cognitive-structural features that give them the specific qualities that enable us to differentiate them from one another. That is, in the example, the affective states in question *include* the adolescents' "interpretations" of the feelings in the pit of their stomachs.

Second, as a consequence, even if in some sense it is acceptable to say that the quality of affects is "determined by" its cognitive-structural development, it is not a *causal* determination. Rather, these cognitive-structural features serve as criteria for identifying and differentiating affective states. Therefore, what is causally responsible for the particular affective states experienced by the adolescents is still an open question. In fact, it is curious that it does not occur to Kohlberg to ask why the adolescents interpret the feelings in their stomachs as they do. He provides no reason for supposing that the answer need not make any special reference to previous affective states or dispositions.

Third, in light of the first two points, it is not clear what Kohlberg means when he says, "The difference in reaction is one in cognitive-structural aspects of moral judgment, not in emotional 'dynamics' as such." Emotion, as affect, includes cognitive aspects of moral judgment if we are talking about moral emotions, or sentiments. It is not clear what we are to understand "emotional 'dynamics' as such" to refer to when it is contrasted to cognitive-structural aspects of moral judgment. If Kohlberg is abstracting some kind of "uninterpreted" feelings in the pit of one's stomach from the experience of the adolescents and referring to these feelings as the "emotional 'dynamics' as such," his point can be granted—but then it should be acknowledged that these feelings are not, in themselves, emotions. Thus, nothing is settled in regard to whether special attention should be given to affective states in explaining moral development, including what factors encourage or inhibit that development.

In regard to this last point, Kohlberg maintains, "Concern for the welfare of other beings, 'empathy,' or 'role-taking,' is the precondition for experiencing a moral conflict rather than a mechanism for its resolution" (1981, p. 175). This is a puzzling passage, given other things Kohlberg says. Advancement from one stage to the next is, according to Kohlberg, facilitated in part by the higher stage's ability to resolve conflicts that cannot be handled adequately by the lower stages. Kohlberg often emphasizes the importance of "empathy," or "role-taking," for advancement from one stage to another. Thus, it is not clear how we can deny that, at least in part, concern for the welfare of others is a mechanism for the resolution of moral conflict. For example, those on the verge of moving from stage 3 to stage 4 might experience conflict between their concern for the welfare of their close associates and their concern for the welfare of other members of their society. Insofar as they acknowledge that, in this context, the proper scope of concern should include all members of their society, they are employing stage 4 thinking. Their concern for the welfare of members of this larger class seems to provide some help in enabling them to adopt a more impartial stance than stage 3 allows, thus aiding them in resolving the conflict.

At this point we must ask what encourages or discourages individuals to alter the scope and nature of their concern for others. There is no doubt that opportunities for role-taking play an important part. Insofar as Kohlberg does acknowledge a gap between cognitive and moral development, he cites the lack of adequate opportunities for role-taking as the decisive factor, but it is not clear that this is the whole story. In fact, in some instances role-taking might inhibit rather than encourage moral development. Consider someone who is envious and resentful of those who have social and economic advantages over his or her position. If the person is basically at stage 2, the resentment will have stage 2 qualities. It is possible, of course, that somehow taking the role of the other will result in stage 3 resentment, but there is no a priori reason to suppose that this is likely. It is not difficult to find examples of individuals who harbor unreasonable envy, hatred, and vindictiveness toward those they believe to be "better off." In such cases role-taking of this sort might well entrench them more firmly in stage 2.

This raises the more general question of the relationship between moral sentiments at the lower stages to one's advancement to the higher stages. Presumably, resentment takes on different forms in the various stages. Those interested in moral education should be concerned with finding out to what extent, if any, resentment in the earlier stages presents an obstacle to the development of the more impartial postures of the later stages. The other morally reactive attitudes such as guilt, shame, and remorse, as well as the more positive attitudes associated with concern for others, should be accorded the same interest.

RAWLS AND KOHLBERG

A comparison of Rawls and Kohlberg will bring out even more basic difficulties with Kohlberg's treatment of affect, problems that go to the heart of his stage theory. Rawls, like Kohlberg, draws from Robert White's effectance, or competence, theory of motivation and formulates what he calls the *Aristotelian principle*, which holds that "other things equal, human beings enjoy the exercise of their realized capacities (their innate or trained abilities), and this enjoyment increases the more the capacity is realized, or the greater its complexity. The intuitive idea here is that human beings take more pleasure in doing something as they become more proficient at it, and of two activities they do equally well, they prefer the one calling on a larger repertoire of more intricate and subtle discriminations" (Rawls 1971, p. 426). The "other things equal" clause is important, as is evident when we consider situations in which other things are not equal.

Consider, first, one of *Newsweek*'s examples from its cover-story on heroes:

Nine-year-old Ralph Heard, Jr., didn't think he was a hero for saving his mother and brother from their burning apartment last year. Neither, it appeared, did anyone else in Atlanta. No local paper reported the fire; a neighbor whom Ralph helped rescue sued for damages because the flames had started in the Heard apartment, and when Ralph returned to Kimberley Elementary School after six weeks in an emergency unit (where it was feared that facial burns had blinded him), classmates jeered at his headmask with taunts of "burnt boy."

Ralph came home in tears most days—sobbing as he never had at the burns that seared 50 percent of his body. But eventually justice triumphed, sort of. After Ralph's mother moved the family to a new school district, a visiting fire marshal noticed Ralph's mask and asked for explanations. The story touched off a string of tardy tributes from a local radio station, the Hartford Insurance Group, Atlanta Mayor Maynard Jackson and even the Governor—who honored him with a special proclamation in the gold-domed capitol.

Still, Ralph hasn't lost sight of the painful surgery ahead or of the painful mockery behind him. "Yes, I'd do it again," he answered a reporter after pondering for several minutes. "But only for my family. Not for anybody else." (August 6, 1979, p. 50)

Ralph's case might be compared with Kohlberg's famous Heinz example. Kohlberg characterizes the highest stage of moral development as insisting that Heinz should be as willing to steal a needed cancer-curing drug for a stranger as for his wife—since, at the highest level of morality, human life as such is valued, not simply the life of a loved one.

What might Kohlberg say of young Ralph's reasoning after his ordeal? Since at one time Ralph actually risked his life to help save a neighbor, this suggests he was at least at stage 3. However, now Ralph says that he would do it again, but only for his family. This, on Kohlberg's view, seems to constitute moral regression, perhaps even to stage 2 (where actual reciprocation occurs, in contrast to the ideal, or imaginative, reciprocation of stage 3). Is this a fair analysis? Ralph's heroic efforts resulted in derision from his classmates and a lawsuit on the part of his neighbor. The derision threatened his self-esteem. Is it not perfectly rational, and morally acceptable, in such a circumstance to refuse to do again something that might have such consequences? What is especially interesting about this example is that Ralph's sensitivity to what his peers think of him (stage 3) triggers his "regression" to stage 2.

Kohlberg's theory does not adequately address problems of this sort, the result of a nearly exclusive concentration on cognitive aspects of moral development. Rawls's theory, on the other hand, can readily account for what happened in Ralph's case. Reciprocation in kind fosters moral development, according to Rawls's psychological principles. Since self-esteem is a primary good (for the reasons given by Rawls), it is quite understandable that Ralph would modify his stance. Not only was there no reciprocation in kind, Ralph was also subjected to humiliation and a lack of gratitude.[5] Rather than betraying a lack of moral maturity on Ralph's part, this example illustrates serious problems in the social environment within which he lives. In short, the problem is much larger than Ralph.

Consider, next, problems with being a Good Samaritan. Herbert Fingarette provides an example:

> They were hurrying to a meeting in a relatively strange part of town. Suddenly, from out of a nearby apartment-house window, a woman began crying for help. My friends were of course startled and frightened. They debated for a few moments whether to go their way or rush to the rescue. The screams continued. The impulse to keep on their way was strong; but they finally decided to go into the house. As they rushed up several flights of stairs, they passed a number of apartment dwellers, standing in the hall at their open doors, listening avidly to the increasingly anguished screams. Frightened and

breathless, my friends at last arrived and banged on the door. To their utter amazement, the woman herself opened it. It was immediately obvious that the well meaning Samaritans had interrupted a glorious family fight. The woman proceeded to deliver a rapid-fire, full-voice lecture on a citizen's right to privacy, on the obnoxiousness of self-appointed Good Samaritans, and on her own good nature which prevented her from reporting the intruders to the police. (1967, p. 143)

Fingarette does not describe the full emotional reaction his friends had to being verbally assaulted. There are two obvious possibilities; one is that they were very embarrassed. This embarrassment is distinct from shame, but it does pose at least a temporary threat to self-esteem. Another possible reaction is indignation at the humiliation to which the woman tried to subject them and her lack of appreciation for their concern for her well-being. Either response connects with self-esteem. The point of this example is that if lending a helping hand is likely to be met with hostility or recrimination, each of us has some understandable reason for being somewhat reluctant to make the effort. Fingarette's essay is addressed to the problem of how to encourage Good Samaritans in a society that has such a variety of ways of discouraging them.

Again, as in the case of young Ralph, the problem seems larger than the particular individuals in question. In cases like these we should not always expect individuals to reason in the manner commended by Kohlberg's stages 5 or 6, and those who reason at earlier stages should not necessarily be regarded as less morally mature than those at stages 5 or 6. Nevertheless, if we believe it is desirable for individuals to reason at Kohlberg's later stages, then we must attend to the social and institutional structures that inhibit as well as enhance moral development.

This last statement might be acceptable to Kohlberg. He says that "the formation of a mature sense of justice requires participation in just institutions" (1981, p. 193). However, his way of putting the matter is problematic. From the standpoint of minorities and women, at least, many aspects of American institutions are not particularly just. No doubt Kohlberg would cite this injustice in explaining why, on his account, so few members of these groups (or any others) reason at his highest level. Obviously Kohlberg and his colleagues have not tested the entire population to verify the claim that most Americans never get beyond stage 4, so we can only speculate about how members of these groups might handle Kohlbergian questionnaires.

Still, suppose Kohlberg's speculations turned out to be largely correct and that, in fact, the preponderance of answers fit into his earlier stages. It seems to follow, given his analysis that these persons lack a mature sense of justice, but this conclusion is not warranted. Compare Kohlberg's conclusion with a remark by Rawls: "But it is also true that it is rational for each person to act on principles of justice only on the assumption that for the most part these principles are recognized and similarly acted upon by others" (Rawls 1971, p. 436). This matches up well with Rawls's psychological principles of reciprocity and the significance he believes we attach to self-esteem and self-respect. Rawls's point is that what can be morally expected from someone may vary with the degree to which his or her social circumstances approximate a reasonably just setting. It seems that, for Rawls, in a seriously unjust society it may sometimes be rational (and morally allowable) for at least some (the victims of injustice) to show partiality toward themselves or those with whom they have close ties, even when this might conflict with principles of justice suited for a more well-ordered society.

How this might plausibly be spelled out is a complicated matter and will not be attempted here. The important point is that Rawls acknowledges that the conditions of actual societies do complicate issues of justice. Yet Kohlberg takes Rawls's model of justice for well-ordered, reasonably just societies and applies it directly to our own. Rawls is more cautious, in that he restricts his discussion (even of the development of a sense of justice) to hypothetical societies that most would agree are clearly more just than our own.

Although Kohlberg concludes that anyone whose reasoning falls short of his stage 5 lacks a mature sense of justice, a more careful investigation requires us to take into consideration the appropriateness of different types of reasoning in the various kinds of circumstances that arise in societies like ours. Since Rawls concentrates on hypothetical, ideally just societies, Kohlberg misapplies his account. Does a judgment that shows partiality toward a group of which one is a member, and resentment and distrust of those outside it, betray something less than a mature sense of justice? Seemingly, Kohlberg would say yes. Rawls would ask us to take a closer look before making a determination.

When we do take a closer look, it is likely that the moral landscape will appear much more unclear and problematic than Kohlberg's account suggests. Before concluding that a shortfall of stage 5 or 6 responses indicates a lack of moral maturation, we must determine to what extent that shortfall is a function of the appropriateness of other sorts of responses. If it is arguable that other sorts of responses are sometimes appropriate, serious doubt is cast on the adequacy of Kohlberg's characterization of moral reasoning in terms of different stages. Instead, we might better talk about different types of reasoning that are appropriate or inappropriate for different kinds of situations. Thus viewed, those who are morally the most "mature" would be those who most consistently use appropriate types of reasoning in different types of situations calling for practical decisions. Insofar as we may be unsure about what *is* appropriate, we are bound to be uncertain to some extent about what constitutes moral maturity. Nevertheless, it seems unlikely that those who should be counted as reasonably mature would, as a matter of course, satisfy Kohlberg's criteria for stages 5 or 6 if broadly representative samplings of their practical decision-making situations are considered. This contention will be developed in the next chapter, which examines Carol Gilligan's critique of Kohlberg.

8
Caring and Justice in Moral Development

> Magda Trocme believes that something is evil *because* it hurts people. Hers is an ethic of benevolence: She need only to look into the eyes of a refugee in order to find her duty.
>
> But her husband had a more complex ethic. He believed that something is evil both because it hurts somebody *and* because it violates an imperative, a commandment given us by God in the bible and in our particular hearts. He had to look up some authority beyond the eyes of the refugee to find that commandment, but having found it, his duty, like hers, lay in diminishing the hurt in those eyes.
>
> —*Philip Hallie*, Lest Innocent Blood Be Shed

Carol Gilligan's *In a Different Voice* (1982) presents a serious challenge to some central features of Lawrence Kohlberg's theory of moral development. After working within the Kohlbergian framework for several years, Gilligan became convinced that it systematically excludes a "different voice." Kohlberg's account emphasizes reciprocity, justice, rights, duties, impartiality, and individual autonomy, or independence. In contrast, Gilligan's "different voice" emphasizes responsibility, care, special relationships, and interdependence. Thus, she contrasts Kohlberg's "ethic of justice" with an "ethic of care."[1]

Although her "different voice" has received considerable attention in its own right, Kohlberg's extensive reply to Gilligan's challenge is still in need of detailed examination.[2] The primary aim of this chapter is to show that Kohlberg's attempt to accommodate Gilligan's perspective within his fails. I will argue that, ironically, Kohlberg's famous Heinz dilemma exemplifies this failure. Although he refers to the Heinz dilemma as a "justice dilemma," I will try to show that it has very little to do with justice. I will conclude with a brief discussion of some of the implications of the Kohlberg/Gilligan controversy for moral education.

KOHLBERG'S REPLY TO GILLIGAN

Kohlberg acknowledges that Gilligan has correctly pointed out that he paid too little attention to the notions of care and compassion in his earlier work. Nevertheless, he maintains that his basic conception of morality as justice can handle any of the moral dilemmas which might be approached from the standpoint of care or compassion. Just what this amounts to is not clear. Several alternatives must be considered.

One possible linking of morality with care and compassion is through "benevolence as a principle." Oddly, Kohlberg subsumes benevolence under justice: "When benevolence is treated as a principle, it is the principle of utilitarianism and is to be considered a part of justice" (1984, p. 227). This statement is a reversal of the classical utilitarian view that justice is but a part of utility, and it ignores the ongoing philosophical debate about whether utilitarianism can provide an acceptable view of justice. Furthermore, this view threatens to trivialize the claim that an ethic of justice can handle dilemmas that might otherwise be approached from the standpoint of care or compassion. If benevolence is regarded as a part of justice, then it seems that "morality" and "justice" are simply being equated, thus reducing all universal moral principles to principles of justice.

In any case, Gilligan does not propose an impartial principle of benevolence as an alternative to Kohlberg's ethic of justice. In fact, she does not propose a comprehensive philosophical theory of morality. Insofar as she offers a theory at all, it is a psychological theory of moral development. As she is no doubt aware, a psychological theory of moral development is bound to rely on some philosophical assumptions; but this need not amount to a comprehensive philosophical theory, such as utilitarianism.

Gilligan attempts to address a neglected psychological orientation to situations which have significant moral dimensions. She identifies cares and concerns people have in particular and often special relationships to others. She sometimes refers to her approach as "contextual relativism," as distinct from a more abstract, universalistic approach. Gilligan does not deny that there is a place in morality for universal, impartial principles of justice, rights, duties, or even utility. Her concern is to show that attempts to categorize the moral thinking of people solely in relation to such principles either distorts or ignores important aspects of the moral thinking of a large number of people, particularly women.[3]

Kohlberg contrasts his "moral point of view" to Gilligan's perspective by distinguishing two senses of the word "moral":

1. The "moral point of view" emphasizes impartiality, universalizability, and the effort to gain consensus with others who are attempting to adopt an impartial, universalizable perspective.
2. The "ethic of personal responsibility" emphasizes relationships of special responsibility to family and friends, without concern for impartiality and universalizability, and without any effort to gain consensus with others. (1984, p. 229)

This contrast seems overstated. Gilligan's perspective can be concerned not to *violate* requirements of universalizability and impartiality. Also, her perspective does concern itself with efforts to gain consensus with at least some others—namely, those believed to be affected by the alternatives under consideration. This is a concern to gain actual consensus among the parties affected rather than the more hypothetical consensus of all reasonable persons that is sought by Kohlberg's "moral point of view." In any case, for Kohlberg, moral development is to be understood in terms of stages marking a progression in the direction of the fullest satisfaction of the criteria specified in the "moral point of view."

Kohlberg apparently believes that the second sense of "moral" captures Gilligan's ethic of care. He claims that this second sense bears three marks of morality:

a. It embraces some concern for the welfare of another.
b. It involves a feeling of responsibility or obligation.
c. It involves an effort to communicate with the other parties involved. (1984, p. 229)

Although Kohlberg acknowledges that this is a perfectly legitimate sense of the word "moral," he is concerned to show that the "moral point of view" can adequately handle the moral issues considered from the second standpoint. How he thinks this is possible must now be considered.

Unfortunately, Kohlberg nowhere provides a clear statement of how he thinks care and justice are related. Consider this passage:

In our view, special obligations of care presuppose, but go beyond, the general duties of justice which are necessary but not sufficient for them. Thus, special relationship dilemmas may elicit care responses which supplement and deepen the sense of generalized obligations of justice. In our standard dilemmas considerations of special relationship are in some sense supplementary since they go beyond the duties owed to another on the basis of a person's rights. . . . Heinz's care for his wife deepened his sense of obligation to respect her right to life. (1984, p. 230)

Heinz's situation is that he must steal a cancer-curing drug if his wife is to be saved. The druggist is charging $2000 for the drug, but Heinz is able to raise only $1000. The druggist is unwilling to lower the price or extend credit to Heinz. A straightforward interpretation of this passage suggests that if Heinz has a responsibility to help his dying wife, it must be grounded in justice (respect for her right to life), regardless of his motivation. If this is what Kohlberg means, then what does he mean when he says that special obligations of care in some sense "go beyond" duties of justice? Perhaps all he means is that caring provides a *motivational* supplement to fulfilling duties of justice, but it does not provide an additional *justificatory* ground for action. If this is what Kohlberg has in mind, it seems that he does not really mean to acknowledge that there is an *ethic* of care. No new obligations or duties are grounded in caring. Rather, the sense of responsibility which is based on caring simply enhances one's appreciation of duties of justice. Viewed independently of justice, this caring might even be called premoral.

In contrast, consider one of Kohlberg's more advanced reasoners. He is characterized as expressing a caring response to his wife's predicament. However, he generalizes his response to include strangers. Not only would he steal a lifesaving drug for his wife if it could be acquired in no other way, he would also do the same for a stranger. He comments, "Jesus tells of the guy at the side of the road and the stranger that helped him. He felt human and that was enough of a bond" (1984, p. 230). From this perspective, the reasoner is assisted in recognizing Heinz's duty of justice to help his wife by imaginatively putting himself in Heinz's situation as a loving husband, but this projection is then somehow generalized to include the stranger. Thus, through imaginative caring for a particular person (the wife), he is able to appreciate a duty of justice to save a stranger as well. Overlooked here is the possibility that he is generalizing, not a duty of justice, but caring. That is, what is generalized is not justice, but benevolence. This example seems to be just one more instance of Kohlberg's general failure to recognize the distinction between universalizability and justice.

There is another possible relationship between Kohlberg's ethic of justice and Gilligan's ethic of care, suggested by Kohlberg's discussion of what should be said about the reasoning of a respondent who is reflecting about whether to divorce her husband. Kohlberg says, "Reasoning at this postconventional level leads to a tolerance about resolution of personal dilemmas of special obligation while at the same time upholding a general framework of nonrelative justice that provides the context within which individually varying personal moral decision making takes place" (1984, p. 232). Although the respondent herself does not characterize her dilemma as moral, Kohlberg does. Yet in apparent contradiction to his prior claim that his ethic of justice can handle the dilemmas of personal responsibility, he concludes that her dilemma cannot be resolved by the "moral point of view" alone. Instead, Kohlberg insists only that such dilemmas be resolved within the general framework of the "moral point of view." Presumably, this means that, although there is some personal latitude about how such dilemmas may be resolved, acceptable resolutions must not conflict with duties of justice which emanate from the "moral point of view."

If this is Kohlberg's position, it allows for an independent grounding of Gilligan's ethic of care and gives it greater moral significance than that of being simply a motivational supplement to Kohlberg's ethic of justice. Once this concession is made, the distinctiveness of Gilligan's perspective can be made more apparent. Although Kohlberg continually characterizes it in terms of special obligations, the notion of obligation is not emphasized by Gilligan. Instead, she talks about caring responses, responsiveness to need, and the acceptance of responsibility. Caring for others often exhibits a much more supportive response than would be expected from those who do only what justice requires of them or what is a matter of obligation. Similarly, many take on responsibilities that exceed ordinary requirements of justice or obligation.

However, the contrast between Kohlberg's ethic of justice and Gilligan's ethic of care must not be overdrawn. Unfortunately, Kohlberg does not sufficiently guard himself against this. Consider one of the ways he contrasts judgments of responsibility and justice judgments: "Judgments which consider fulfilling the other's need when not based on a right or claim—or where it is not a matter of preventing harm—are responsibility judgments. [Considerations of welfare based on right or claim—or where it is a matter of not harming another's welfare—are justice judgments.]" (1984, p. 234). This does not leave much for Gilligan's ethic of care. Respecting rights, preventing harm, and not causing harm are all considered justice judgments. Promoting good, as distinct from preventing harm and the avoidance of causing harm, is all that is left. Not only is this an implausible way of distinguishing justice and responsibility judgments, it is also in direct contradiction to Gilligan's characterization of her ethic of care. She continually emphasizes that those who share this perspective are concerned not to harm others and to prevent the occurrence of harm and suffering.

Thus, some overlapping between the prescriptions is likely to emerge from the perspectives of Kohlberg and Gilligan. However, this does not mean that the basis of those prescriptions is identical. Insofar as harming others is seen as unjust, or a violation of rights, an ethic of justice will oppose such harms. So will Gilligan's ethic of care, but without necessarily grounding the opposition in an appeal to justice or rights. The contrast between the two perspectives might be illustrated in this way. If I see two cats fighting, I might intervene in order to prevent them from harming each other. I am trying to prevent harm and suffering, but I am not trying to prevent injustice; nor is it necessary to invoke the notion of rights in order to make intelligible the moral appropriateness of my response. Those who think that the concepts of justice and rights apply to cats as well as humans might object. My point is not to deny that such concepts could apply; rather, it is that such concepts need not apply. Similarly, although it may be appropriate to object to the injustice of not preventing certain harms to human beings, one may focus instead simply on preventing the harms.

THE HEINZ DILEMMA

I now turn to a more detailed analysis of Kohlberg's widely cited Heinz example. He classifies this as a justice dilemma but actually says remarkably little as to what makes this a dilemma about *justice*. One aspect of the situation that concerns justice is the behavior of the druggist. We can ask, first, whether the druggist is charging a fair price for the drug. Second, we can ask whether the druggist is being unfair in his unwilling-ness to let Heinz delay full payment for the drug. However, the dilemma concerns what Heinz should do, not what the druggist has done.

Still, questions about whether the druggist is unfair, or unjust, may be relevant to Heinz's deliberations. If Heinz concludes that the druggist is not being unfair in any sense, he must decide whether it is justifiable to steal the drug from someone else who is fully entitled to retain the drug until offered the price he is asking. If Heinz concludes that the druggist is being unfair, he still must ask whether the druggist is nevertheless act-ing within his legal and moral rights in retaining the drug. However these questions are answered, Heinz may ask whether it would be un-fair, or unjust, for him to steal the drug.

Assuming that Heinz does ask this last question, it might be thought that if he decides that he should steal the drug, then he thinks that steal-ing is what justice requires of him. But this need not be the case. He might think that stealing the drug is unjust, either because he does not believe that the druggist is being unjust or because he thinks it is unjust to steal even from an unjust person. Despite his belief that he is acting unjustly, Heinz might steal the drug because of his love for his wife.

Such a response would be characterized by Kohlberg as at best stage 2 or 3 reasoning. A stage 6 reasoner, according to Kohlberg, would con-clude that Heinz should steal the drug for his wife, and he should steal the drug for a stranger as well. In either case the moral grounding is the same for a stage 6 reasoner. The right to life takes priority over the right to property. The dying person, whether wife or stranger, has a right to life, correlative to which is Heinz's duty to steal the drug. This, for Kohlberg, is justice reasoning at the highest level: There is the fullest rec-iprocity, as reflected in the complete correlativity of rights and duties.

Kohlberg characterizes one of his stage 5 respondents in the following way. While acknowledging that the right to life takes priority over the right to property, this respondent also expresses "a related sense of care between connected selves" in discussing the husband's duty to his wife (1984, p. 228). Kohlberg adds, "There is a commitment to another per-son; marriages being a kind of thing like something in two bodies, and in that sense there is a responsibility; she can't do it for herself. It's like an extension of yourself" (1984, p. 228). It is curious that Kohlberg interprets this response within his justice perspective rather than within Gilligan's perspective of care and responsibility. The intimacy of the relationship described by the respondent does not seem adequately captured by the language of rights, duty, obligation, or contract, the concepts which most readily come to mind in the context of Kohlberg's ethic of justice.

Yet Kohlberg recasts this respondent's remarks in terms of justice. Not only does the respondent acknowledge a duty of justice to Heinz's wife, he is also able somehow to generalize to others: "Being high in justice stage, this respondent is also able to universalize the special relations of caring to a stranger" (1984, p. 229). What evidence does Kohlberg offer for this? The respondent says: "Jesus tells of the guy at the side of the road and the stranger that helped him. He felt human and that was enough of a bond." What, one might ask, has this to do with justice? Care is extended to the stranger as well as to the wife. Still, it cannot be assumed without argument that generalized care is based on considerations of justice. Kohlberg's respondent refers to a bond among human beings, but there is no clear indication that this is a bond of justice. It is expressed as a kind of shared humanity ("He felt human . . .").

Kohlberg's reconstruction seems to be basically that a stage 3 respondent might well urge Heinz to steal the drug for his wife, but not for a stranger. This would show that the respondent is more concerned about the special relationship between Heinz and his wife than about the demands of justice. It is a caring rather than a justice response. The stage 5 reasoner is also giving a caring response, but in a different way. The stage 5 respondent also extends his care to a stranger, suggesting to Kohlberg that the basic response to both the wife and the stranger is concerned with justice. Caring arouses the sense of justice of the respondent. Imagining himself to be Heinz, he recognizes his duty to save his wife because he cares for her. Being high in justice reasoning, he now realizes that this duty is based on justice, not simply on his particular caring relationship to his wife. Thus, he recognizes that (in all fairness) care should be extended to strangers as well. Although caring provides a *psychological* ground for the recognition of the duty to save his wife, the *moral* grounding is justice—the fully reciprocal relationship between rights (to life) and duties (to prevent the loss of life).

However, if one concludes that Heinz should be willing to steal the drug for a stranger as well as for his wife, the underlying principle need not be the same. Heinz might think he should steal for his wife because of their special relationship. He might think he should steal for the stranger because he is in a position to do so, and he feels a responsibility to save the stranger's life—not from love, but from concern for a fellow human being.

That this is a difference that can make a difference is apparent if we consider some variations on the Heinz example. Suppose that Heinz has an alternative to stealing the drug. He can sell a valued family heirloom or the family car, or he can give up the $2000 he and his wife have been saving for many years so that they can take an extended vacation together. In any of these cases it might be expected that Heinz would be willing to come up with the needed money for his wife. Would we expect him to do likewise for a stranger? If Heinz has a duty of justice to steal the drug for his wife or a stranger, doesn't he have a duty of justice to sell the heirloom or the family car, or to give up the savings, if these are available alternatives? Yet few would say that Heinz would be unjust if he were unwilling to do any of these things in order to save a stranger; nor would they likely think that Heinz had any serious moral shortcomings if he were unwilling to do any of these things (or, more likely, if these options never even occurred to him).

Would he be unjust if he were unwilling to do any of them in order to save his wife? Although such unwillingness seems to betray some sort of moral shortcoming in Heinz, it is not at all clear that he is being *unjust* (as distinct from uncaring, unsupportive, or the like). Special responses are appropriate to special relationships. Thus, the moral relationships between intimates can be importantly different from those between strangers—even when, as in the instance of Kohlberg's stage 5 respondent, one is prepared to aid either an intimate or a stranger. Of course, one must be careful not to overstate these differences. There are situations in which special relationships should be ignored because of requirements of impartiality. When an avoidable conflict of interest is involved, there can even be a requirement that intimates be excluded from consideration (for example, in certain hiring situations) or from rendering judgment. However, this is not true of the Heinz example or its variations. Underlying Kohlberg's failure to acknowledge the relevance of special relationships in the Heinz example is confusion about what it means to value life over property and to respect the right to life. This confusion must now be addressed.

VALUING LIFE

Most would acknowledge that human life is, in some sense, to be valued over property. Most, too, would acknowledge that human beings have a right to life, at least in the sense that, barring exceptional circumstances, we should not take the lives of others and that we should prevent the death of others when it requires no great risk or sacrifice to do so. Some are willing to take substantial risks or make great sacrifices in order to prevent the death of others. From a justice perspective, such persons do more than can reasonably be required. Failure to take such risks or make such sacrifices is not unjust. Nor, barring special situations (e.g., those involving police officers), is this a neglect of duty or obligation. From a rights/duty perspective, taking substantial risks or making great sacrifices in order to prevent the death of others is characterized as supererogatory, "above and beyond the call of duty."

The notion of the supererogatory will be discussed at length in Chapter 9. For now it will be sufficient to note that from the perspective of Gilligan's "ethic of personal responsibility," or "ethic of care," those willing to take substantial risks or make great sacrifices are characterized differently. The supererogatory is linked with duty. Although those who care for others or simply accept responsibility to help those in need may do more than duty requires, they do not necessarily view themselves as doing their duty plus a bit (or a lot) more. In fact, particularly when love or friendship is involved, attention to rights, duties, and obligations often marks tension in the relationship.

It is against this background that issues concerning the value of life vs. property and the right to life should be understood. If Heinz were unwilling to sell his $2000 stamp collection in order to save his wife, his priorities certainly would be questionable. What if he were unwilling to sell his $2000 stamp collection in order to save a stranger's life? Would this show that Heinz does not value life over property and that he does not respect the right to life? Someone answering in the affirmative might say, "Evidently Heinz thinks that human life (as distinct from his wife's life) is worth less than $2000." Yet we do not expect people to give up their prized possessions whenever doing so will result in the prevention of a death. We do not even expect them, as a matter of course, to give up less valued possessions or entertainment in order to prevent a death. For example, instead of going to a restaurant, one could give the money to a relief fund in order to save a life. Even those who give generously to the relief fund presumably could give even more if they were willing to reduce recreational and entertainment expenses a little more. At some point, however, they cannot reasonably be expected to give more, even if some actually do give more.

What should we say of those who could give five dollars more to save a life but who do not? That they value property over life? That they value human life at less than five dollars? However welcome the additional five dollars might be, such a conclusion would be unwarranted. How much money one is or is not willing to part with in order to prevent the loss of life should not be equated with placing a dollar value on human life. Rather, it is more an indicator of one's willingness to assume responsibility for doing something to prevent the death of another, and it is not a very reliable indicator, since those who could afford an additional five dollars must be viewed under different background conditions. (For example, some have already given more than others, some have greater financial obligations than others, and so on).

We must ask what background conditions would make plausible Kohlberg's view that a stranger's right to life holds an equal moral claim on Heinz to that of his wife. Given that stealing is the only option apparently available, it is difficult to see what conditions could make this plausible. Stealing would certainly place Heinz at high risk. In fact, it is difficult to see why Kohlberg would say that anyone's right to life imposes a duty on anyone else to steal from the druggist in order to save a life. It is precisely Heinz's special relationship to his wife that enables us to understand why he might feel impelled to steal the drug, but this makes no appeal to an abstract, generalizable right to life.

Furthermore, even in those instances in which it can be said that one has a duty of charity to help those (unknown others) in need, it does not follow that the needy have a right to help from the specific person who has the duty to help. Thus, there seems to be a confusion in Kohlberg's claim that rights and duties are fully correlative at his highest stage of reasoning. Finally, we might consider the flatness of Heinz's appeal to the right to life should he reason at Kohlberg's highest level. Suppose Heinz, after stealing the drug to save his wife, were to explain to her, "I know I had to break the law in order to get the drug for you, but I would have done it for anyone. After all, everyone has a right to life."

UNIVERSALIZABILITY AND REVERSIBILITY

It has already been noted that universalizability and reversibility are essential features of Kohlberg's "moral point of view"—as, indeed, they are of most contemporary moral theories. Kohlberg's treatment of these two ideas needs to be examined in some detail at this point. The universalizability requirement is that justifiable moral judgments are generalizable to similar persons in similar situations. The reversibility requirement is that one must find one's moral judgment acceptable whether one is on the receiving or the giving end of the judgment. (Notice that this does not mean that one would *want* to be on the receiving end—only that one would find it morally acceptable.)

These two requirements are, for Kohlberg, not only necessary for all justifiable moral judgments, they are also requirements of justice. They require impartiality at the level of principles. That is, we must have impartially justifiable principles, ones that can apply to all similar persons in similar situations. However, impartially justifiable principles should not be confused with principles of impartiality, that is, principles that require us to treat people impartially. An impartially justifiable principle might in many kinds of circumstances approve partiality to friends or loved ones. A principle of impartiality rules out such partiality (for example, in a court of law, or in employment policies). Unfortunately, Kohlberg does not always bear this distinction in mind.[4]

Principles of universalizability and reversibility are requirements of moral consistency, so violations of these principles are commonly regarded as unjust, or unfair. Kohlberg seems to confuse the requirement that justifiable moral judgments not be unjust with the notion that justifiable moral judgments are judgments of justice. This confusion is evident in his attempt to assimilate the generalized principle of benevolence to justice by claiming that benevolence as a principle is a part of justice. Thus, as we have already seen, Kohlberg characterizes utilitarianism as a part of justice.

However, even though a moral judgment which fails the tests of universalizability and reversibility may be unjust, it does not follow that a moral judgment that passes these tests is a judgment of justice. There are two possible reasons why Kohlberg may not notice this. The first involves a possible misunderstanding of John Rawls's *veil of ignorance*, a device used by Rawls to derive fundamental principles of justice (Rawls 1971). The second results from a failure to appreciate fully that frequently the tests of universalizability and reversibility *underdetermine* moral choice. That is, several incompatible choices may be able to pass these tests.

Let us first consider Rawls's veil of ignorance. Rawls asks us to imagine an original position, a hypothetical situation in which we are deprived of certain specific kinds of information about ourselves and our circumstances which typically influence our practical judgments. While under the veil of ignorance, we do not know whether we are male or female, what our race is, whether we are rich or poor, well or poorly educated, employed or unemployed, and so on. On the other hand, we are permitted general knowledge about human nature, social dynamics, political behavior, and economic theory. Furthermore, we are to imagine ourselves to be highly self-interested. (We will not settle for less personal happiness if more is available to us.) Placed under these constraints, we must try to agree on the basic principles of justice which should be used to evaluate the fundamental structure of our social and political institutions.

It is clear that the veil of ignorance is intended to minimize bias by depriving us of just the sorts of knowledge that tend to slant our judgments in favor of ourselves and those we care about. However, Rawls is careful to point out that he intends his veil of ignorance to be used only when deliberating about the fundamental principles to be used in evaluating the basic structure of society. Unlike Kohlberg, he does not attempt to use this device in deliberating about individual moral choice in everyday affairs. Given his limited context, it is understandable that Rawls would think of the resulting principles as principles of justice. The parties in the original position over which the veil of ignorance is imposed are understood to be potential supporters and beneficiaries of the institutions and practices that are to be evaluated. One would expect reciprocity to be fundamental to such a cooperative scheme.

But, as Rawls recognizes, extending the veil of ignorance to everyday choices leads to complications. One is that cooperation and reciprocity may have less clear application. This is particularly so in the case of the Heinz dilemma, which is not concerned with the question of what one might rightly expect in return for giving support to the basic structure of society. Rather, it is a question of what one should do (and why) in response to the unfortunate plight of someone in desperate need of help. Rawls's veil of ignorance focuses on individuals voluntarily promoting a social scheme which promises them something in return for their support. Here the questions are, what can fairly be required from each, and what can one fairly expect in return?

Such questions of fairness do not seem clearly applicable to Heinz's relationship to the stranger, nor should they be presumed to be the operative notions in Heinz's relationship to his wife. In neither case do we need to suppose that any notion of reciprocity, actual or ideal, is operative. If Heinz thinks it would be appropriate to steal the drug for a stranger, presumably he would think that a reversal of roles would also be acceptable (even though he might not have an expectation that a stranger would actually do the same for him). But it does not mean that this ideal reciprocity provides the basic reason for stealing the drug. Stealing the drug might be judged appropriate simply because someone is in desperate need. Consistency requires universalizability and reversibility, but it may be the response to need that is fundamental.

Heinz's willingness to steal for his wife involves other considerations. Even if Heinz would expect his wife to steal the drug for him if the roles were reversed, this may have little, if any, bearing on his willingness to steal for her. He may steal the drug because his loved one is in desperate need of help. If he believes she loves him, he might expect her to do the same if the roles were reversed. This is quite distinct from his believing that he should steal the drug because she would do the same for him. Again, justice, or fairness, is not the issue.

On the face of it, stealing has much to be said against it. However objectionable the druggist's pricing of the drug might seem, there is no suggestion in the Heinz dilemma that the druggist is not legally entitled to exact such a price. Most do not regard breaking the law as morally indifferent in and of itself. Furthermore, if the drug is stolen, it is not available to someone else who could afford it. (Presumably the druggist would not ask such a price if he thought he could not sell it. If the supply is limited, then possibly someone else in need will be left out.) Also, of course, Heinz places himself at great personal risk by engaging in theft. Finally, there is likely to be some doubt about the effectiveness of the drug even if it is available to Heinz's wife or a stranger. These are all substantial reasons for Heinz's reluctance to steal the drug, even for his wife.

Given all this, what grounds can there be for thinking that stealing the drug could be a requirement of justice? In the case of the stranger, there seem to be none. The stranger might wish that Heinz would steal the drug; and Heinz might think that, were he in the stranger's shoes, he would wish that the stranger would steal the drug for him. (In both cases this is only a "might." They might not wish that someone would break the law to save them.) It is not plausible to hold that justice or the right to life imposes a duty on anyone to steal the drug for a stranger. Even if a stranger felt that his right to life were being violated by not having access to the drug, he could hardly complain that Heinz was violating that right by not stealing the drug. The violation of his right to life would fall either on the druggist or perhaps on structural injustices of a society which make such a drug unavailable for those who cannot afford it.

It might be thought that justice is relevant to the question of whether Heinz should steal the drug for his wife. However, even if one is inclined to say that Heinz should steal the drug for her, it is implausible to ground this claim in justice. Certainly the vow of marriage, or even a written contract of marriage, is not sufficient to show that Heinz would be unjust to his wife if he were not to steal for her. Even if it is acknowledged that certain moral obligations flow from marriage vows or a contract of marriage, neither stipulates or implies that the marriage partners are morally obligated to steal for one another. The history of the relationship between Heinz and his wife might well make intelligible Heinz's conviction that he must steal the drug, but this conviction is more likely an expression of his love for his wife than his sense of justice. The upshot is that, ironically, if one is convinced that Heinz should steal the drug for a stranger, what one should really advocate is a broadening of Gilligan's ethic of care to include strangers as well as intimates. Contrary to Kohlberg, it is not a higher level of justice reasoning which is required. It is an extension of care.

Kohlberg's employment of the notion of "moral musical chairs" might seem to suggest otherwise. He suggests that we test our moral judgments by asking if we would find their implications acceptable regardless of which position we might imagine ourselves to be in. He concludes that the druggist would not be able to pass the test. Were the druggist to imagine himself in the position of the wife, he would find the consequences unacceptable. The test of "moral musical chairs," Kohlberg thinks, would show the druggist that his position does not meet the requirement of reversibility.

Assuming that the druggist cannot meet the test of reversibility, it could be concluded that the druggist's position is unjust. However, several other observations should be made. First, it still may be the case that what is most objectionable about the druggist is not that he is unjust, but that he is uncaring. Second, although the druggist may be unjust, it does not follow that Heinz is unjust if he does not resist that injustice by stealing the drug. Third, the basic question here is not whether the *druggist's* position is reversible. It is whether *Heinz's* not stealing the drug is reversible.

The problem for Kohlberg is that, even if stealing the drug is reversible, so is not stealing the drug. That is, "moral musical chairs" underdetermines moral choice in this case. It is not clear that either choice fails to meet the requirements of universalizability or reversibility. This is why it is a mischaracterization to refer to the Heinz dilemma as fundamentally a dilemma of justice. At most, considerations of justice constrain choice in favor of the druggist, but it is not a duty of justice on Heinz's part which might override justice to the druggist. Rather, it is a caring other-regard, whether this is the special love of one person for another or a more general form of benevolence.

MORAL DEVELOPMENT AND MORAL EDUCATION

This final section will explore some of the implications of the preceding discussion for how the moral development of children should be understood, and, in turn, the importance of this understanding for moral education. First, it should be recalled that, according to Kohlberg, it is not until a child has advanced to stage 3 that he or she sheds self-centered concerns to any significant degree. Stages 1 and 2 are highly egoistic as well as egocentric. When nonegocentric other-regard surfaces at stage 3, it is limited to loved ones, friends, or associates whom one wishes to please. The reasons for the limitations of these first three stages are cognitive and social. Cognitively the child is not yet ready for the kind of logical thinking presupposed by an understanding of social and institutional relationships included in stage 4 "law and order" reasoning. Socially the child's experiences are too restricted to embrace the society-wide concerns of stage 4 or the more universal concerns of stages 5 and 6.

Since, according to Kohlberg, stage 3 reasoning typically does not occur until the child is six or seven years old, those who take this theory seriously are not likely to include in their observations of moral development manifestations of care and compassion in very young children. Yet, as Martin Hoffman (1976) and William Damon (1988) point out, children as young as eighteen months sometimes exhibit a kind of empathy which suggests, not only that they care about the plight of others, but also that, in familiar settings, they can understand others in a nonegocentric manner. Since Kohlberg's account is wedded to the view that moral development consists in the gradual, stagelike development of a moral logic of reciprocity, it should not be surprising that much falls through the cracks.

For example, if a young child rescues a bird from an attack by the family cat, it is difficult to see how this behavior might fit within Kohlberg's account. We need not suppose the child has even implicitly considered what justice, duty, or the rights of others require of him; and it is implausible to read some form of reciprocity into the situation. Furthermore, since such behavior is not a response to a moral dilemma and is typically nonverbal, most likely it would be ignored by Kohlbergians. Yet, insofar as such early manifestations of generalized benevolence are precursors of valued adult benevolence, they should be noticed and supported. If we assume that sympathetic understanding does not surface until the child is well into school years, we will fail to notice and reinforce early caring responses—or we will recast them as forms of behavior designed to avoid punishment or to receive something in return. Thus, opportunities to encourage the further development of caring and compassionate responses will be missed, and possibly the child will come to understand his or her responses in similarly limited ways.

Hoffman's account of the origins of genuine regard for others ("altruism") is based on sympathetic understanding rather than reciprocity. Thus, the child's regard for others is implicitly general from the outset. Interestingly, this generality is grounded in the infant's initial inability to differentiate itself from others—thus responding to the sounds of distress made by others as if they were its own. Unlike Kohlberg, Hoffman does not have the problem of having to show how children move from being basically egoistic to having altruistic concerns. Gilligan's view has a similar virtue.

Unfortunately, Kohlberg's Heinz example is not well designed to test the generality of one's other-regard. In fact, by putting Heinz at risk of being caught, the odds are increased that the replies of those interviewed will suppress empathy for his wife. However, a somewhat different example might show how implausible it is to suppose that even rather young children are incapable of generalized benevolence:

> Little Tammy and her best friend are walking along a country road. A car swerves off the road and hits Tammy's friend. Her friend is badly hurt, but the car keeps on going. Although there are no

houses nearby, there is a pay telephone. But neither Tammy nor her friend have any money. Just then another child is walking by. Tammy asks if she can borrow a quarter to phone for help. The other child replies: "I've worked hard for my money. I'm going to the store to buy a toy I've wanted for a long time; and I have just enough money." As the child talks he protectively puts his hand in his pocket. Tammy notices that a quarter has dropped from his pocket and is caught in the child's pantleg. If she bends over to tie his shoes, Tammy could probably steal the quarter without the other child noticing. Should Tammy steal the quarter? Suppose the injured child were a stranger to Tammy. Should she steal the quarter to help the child?

It seems highly implausible that many children who could understand the story would say that Tammy should not steal the quarter for her best friend. Would many of these children say Tammy should not steal it for the stranger? No doubt Tammy's feelings would differ somewhat in the two cases, as would her reasons for stealing the quarter, but it is hard to believe that many children would lack benevolent concern for the stranger.

At least in this instance, it seems that even young children can recognize that life is more important than property and that preventing death or relieving serious injury can supersede the law. Yet such responses find no comfortable place within Kohlberg's stage theory of justice reasoning. Oddly, on Kohlberg's theory, an older child (or fanatical adult) who insists that it is wrong to steal under any circumstances, since it is against the law (and society needs laws, and so on), would seem to exhibit more mature moral reasoning than the five-year-old who would unhesitatingly steal the quarter to call for help.

Even more odd is Kohlberg's apparent insistence that children who confidently resort to the law and order reasons available in stage 4 to resolve moral perplexity are reasoning at a more advanced stage than children who, because of their concern to avoid harm to others and their relationships, are seen to vacillate uncertainly between conflicting choices. It is morally important to have an understanding of the complexity of social, legal, and political structures in resolving certain moral perplexities. However, appealing to prevailing laws, regulations, and practices can also facilitate decision making at the cost of concern for the parties affected. It is not obvious that the unreflective appeal to rules is a moral advance over developing greater sensitivity to the interests and concerns of those affected by the decisions which are made.

One of the strengths of Gilligan's alternative account is that it emphasizes how sophisticated one's understanding of circumstances must be if one is to determine how the well-being of others (and their relationships to one another) can be affected by the choices we make. Unfortunately, greater sensitivity to such matters often results in greater uncertainty about what one should do. Some may take comfort in established rules which seemingly dictate clear resolutions. As Kohlberg's stages 5 and 6 reveal, this is an illusory comfort—to be shed when one advances to the level of critical morality. For Kohlberg, this critical level involves the acceptance of universal principles of justice, rights, and duties. However, according to Gilligan, lost in the account are the thoughtful reflections of those whose moral orientation pivots more around concepts of care than of justice. Falling short of both the conventional law and order reasoning of stage 4 and the more universalistic justice reasoning of stages 5 and 6, these reflections are indiscriminately consigned to stage 3 concerns to please others and receive their approval.

If Kohlberg's theory did not rest on the assumption that stages 4, 5, and 6 are more adequate than stage 3, perhaps this consignment would not be so objectionable. Yet Kohlberg's characterization of stage 3 reasoning makes care and compassion seem so narrow and unreflective that, by default, the later stages seem more developed morally. One of Gilligan's tasks is to show that Kohlberg has vastly underestimated the complexity and strength of an ethic of care. This underestimation has resulted in a theory of moral development which not only fails to do justice to benevolence, but which also fails to do justice to justice. On any plausible theory of justice, ours is a world with vast injustice, a world where many who are responsible for bringing about injustice are not likely to make any serious effort to reduce it. This default by the agents of injustice does not automatically shift an additional burden of justice to those who are concerned that our world be more just, as the Heinz example illustrates. Even if it is unjust for the druggist to withhold the drug from the cancer victim, it does not follow that it is unjust for Heinz not to steal it.

Still, the Heinzes of this world might accept an additional moral burden in order to compensate for injustices perpetrated by others. Whether they should steal in order to do this is, of course, debatable. However, in general, there are many lawful means for attempting to redress the wrongs done to others, even if none seem available in the Heinz example. If someone who is not responsible for causing an injustice nevertheless acts in behalf of the victims of that injustice, he or she has the virtue of justice to a much higher degree than someone who is concerned only not to cause injustice. A person who has the virtue of justice to this higher degree is not merely fulfilling his or her duties of justice. Here, it seems, we have an overlapping of the virtues of justice and benevolence, but here the virtue of justice transcends what we can demand from one another as a requirement of justice. If there are moral requirements here, they are requirements of benevolence; and there is enough injustice to combat in this world that one could exceed these requirements of benevolence and still not eradicate injustice.

There are forms of benevolence that are addressed to concerns quite other than justice. Consider a recent Dear Abby letter:

> DEAR ABBY: I am a healthy 27-year-old male and have carried an organ donor card since I was 16. However, it seems a shame that I must die before my kidneys can help someone.
>
> With so many people desperate for a kidney, why can't a living person donate one to a stranger? I would be happy to give one of my kidneys to help a person lead a normal life.
>
> Do you know of anyone who would consider a gift of life from the living?
>
> ANONYMOUS IN WISCONSIN[5]

It is perhaps an important commentary on the morality of our time that the first response many have to this letter is to ask whether the writer needs psychological counseling. Perhaps he does, but why should this be our first thought? "Normal" people just aren't like that, we insist. Like what? The letter writer, let's call him George, regards himself to be healthy. No doubt he thinks he will be able to live a normal life with only one kidney (since he thinks the recipient would be able to live a normal life with only one kidney). He is willing to put himself at higher risk in order to provide "a gift of life from the living." Most people would be unwilling to take such a risk. What follows from this?

Do we find it so difficult to accept George's altruism that we are convinced that he must have some sort of deep-seated problem (for example, irrational guilt feelings from his past, a latent death wish, or a desperate sense of inadequacy)? To her credit, Abby does not raise such issues in her response. She praises his "exceptional generosity" but replies that the National Kidney Foundation, for various reasons, does not encourage "unrelated, living kidney donations." However, Abby does provide her readers with information about how they can become organ donors upon death. Interestingly, this information immediately follows her commendation of George ("Bless you for your exceptional generosity.") She does not argue that acquiring a donor card is a requirement of justice, that respect for the right to life demands this, or that, in any sense, one has a duty to become an organ donor. This, too, would be an act of generosity. At the same time, most would agree, it would be morally commendable.

George has already exhibited this more modest generosity by acquiring an organ donor card at age sixteen. Is there something pathological about acquiring an organ donor card at age sixteen? Perhaps George did this in hopes that others would do likewise, so that, should he ever be in need, an organ would be available for him, but this hardly seems necessary. His act of acquiring the card required no serious sacrifice (a few minutes' time to fill out the form and sign the card). As an act of generosity it seems perfectly intelligible in and of itself. Yet where does it fit into Kohlberg's account of moral development? And what were its precursors in George's earlier years? If we leave aside the elements of reciprocity, justice, rights, and duties which dominate Kohlberg's account, what is left to account for George's concern?

If we consider George's willingness actually to give up a kidney while he is alive, Kohlberg's theory is placed under even greater strain. Yet, notice: George says he would be happy to give up a kidney to help another lead a normal life. No doubt he realizes that he is in the minority. Can he universalize his position? Surely he can in this sense: He would not *object* to anyone else (similarly healthy) volunteering the same, but he need not be seen as thinking that others *ought* to do as he is willing to do. (Whether he can coherently think that *he* ought to volunteer his kidney without thinking that others ought to as well is another matter—one that will be taken up in Chapter 9.)

Perhaps some think George goes too far. Even if that were conceded, surely we must agree that it would be desirable for people to be more giving than justice requires. How are we to encourage this? Adherence to Kohlberg's framework is not likely to suffice (both because of what is likely not to be noticed and because of the concepts emphasized themselves). If caring responses are given equal billing with justice responses, we may turn out a few Georges along with more who are willing to sign donor cards. Isn't it better to risk spawning a few who go too far in their generosity rather than have too many who are unwilling to go even an inch of the "extra mile"?

We need to ask what elements of moral education are likely to encourage the emergence of sixteen-year-olds like George, who, even if they aren't willing to give up a kidney while alive, are willing to give without the promise, or even likelihood, of return—and without having to be convinced that it is their duty (correlative to which is a right to life). Kohlberg's account, unlike Gilligan's, is not very promising here. Gilligan is not hamstrung by the problem of egoism and reciprocal logic in the earliest years. Without denigrating reciprocity, an ethic of care can surpass it.

9

Personal Morality

Often moral praise is an interpretation, a grid laid upon the facts by an outsider's hand. An outsider may see goodness or decency "in" an action, as an integral part of, say, Magda's invitation to the police to join them at the big dining table, but the doer of the deed, who often acts on the spur of the moment, see nothing "moral" or "ethical" in that deed. For Magda Trocme and most of the other people of Le Chambon, words of moral praise are like a slightly uncomfortable wreath laid upon a head by a kind but alien hand.
—*Philip Hallie*, Lest Innocent Blood Be Shed

This chapter addresses the question of whether there is a personal dimension of moral life that extends beyond the reach of ordinary interpersonal moral requirements and demands. My answer is that there is, and that this should be grounded in respect for personal integrity and autonomy. Although its boundaries may be imprecise, this sphere of "moral privacy" is a fundamental part of moral life. Further reflection on differences between Kohlberg and Gilligan suggest important issues in need of attention.

At the close of Chapter 8 I suggested that, without denying the importance of reciprocity, an "ethic of care" can surpass a Kohlbergian "ethic of justice." However, it can do so, it seems, only by sacrificing much of the conceptual tidiness sought by Kohlberg. As we have seen, Kohlberg's view is that moral development moves in the direction of a fully reciprocal relation between rights and duties. However, the care orientation Gilligan describes places much greater emphasis on acceptance of responsibility and responsiveness to perceived needs than on reciprocal rights and duties. Her view suggests greater variability of two sorts.

First, less constrained by a logic of reciprocal relations, care-oriented persons often may have little interest in drawing a distinction between the interpersonal requirements of duty and more self-imposed requirements.

They may view themselves as basically responding to needs, doing what they think they ought to do, and the like. Others, however, may see them as doing more than anyone can reasonably require, or even expect.

Second, often those who are more care oriented make greater moral demands on themselves than they do on others. There are many possible explanations of this, but it is not simply a matter of their knowing their own character and circumstances better than anyone else does—for they might not. Nor is it simply a matter of their not knowing the character and circumstances of others well enough—for they might. In large part, it may reflect a more general reluctance to be "judgmental." Some matters, it may be thought, are simply no one's (moral) business but the agent's.

However, the desire to avoid being "judgmental" does not necessarily include a reluctance to judge oneself. We can hardly claim that judging ourselves is none of our (moral) business. Still, it may be objected, moral judgments are universalizable. If I judge that I ought to do x, consistency requires me to judge that any relevantly similar person, in relevantly similar circumstances, also ought to do x (or something like it). I may not know specifically to whom this should be addressed; but, unless I hold the implausible belief that I am unique in a morally relevant sense, I am judging others as well as myself. How can I avoid being "judgmental" to at least some extent? Perhaps I should simply refuse to evaluate other people's conduct except in regard to minimally decent behavior. Anything beyond that makes me uneasy and uncertain. Yet if I am reluctant to judge that others ought to act as I am inclined to think I should, how can I have any confidence in ascribing responsibility to myself?

There may be occasions in which my reluctance to ascribe responsibility to others should make self-ascription doubtful as well, but this is not always so. The problem, then, is to give an accounting without getting bogged down by difficulties such as those just described. The solution, if there is one, lies in broadening our understanding of morality beyond quasi-juridical conceptions of justice, duties, obligations, and rights, just as J. O. Urmson urges in his widely discussed "Saints and Heroes" (1958).

JURIDICAL MORALITY

Urmson reminds us in his essay that there is much more to morality than "rock-bottom duties which are duties for all and from every point of view, and to which anyone may draw attention" (1958, p. 204). Understood this way, moral duties have a quasi-juridical status. Joel Feinberg observes that the target of Urmson's criticism is the fundamental error of uncritically accepting "jural laws and institutional 'house rules' as models for the understanding of all counsels of wisdom and all forms of human worth" (1970, p. 3). Certainly recent writings in moral philosophy have heeded Urmson's and Feinberg's advice, even among those who stretch the concept of duty to embrace virtually all of morality.[1]

In making his case that morality includes more than the quasi-juridical, Urmson concentrates on saintly and heroic actions. He gives special attention to those saintly and heroic actions that, juridically speaking, are "above and beyond the call of duty." Such actions are commonly referred to as supererogatory. Urmson now regrets having used this term, which he thinks is basically a theological one (1988, pp. 167-68). His most famous example, St. Francis preaching to the birds, is itself more theological than moral. It is not so much the theological aspect of the supererogatory that now bothers Urmson as the extraordinariness of the supererogatory. To focus narrowly on the supererogatory in contradistinction to the juridical notion of moral duty "is to ignore the vast array of actions, having moral significance, which frequently are performed by persons who are far from being moral saints or heroes but which are neither duties nor obligations, nor involve conformity to principle as I use that term" (1988, p. 168).[2]

Urmson provides several examples of actions that are not "rock-bottom" moral duties or obligations, but do not qualify as supererogatory either:

> As well as acts of moral saintliness and heroism, this class includes many much humbler types of action within the reach of all of us. There are various types of action which we might call kind, considerate, chivalrous, charitable, neighbourly, sporting, decent, or acts of self-denial and self-abnegation; actions so described are in many circumstances neither duties nor obligations; to fail to do them would not be positively wrong (though, perhaps, unneighborly, unkind, etc.), nor are they dictated by what I call principle. (1988, p. 168)

These humbler types of action are not reducible to the supererogatory or to each other. Nevertheless, what they have in common is that they exceed what we can reasonably demand from one another as a matter of strict duty or obligation.

In "Saints and Heroes" Urmson refers to that which exceeds "rock-bottom" duties as the "higher flights of morality." However, this is not meant to suggest that it is uncommon for us to ascend to these "higher flights." That may be so with the supererogatory, but not with simply going beyond what others may legitimately demand from us as a matter of duty or obligation. Urmson adds that "we may look upon our duties as basic requirements to be universally demanded as providing the only tolerable basis of social life. The higher flights of morality can then be regarded as more positive contributions that go beyond what is universally to be exacted; but while not exacted publicly they are clearly equally pressing *in foro interno* on those who are not content merely to avoid the intolerable" (1958, pp. 216-17).

In this passage Urmson draws a fundamental contrast between third- and first-person moral perspectives. From a third-person perspective, there are "rock-bottom" duties and obligations, the fulfillment of which may be universally demanded or exacted. But we often demand more of ourselves (*in foro interno*) than others feel entitled to demand of us. For example, others may regard John's generous contribution of time and effort to a particular community project as extremely praiseworthy, but though they regard his actions as morally commendable, they will not reproach him if he is less generous with his time and effort. They will not think that he has failed to do what he ought to have done if he does less.

However, John's perspective, we may suppose, is quite different. He does not think of his contributions to the community project in terms of generosity at all but sees a need for the project and volunteers his time and effort. Embarrassed by the praise others bestow on him, he thinks that contributing to the project is just what he ought to be doing, and he would reproach himself morally if he were to slacken his efforts. As for others, he will not judge—not even if they slacken their efforts.

So, at least in regard to this activity, John offers some resistance to the widely accepted idea that one should universalize judgments about what one ought to do. On matters like this (but not on all matters) John's view is: "I think I ought to give my time and effort to this project. Others must decide for themselves." Whether this is a serious problem for the principle of universalizability is a matter to be explored in this chapter. However the principle of universalizability fares, it seems clear that room must be made for a distinction between moral demands that may be interpersonally demanded of one another and those that are personal and may be made only of oneself.

PERSONAL MORALITY

Urmson's most unusual example is that of Francis of Assisi preaching to the birds, an instructive example precisely because it is so unusual. There is good reason to resist applying the principle of universalizability to Francis's perspective. At the same time, it is implausible to deny that his attitude expresses what is, for him, moral conviction. Although his attitude is unusual, it can help clarify the idea that we should acknowledge a personal dimension of morality that extends beyond the reach of interpersonal moral demands.

This is not to say that such a personal morality is free from the constraints of interpersonal morality. Universalizability applies in that for anyone who adopts a personal moral perspective, he or she must find it acceptable for any relevantly similar person to adopt a similar personal perspective. This is universalizability in a *weak* sense, but the notion of acceptability does not express the imperativeness of the personal perspective of the agent. If Francis finds it acceptable for others to believe that they, too, ought to preach to the birds, it does not mean that *he* believes they ought to preach to the birds. That, he might say, is entirely up to them. Yet he does not view his own preaching to the birds as optional. In this sense he does not demand from others what he demands from himself; he resists universalizability in a *strong* sense. And, as we shall see, it is this strong sense that philosophers such as R. M. Hare endorse.

Francis's companions praised and admired him for preaching to the birds, but he reproached himself for not having preached to the birds sooner. Urmson contrasts this with straightforward breaches of duty:

> First, Francis could without absurdity reproach himself for his failure to do his duty, but it would be quite ridiculous for anyone else to do so, as one could have done if he had failed to keep his vows, for example. Second, it is not recorded that Francis ever reproached anyone else for failure to preach to the birds as a breach of duty. He could claim this action for himself as a duty and could perhaps have exhorted others to preach to the birds; but there could be no question of reproaches for not so acting. (1958, p. 204)

Why would it be ridiculous for others to reproach Francis if he were to fail to preach to the birds? And why would it be ridiculous for Francis to reproach others if they do not preach to the birds? The answer to both questions is that interpersonal reproach should be reserved for failure to satisfy interpersonal moral requirements. If there is any moral requirement to preach to the birds, it is strictly self-imposed and, therefore, personal. It is no one else's (moral) business. At the same time, it is desirable to respect the perspective of those who morally demand more of themselves than others reasonably, or even sensibly, can. Others may view actions that are "beyond the call of duty" as optional from a moral point of view, but this is not necessarily how those who undertake such actions view them. Urmson observes:

> Such actions do not present themselves as optional to the agent when he is deliberating; but, since he alone can call such an action of his a duty, and only from the deliberative viewpoint, only for himself and not for others, and not even for himself as a piece of objective reporting, and since nobody else can call on him to perform such an act as they can call on him to tell the truth and to keep his promises, there is here a most important difference from the rock-bottom duties which are duties for all and from every point of view, and to which anyone may draw attention. (1958, p. 204)

Urmson's passage makes an important distinction between first- and third-person perspectives. Does it adequately reflect the first-person perspective of those who go "beyond the call of duty"? Urmson says that, even for such an agent, it is not a matter of "objective reporting" that he or she is doing what duty requires.

We must ask from what vantage point this "objective reporting" is done and what implications this point has for an agent's perspective. If "objective reporting" means only what would be reported from the standpoint of a third person, it need not have any disturbing implications for the agent's perspective. However, Urmson apparently means something more; for him, the agent, too, will agree that, strictly speaking, he or she has no duty to do that which exceeds our "rock-bottom, basic duties." It is only during deliberative moments just prior to acting that the agent will feel any additional pull of duty.

This suggests that Urmson thinks these attitudes are somewhat misguided although he does wish in some sense to respect the attitudes of those who, like Francis, demand more of themselves. We can ask two questions at this point. First, just what is it about an agent's attitude when deliberating just prior to action that is supposed to be misguided? Second, is it really true that it is only during such deliberative moments that an agent has this supposedly misguided attitude? Contrary to Urmson, the answer to the second question is no. If Urmson's diagnosis of Francis's attitude as somewhat misguided is accepted, the diagnosis will cut more deeply than Urmson suspects. However, I will try to show that there need be nothing misguided about such attitudes.

If, at the moment of deliberation, Francis thought he had the sort of "rock-bottom," basic duty to preach to the birds that anyone is warranted in ascribing to others, then certainly his attitude would have been misguided, but this is decidedly not how Urmson portrays Francis's perspective. There is no suggestion that Francis at any time entertains the idea that anyone else has a similar duty, or even that others would be warranted in reproaching him for failing to preach to the birds. Only *self*-reproach is advanced as appropriate. Perhaps what Urmson has in mind is that, in an objective moment, Francis would have to agree that he does not really have a duty to preach to the birds, at least not a "rock-bottom" duty. Thus, Urmson says:

> It is part of the notion of duty that we have a right to demand compliance from others even when we are interested parties. I may demand that you keep your promises to me, tell me the truth, and do me no violence, and I may reproach you if you transgress. . . . A line must be drawn between what we can expect and demand from others and what we can merely hope for and receive with gratitude when we get it; duty falls on one side of this line, and the other acts with moral value on the other, and rightly so. (1958, p. 213)

It is useful to make some such distinction, and marking it with a quasi-juridical notion of duty has something to be said for it.[3] However, it is not clear just how acceptance of this restriction of the notion of duty affects the analysis of Francis's position.

Francis could acknowledge, even in deliberative moments just prior to action, that he has no duty to preach to the birds, but he might go on to insist that he *ought*, nevertheless, to preach to the birds and that he would morally reproach himself were he not to do so. The notion that one ought to do something is not restricted to quasi-juridical notions of duty and obligation. This is clear when there are conflicting duties and one ought to act contrary to one of them (though not necessarily without qualms). And, as Feinberg points out, there may be situations in which one ought to do something without there being any question of duty at all (1970, p. 6). If someone politely asks me what time it is, it seems reasonable to say that I ought to tell them (if I know). But it is not necessary to add that I have a duty to do so.

Assuming that Francis's attitude can be adequately represented by substituting "ought" for "duty," we can return to Urmson's analysis of how Francis regards preaching to the birds. Urmson clearly is right in saying that, in his deliberative moments, Francis does not regard preaching to the birds as optional. It also seems plausible to suppose that Francis does not regard it as optional at other times either. That is, Francis seems to have a settled disposition to think he ought to preach to the birds, just as he has a settled disposition to accept Urmson's "rock-bottom" duties. Although third persons might appraise these dispositions differently in Francis, it is not clear that he does—at least not in himself.

If this is right, then if we are to respect the attitude of someone like Francis, we must place that attitude within his or her moral character, rather than treat it merely as a temporary rush of moral sentiment in deliberative moments. Since Urmson concedes that Francis can without absurdity reproach himself for failing to preach to the birds, he should concede this point as well.

Thus we cannot expect "ought" to vanish for Francis even when he reflects about preaching to the birds. This does not deny that there is an important difference between Francis's attitude about the birds and Urmson's "rock-bottom," basic duties. If "objective reporting" implies taking a third-person perspective regarding what one ought to do, Urmson is right in saying that Francis cannot, as a piece of objective reporting, judge that he ought to preach to the birds, precisely because Francis's perspective here is admittedly and peculiarly first person.

However, it is just this last point that is puzzling. It seems to conflict with the widely accepted view that moral judgments must be universalizable. In this instance, the universalizability thesis holds that, at least in principle, moral oughts apply to classes of individuals and circumstances, rather than to uniquely specified individuals and circumstances. For example, if Francis judges morally that he ought to preach to the birds, consistency requires him to judge that relevantly similar persons in relevantly similar circumstances also ought to preach to the birds. But Francis resists making such judgments about others.

There is no indication in Urmson's account that Francis's resistance is based on any supposition on his part that he is the sole member of a class of relevantly similar persons in relevantly similar circumstances. We need not assume that Francis thinks of himself as having been (uniquely) commanded by God to preach to the birds, or that he (and he alone) has made a special commitment to God, the birds, or anyone else. Francis seems not in the least concerned about whether others have been so commanded or have made such commitments.[4]

In short, Francis's attitude toward preaching to the birds seems to fly directly in the face of standard versions of the universalizability requirement. Whether this attitude can be made intelligible and defensible will now be considered. The next section tries to make more fully intelligible just what an attitude like Francis's consists in and is followed by a discussion facing directly the challenge of the requirement that moral judgments be universalizable.

GUILT AND SHAME

One way of trying to clarify different moral concepts and perspectives is to look at the morally reactive attitudes and feelings with which they are typically associated. Guilt and shame, for example, differ significantly in this regard. In fact, it is shame rather than guilt that is most closely associated with those aspects of morality that move beyond Urmson's "rock-bottom," basic duties in the direction of the supererogatory.

Herbert Morris (1976) makes some helpful distinctions between moral conceptions centering around feelings of shame and those centering around guilt. Although fully aware that both guilt and shame are likely present to some degree in any society, Morris outlines two perspectives that can serve as hypothetical models for differentiating guilt and shame as moral concepts. He refers to these models as *shame morality* and *guilt morality*.

In a shame morality, according to Morris, conduct is evaluated in terms of how one compares or contrasts with a model identity. Morris provides "You don't find your bigger brother doing that!" and "That is what a pig would do" as illustrations of shaming techniques sometimes used in the moral education of children. However, many criticize such techniques as too severe, since they focus as much on a child's identity as on his or her behavior. That is, many object, this cuts too deeply. In contrast, a guilt morality criticizes conduct in terms of disobeying orders or violating rules.

Morris's second contrast is related to the first: the crucial concept associated with shame is failure or shortcoming; with guilt it is violation. Morris sums up by saying that shame morality is a scale rather than a threshold morality. With shame there is the notion that one may have gone some way toward achieving an ideal, but not all the way. Shame is associated with the failure to achieve an ideal or perfection, some maximum. With guilt, it is a minimum that has not been met.

The next contrast relates directly to that which exceeds "rock-bottom," basic duties. Morris says that "shame, unlike guilt, is not essentially tied to fault. Fault is connected with blame and blame is connected with failing to meet demands that others might reasonably place on one because they would place it upon themselves in like situations. Shame, however, may arise through failure to do the extraordinary. We may feel either guilt or shame in behaving as a coward; we may feel shame and not guilt in failing to behave as a hero" (1976, p. 61). The possibility of feeling shame at failing to behave as a hero suggests that Morris takes issue with the more common view that shame requires an actual or potential audience—that shame is felt only at what we think others would find shameful in us. This is an important point, one to which I will return shortly.

Next, Morris holds that what is valued in a shame morality is an *identity* of a certain kind; in a guilt morality what is valued is a set of *relationships* with others. Thus, in a guilt morality there is an emphasis on meeting one's duties and obligations to others and attempting to restore the relationship when one has failed to fulfill one's duties or meet one's obligations. In a shame morality what is at stake is the sense that one is a worthy person. Shame calls for becoming the kind of person who is worthy in one's own eyes or the eyes of others. Guilt, on the other hand, focuses more on specific transgressions, without there being any necessary implication that what is at stake is the kind of person one is. Since one's sense of worthiness may in large part depend on how one thinks he or she is esteemed by others, it is clear that shame, as well as guilt, can be concerned with interpersonal relationships. With shame the concern may be to be worthy in the eyes of others. With guilt the concern is to restore or repair a relationship.

Morris's concept of a morality based on guilt bears strong similarity to our concepts of legal relations. In fact, he explicitly makes such a comparison. As in law, a guilt morality is concerned with maintaining a minimally acceptable level of conduct. The concept of duty, in the sense that has a correlative concept of a right, is at home in a guilt morality. Thus, we should expect the concept of guilt to be at home in Urmson's discussion of "rock-bottom," basic duties. In such a context, unlike in a shame morality, says Morris, "there is an absence of concern with motives, with purity of heart, grandeur of soul" (1976, p. 61).

Finally, Morris concludes, "Shame will arise when our concern is achieving more than a minimum, when our concern is that individuals realize to the fullest what they have within them, when what one is takes priority over a nice balance in relations with others with respect to particular types of conduct" (1976, p. 61). Although Morris is right to emphasize that shame is concerned with more than merely meeting standards of conduct prescribed by duty or obligation, he somewhat overstates what is involved in shame. Shame may pivot around the failure to satisfy maximal ideals of excellence, but it need not. It may be directed at something less, even while focusing on more than merely meeting standards of conduct prescribed by duty or obligation.

John Rawls's (1971) reflections on guilt and shame make this clear. Rawls roughly agrees with Morris that guilt is associated with failure to satisfy standards of conduct prescribed by duty or obligation. Rawls associates guilt primarily with principles of justice and rightness. One feels guilt for having failed to do what is just or right. However, there is also a liability to experience shame because of failure to satisfy these same principles. According to Rawls, we may prize certain excellences of character that are directed to the fulfillment of these basic moral requirements. If we do prize these excellences, then expressing them in our conduct will be a condition for our sense of self-worth. The virtues that make up excellences related to principles of justice and rightness are regarded by Rawls as good both from our own standpoint and the standpoint of others. He says, "The lack of them will tend to undermine both our self-esteem and the esteem that our associates have for us. Therefore indications of these faults will wound one's self-respect with accompanying feelings of shame" (1971, p. 444).

Insofar as shame is bound up with virtues related to principles of justice and rightness, Rawls seems to accept the appropriateness of interpersonal reproach. In regard to these principles it is understandable that shame is linked to an actual or potential audience—an audience of those who are similarly held accountable. Similar remarks could be made about the relationship of shame to Urmson's "rock-bottom" basic duties and Morris's minimal standards of duty within a scheme of reciprocal rights and duties that are necessary for maintaining a proper balance of freedom. The reproach associated with shame is directed not only at conduct, but also character, linking shame with the concept of goodness. The reproach associated with guilt is directed primarily at conduct and is more readily linked with the concept of rightness. Rawls comments, "In general, guilt, resentment, and indignation invoke the concept of right, whereas shame, contempt and derision appeal to the concept of goodness" (1971, p. 484).

Morris notes that typically it is less clear what overcoming shame requires from us than what overcoming guilt requires. Shame cuts more deeply, typically raising questions about what kinds of persons we are and ought to be. That is, shame raises fundamental questions about our identity, whereas guilt more typically calls for changes in conduct without thereby calling for changes in character. This difference helps explain why, as Morris and Rawls both note, shame is often associated with concealment (even from oneself), whereas guilt is often associated with confession.

If shame does cut more deeply than guilt, it is understandable that we exercise greater caution in attempting to evoke shame in one another. Not only does shaming impose a greater burden, it presumes greater knowledge of others. It is one thing to object to another's behavior on a particular occasion, but it is quite another to object to his or her character. It may be quite clear whether one has or has not violated a basic moral requirement. However, it is likely to be much less clear what this indicates about one's moral character—and whether a change at this level can reasonably be urged. Furthermore, as we move from Urmson's "rock-bottom," basic duties in the direction of moral excellences, the appropriateness of interpersonal, moral demands becomes more questionable. Since we experience moral shame as a kind of demand (and a rather severe one at that), interpersonal attempts to evoke shame become more questionable. We may speak of a decent moral minimum in regard to character as well as conduct, yet we do not have to ascend to the level of moral excellences before we have reason to exercise caution in finding fault with one another's moral character.

Although Rawls does confine most of his attention to moral goodness in relation to concepts of justice and rightness, he does comment more broadly on its relation to shame. He notes that "a breach of any virtue may give rise to shame; it suffices that one prizes the form of action among one's excellences. . . . Thus, in particular, the moralities of supererogation provide the stage for shame; for they represent the higher forms of moral excellence, the love of humankind and self-command, and in choosing them one risks failure from their very nature" (1971, p. 484). Rawls insists that a complete conception of morality must find a significant place for both guilt and shame. He also seems to hold that, while guilt and shame are both related to principles of justice and rightness, only shame can be related to the higher forms of moral excellence, including the supererogatory.

If, as many insist, shame does require an actual or potential audience, Rawls would be mistaken in connecting shame with the supererogatory because he also agrees that failure to do the supererogatory does not warrant the reproach of others. Indeed, it would be unusual for someone actually to reproach another person for failure to do something supererogatory. That is, the requisite audience, actual or potential, is simply not available; and this is as it should be.

Nevertheless, people like Francis do reproach themselves for failure to do what others may regard as supererogatory. If it is not shame that Francis would feel when reproaching himself, it is something very like shame. Or at the very least, we must agree that it is more like shame than guilt. His sense of self-worth is at stake, at least when his self-reproach is severe. We might say that what is at stake is his sense of his own worthiness, not in the (actual or potential) eyes of others, but in his own eyes—and in regard to his own, quite personal ideals.

In any case, quite apart from the very unusual case of St. Francis, it is clear that many people do require more of themselves morally than they require of others—as well as more than others may justifiably require of them, and this is not an insignificant aspect of their moral lives. A full understanding of their moral integrity needs to find a place for this moral "extra." Thus we must ask whether respect for the integrity of such persons requires us to grant them a sphere of moral privacy—a sphere within which they are free from the censure of others in regard to the moral ideals to which they commit themselves. This sphere could be limited by Urmson's basic duties, Rawls's principles of justice and rightness, or Morris's minimal reciprocal rights and duties. We need not stand by without urging caution to those who demand more of themselves in self-destructive, self-deprecating ways.[5] Aside from such limitations, why not reserve for individuals a sphere that, we might say, is their own moral business and none of ours?

Rawls says that his theory of justice is grounded in notions of reciprocity in which "neither concern for others nor for self has priority, for all are equal; and the balance between persons is given by the principles of justice" (1971, p. 485). But, he continues, "where this balance moves to one side, as with the moralities of supererogation, it does so from the election of self, which freely takes on the larger part." If this is so, then it seems reasonable for us to say that our freely taking on the larger part should free us from having to concern ourselves with universalizability in those higher flights of morality that exceed (but do not transgress) the requirements of basic duty. This will now be argued.

A PERSONAL "OUGHT"

R. M. Hare's (1963) principle of universalizability is a representative version of the moral requirement that similar cases be judged similarly. If I judge morally that I ought to do a certain thing, I must judge that any relevantly similar person in a relevantly similar situation ought to act similarly. Of course, I may be uncertain about whether others are relevantly similar to me, or whether their circumstances are relevantly similar. So, judging that I ought to do something need not in practice commit me to making a similar judgment about any other particular person, but it does in principle. To see the kinds of constraints on moral judgment Hare's principle imposes, it will be useful to examine in some detail one of his examples, which focuses on someone's ideal of human excellence. Although this is not an other-regarding ideal, similar observations can be made about ideals that are other-regarding.

Hare asks us to consider a man with an ascetic ideal of human excellence that includes jogging every day before breakfast. This ideal might be held in a variety of ways. For example, Hare suggests, "It is perfectly possible for an ascetic person, who is thinking solely in terms of his ideal of human excellence, to say that everybody (or at least all males between 14 and 40) *ought*, like himself, to go for a run every day before breakfast" (1963, p. 152). But, Hare continues, "It is only if he is the sort of ascetic who wishes to legislate that others should become ascetics, that he will express himself in terms of 'ought,' and thus commit himself to adverse judgments on those who stay in bed" (1963, p. 152). Of course, it is understood that such adverse judgments extend only to those who are relevantly similar in relevantly similar circumstances. And, even within this sphere, there may be functionally equivalent ways of fulfilling the ascetic ideal. That is, it may not be only jogging, or jogging before breakfast, that would satisfy an ascetic ideal of human excellence.

However, it should be borne in mind that, for Hare, the moral "ought" must be applied to a class of individuals; and those who accept the moral "ought" as applying to them are disposed to have an attitude of reproach, not only toward his or her own failure to live up to the prescribed "ought," but also toward the failure of others for whom the "ought" is prescribed.[6] It should be recalled that those like Francis reproach their own failures, but they extend neither an "ought" judgment nor reproach to others concerning such actions. The "ought" of Francis, then, seems to be uniquely personal. This means that, for Hare, it cannot be a moral "ought." How then, we must ask, should it be understood? We need to return to the jogger to see what Hare might say.

If I wake up each morning thinking I ought to run before breakfast, must I commit myself to any judgment at all about what anyone else (however similarly situated) ought to do before breakfast, or at any other time? Suppose I simply have a personal ideal of fitness, and I have no concern to advance an ideal for anyone else. Hare provides an analysis of such a point of view:

> There is also another use of 'ought', in connexion with ideals, which may seem more harmless. A man who has adopted the ideal of physical fitness, which requires him to run before breakfast, may say of himself that he ought to get out of bed now—or even, if he is weak-willed, that he ought to have got out of bed half an hour ago. But this may be only a hypothetical 'ought'; he may mean merely that if he wants to live up to his ideal, he ought. . . . This would not commit him to any moral judgment on those who do not have such an ideal. (1963, p. 154)

This hypothetical "ought" is not a moral "ought." Apparently, for Hare, the price of not judging others here is that one refrain from moral judgment altogether.

However, it may not be enough for me to judge that I ought to run before breakfast *if* I want to live up to my ideal; I might also judge that I *ought* to want to live up to my ideal. Perhaps part of my ideal self is that I keep my resolve about such matters. This cannot be analyzed as yet another hypothetical "ought." Rather, it would be an expression of the way in which the ideal is held. Whether this is a matter of moral concern on my part depends on whether failure to live up to my ideal is likely to be followed by moral self-reproach, which seems to be psychologically possible in cases like this. It clearly is in cases like that of Francis. If this were my psychological disposition, then, on Hare's view, logically I must be committed to judgments of reproach about others.

Assuming that I wish to resist even covertly reproaching others for not running before breakfast, the only consistent way for me to hold back reproach would seem to be to insist that there is a third sense of "ought" which would allow that, in certain circumstances, I can make moral judgments about what I ought to do without any implications about what I must think others ought to do. Hare replies, "Thirdly, there is the concept ought$_3$, which is prescriptive, but not universalizable. Since I do not think that the word 'ought' is actually ever used in the sense of 'ought$_3$', I should prefer to use some other word to stand for this concept (e.g., some word defined in terms of 'want' or the plain singular imperative)" (1963, p. 165). Yet this returns us to the nonmoral, hypothetical "ought."

My suggestion is that, whatever we might want to say about the personal ideals of joggers, the perspective of someone like Francis can be fully respected only if it is acknowledged that something like an "ought$_3$" has an appropriate place within morality. The logic of such an "ought" can be expressed in the following way: (1) I ought (morally) to do x. But I make no judgment whether anyone else ought to do x, or anything like x—no matter how much like me that person might be or how similar the circumstances. Now, if Jane and Kathy are sufficiently alike in all relevant respects and circumstances, it follows (trivially) that if Jane judges, "I ought (morally) to do x," Kathy will judge, "I ought (morally) to do x," where "x" refers to a kind of action. They will make similar judgments just because they are so much like each other, but from this it does not follow that they will judge each other.

That is, (1) does not require Jane to judge, "Kathy ought to do x." This is so even if Jane knows that Kathy makes this judgment about herself, and even if Jane knows that she and Kathy are as alike in character and circumstance as two people could be. That is, (1) does not require Jane to make any judgment at all about what Kathy ought to do.

This means that (1) must be distinguished from the following: (2) I ought (morally) to do x. But it is not the case that (Kathy), who is like me in all relevant respects concerning character and circumstance, ought to do x. Clearly (2) does threaten to have the kind of inconsistency that Hare argues departures from the Principle of Universalizability entail. For it does seem inconsistent for Jane in the case of (2) to affirm that she ought to do x but deny that Kathy ought to do x. Still, not making a judgment about whether Kathy ought to do x is not the same as denying that Kathy ought to do x, and this is the difference between (1) and (2).

Of course, to say that there are circumstances in which it is appropriate for someone to have the sort of attitude expressed in (1) is not to specify what those circumstances are. I have no general account to offer, but the kinds of examples of supererogation presented by Urmson seem to qualify.[7] In those examples, doing what is supererogatory does not require violating any of his "rock-bottom," basic duties. All of his examples seem to fit comfortably within the range of what, from a third-person perspective, we find morally permissible for behavior. Yet if we say only this, much of the richness of our moral concepts is lost. Once we begin to consider the variety of moral concepts within the realm of the permissible, the importance of preserving some basic distinctions between first and third perspectives becomes apparent.

Further consideration of first-person perspectives illustrates this. I have claimed that Jane can quite consistently and appropriately judge that she ought to do x (which is, say, a supererogatory act) while at the same time drawing back from making a similar judgment about Kathy. However, it is also quite consistent for Jane to urge or exhort Kathy to do x and to judge that it would be morally good for Kathy to do so. But it is just at this point that an important distinction between Jane's concept of what she morally ought to do and the concept of moral goodness must be emphasized.

Consistent with a third-person view of the supererogatory, Jane can judge that it would be morally good, admirable, or praiseworthy for Kathy to do x, even though there is no suggestion of reproach if Kathy does not do x. It might be suggested that the only difference between Jane's attitude toward Kathy doing x and doing x herself is this: In both instances Jane judges that it would be morally good to do x, but she reserves reproach for failure to do so only for herself. Thus, we need only the concept of moral goodness plus the concept of self-reproach. A special concept of a personal, moral "ought" is not needed.

However, it seems we need a concept of a personal, moral "ought" after all. Judgments of moral goodness do not by themselves make intelligible either attitudes of self-reproach or reproach for others. This is especially clear with typical cases of supererogation. Everyone can agree that supererogatory actions are morally good, whether performed by oneself or another. Most would not be willing to judge that others are morally required to do what is, admittedly, supererogatory. Such actions, they might say, are not only "above and beyond the call of duty," they are beyond anything we can reasonably require of others. Yet many, if not most, people have a similar attitude toward supererogatory actions they might themselves perform. That is, their attitude might be, "It would be a good thing for me to do this, but I will not reproach myself if I do not do it."[8] It is not that those who have this attitude do only what they believe is morally required of them; the point is simply that they do not think of such actions as morally required—not even self-imposed moral requirements.

Nevertheless, some people, with Francis being an extreme case, do think it is morally imperative for them to do those things that others think of doing only in terms of moral goodness. This difference in attitude is itself an important part of what we find morally estimable in them. But it is just this difference that is captured by an "ought$_3$"—a personal, moral "ought" that expresses a moral ideal beyond that we believe we have a right to impose on one another. The attitude expressed by this "ought$_3$" carries with it a liability to self-reproach for failure to satisfy its demands, demands which come from within the person. Yet moral goodness alone cannot account for this self-imposed moral imperative.

We might wish that there were more people whose integrity is bound up with self-imposed moral imperatives that go beyond what we can reasonably demand from each other. We might even try to devise ways of reinforcing one another's potential to become such persons (through example and encouragement rather than reproach). This could play an important part in the moral education of children. Even if we believe that St. Francis is too extreme or unusual to serve as a model, there is no shortage of less extreme models for emulation that might be reinforced.

PERSONAL INTEGRITY AND AUTONOMY

As already noted, Rawls thinks of the supererogatory as a part of morality that is associated with self-reproach (as expressed through shame) insofar as it arises "from the election of the self, which freely takes on the larger part" (1971, p. 285). In "Saints and Heroes" Urmson (1958) claims that a utilitarian theory can best accommodate this dimension of morality. Michael Clark (1978) argues against this, claiming that the independent value of autonomy best explains why we should allow that there are genuinely supererogatory actions, actions clearly exceeding what we have a right to demand of one another as a matter of duty or obligation.[9]

Clark does not address himself to the question of whether it is appropriate for individuals to take up the attitude, like Francis, that they ought to do that which others regard as supererogatory. Clark's main concern is to establish that, unless a distinction is preserved between the mandatory and the meritorious at the interpersonal level of morality, respect for the autonomy of individuals is undermined. To respect that autonomy requires us to acknowledge that there is a sphere of moral choice within which individuals have the right to do or not do that which is morally meritorious without fear of moral censure. Clark's worry about certain forms of utilitarianism is that the meritorious and the mandatory become indistinguishable, since one is morally required to maximize goodness.

Even if utilitarianism can meet Clark's objection, I find his independent appeal to respect for autonomy attractive and would add the following. If, because of the independent value of autonomy, one has the right to do the meritorious or to refrain from it, then one also has the right freely to adopt a perspective in which one requires of oneself, but not of others, that meritorious actions be performed. This perspective reserves a place for attitudes of those, like Francis, who make moral demands of themselves while refraining from judging similarly of others.

Of course, as Urmson points out, the actions of a Francis are thought of as saintly, and the action of the soldier falling on a grenade to save his companions is thought of as heroic. Such actions do not by any means exhaust the kinds of actions we find morally commendable but which exceed our basic duties. In addition to saints and heroes, Urmson says, we also have "cases of disinterested kindness and generosity, for example, that are clearly more than basic duty requires and yet hardly ask for the high titles, 'saintly' and 'heroic'. . . . It is possible to go just beyond one's duty by being a little more generous, forbearing, helpful, or forgiving than fair dealing demands, or to go a very long way beyond the basic code of duties with the saint or hero" (1958, p. 205). Once we move away from the saint or hero, we move in the direction of the vast majority of moral agents. Just where they should be placed on the scale outlined by

Urmson varies enormously. Assuming that it is somewhere beyond a concern simply to meet one's basic duties, Morris's notion of a scale morality of shame at not going beyond the demands of basic duty comes into play.

What role does the concept of a personal, moral "ought" (an "ought$_3$") play here? This is a large question, and no general answer may be available. Yet it does seem to warrant a significant role, even if we allow a place for interpersonal forms of reproach for failing to do more than is required as a matter of "rock-bottom," basic duty. Urmson says that the basic duties concern requirements for tolerable social life. They specify what we may justifiably demand of one another morally. Given this, "the higher flights of morality can then be regarded as more positive contributions that go beyond what is universally to be exacted" (1958, p. 216).

However, there are forms of moral reproach that do not presuppose that one has failed to do what we may exact from one another. For example, we may say of someone that he or she was unkind without thereby implying a failure to fulfill a "rock-bottom," basic duty. Normally this would be taken as a kind of reproach. Nevertheless, it is distinct from not extending kindness to another in circumstances where extending kindness may have been possible, but only by making some sacrifice that we cannot reasonably expect others to make. Here we may rightly be unwilling to say of someone who does not extend kindness that he or she should be in any way reproached. Those who are kind in such circumstances are meritorious, yet, might well see themselves differently. For them, doing what they did may have seemed, as Urmson puts it, as "pressing *in foro interno*," as the most pressing universal demand.

Virtues that are praiseworthy because they go beyond the demand for meeting "rock-bottom," basic duties pose a special problem in regard to first- and third-person perspectives. Precisely because of their praiseworthiness, they can be seriously altered, or even corrupted, through their *self*-conscious acknowledgment. For example, suppose John is more generous than most—certainly more so than anyone has a right to expect. We may say this of John, but what does he say of himself? He may regard himself as doing as he ought—responding supportively to the needs and interests of others. He could not live comfortably with his conscience if he did any less. In fact, he might even reproach himself for not doing more. But let us suppose that he is not interested in judging others by his self-imposed standards. Shall we try to set John straight?

We might try to get him to see himself as others do—as exceedingly and admirably generous. If he accepts, then his generosity becomes self-flattering, if not self-righteous: "I'm a really generous person—I do so much more than anyone has a right to expect from me!" Furthermore, thus straightened out, he may now regard as optional what he previously felt pressed *in foro interno* to do. Alternatively, John might raise his standards for others. Not only does he think he ought to be as giving to others as he is, so ought everyone else (at least those who are relevantly similar in character and circumstance). Now John's generosity may seem both self-righteous and officious.

If this is what a thoroughgoing acceptance of universalizability requires, it is a heavy price to pay—and unnecessary. Only a weak sense of universalizability is required. To be consistent, John should not object to others acting as he does. That is, he should find this morally permissible, but it is not necessary for him to go further and insist that others *ought* to act as he does. This last move invites problems with virtues that render moral agents praiseworthy. Insofar as such virtues constitute an important part of the integrity of those who possess them, it is important to understand how these virtues may be expressed in thought and action without subverting that integrity.

To avoid this danger, it is necessary to loosen somewhat the stranglehold of a thoroughgoing idea of universalizability. Universalizability certainly is properly at home in those areas of morality that are concerned with basic duties and obligations we have to one another, or with principles of justice and rightness. Still, as Urmson insists, duty, permissibility, and wrongness are only a part of moral life. Beyond this, universalizability has a more problematic status and should not be taken as a moral given.

10
Autonomy, Reason, and Sentiments

At times it seems as if arranging to have no commitment of any kind to anyone would be a special freedom. But in fact the whole idea works in reverse. The most deadly commitment of all is to be committed only to one's self. Some come to realize this after they are in the nursing home.
—*John MacDonald's Travis McGee*, The Lonely Silver Rain

I have argued that the importance of recognizing an area of morality that is basically personal rests, in part, on the value of autonomy. However, autonomy has recently come under severe criticism, particularly from those sympathetic to Carol Gilligan's reflections on moral psychology. Insofar as autonomy is associated with the radical separateness and independence of individuals, it is vulnerable to such criticism; but this is not the only way of understanding autonomy. Other interpretations are much more receptive to Gilligan's "ethic of care," while at the same time preserving autonomy's central role in moral life, as this chapter will attempt to show.

AUTONOMY AND CARE

The importance we attach to autonomy is evident in many different areas of human life. For example, in medical practice and human experimentation the importance of obtaining informed consent is widely accepted. If I go to a physician, I expect, as a matter of right, to be informed of medical options available to me and their likely consequences. My informed consent should be sought for any forms of treatment that have implications for what I value. Assuming I am of "sound mind," my competence to make responsible choices is to be presumed. The resentment that many feel at being treated paternalistically in medical contexts suggests a connection between autonomy and one's sense of dignity.

The transition from childhood to adulthood provides another example. As all parents are painfully aware, children become more and more impatient to be treated as autonomous as they move from early childhood, through adolescence, and toward adulthood. Parental reluctance may be grounded in fear that the child is not yet ready to decide responsibly, and it may reflect a concern that the child not make choices now that will incapacitate him or her for autonomous living later. Of course, this reluctance may be viewed by the child as unfair, excessively protective and restrictive, and as a fit object of resentment.

It may seem obvious that autonomy deserves the pride of place it is typically given in our everyday lives and in contemporary theories of morality, but autonomy is not everything. Integrity, commitment, loyalty, empathy, compassion, considerateness, and benevolence are also valued. Some believe that there is an inherent conflict between autonomy and these other morally desirable qualities. It is important to examine such concerns to see to what extent, if any, autonomy and other morally desirable qualities can live comfortably together.

Gerald Dworkin (1976) effectively poses the problem.[1] Noting that servile lackeys and those who blindly conform to group pressure seem to be prime examples of persons who lack substantive autonomy, he concludes that, for the same reasons, the compassionate, loyal, or moral person also lacks substantive autonomy: "For the compassionate or loyal or moral man is one whose actions are to some extent determined by the needs and predicament of others. He is not independent or self-determining. Again, any notion of commitment (to a lover, a goal, a group) seems to be a denial of substantive independence and hence of autonomy. There seems to be no way of conceptualizing substantive independence which avoids this classification" (1976, p. 26). Dworkin goes on to suggest that it is possible that "the compassionate man is less autonomous than the selfish one." This possibility, if it is one, is quite disarming, for it suggests that, far from being the mark of a full moral agent, substantive autonomy is incompatible with being a moral agent.

However, Dworkin's remarks exaggerate matters in two respects. First, it is not clear that a selfish person is more autonomous in any substantive sense than a compassionate, loyal, or moral person. An exclusively and possessively self-interested person is no less in the grip of his or her passions than the compassionate, loyal, or moral person, and such a person has no more chosen to be selfish than others have chosen to be compassionate, loyal, or moral. Although the exclusively selfish person cannot be said to have moral commitments, he or she is no less slavishly committed to "self" than a servile lackey is to another. Second, Dworkin exaggerates the similarity between being a servile lackey or unreflective conformist and being a compassionate, loyal, or moral person. One can be reflectively compassionate, loyal, or moral. There is no need to abandon judgment and become blindly compassionate or loyal. A certain degree of critical reflection is normally thought to be one of the marks of a morally autonomous person.

Nevertheless, Dworkin is right in pointing out that, for the most part, our convictions, motivations and principles are not "self-selected." Still, he adds, "If the autonomous man cannot adopt his motivations *de novo*, he can still judge them after the fact. The autonomous individual is able to step back and formulate an attitude towards the factors that influence his behavior" (1976, p. 24). This means that autonomy has less to do with whether one has originally chosen to be a certain kind of person than with the kind of person one now is. Yet the kind of person one now is has a great deal to do with one's ability to evaluate fundamental convictions, motivations, and principles.

Clearly, certain rational capacities are necessary for such evaluation. It is the notable absence of any significant exercise of these rational capacities that inclines us to agree that servile lackeys and unreflective conformists lack substantive autonomy. As we shall see, compassion, loyalty, and moral conviction do not preclude the significant exercise of these capacities. In fact, I will argue that they are necessary for effective *moral* autonomy.

The issues raised by Dworkin relate to the Kohlberg/Gilligan controversy. For Kohlberg, autonomous moral reasoning is a mark of the most advanced level of moral thinking. Moral principles are to be self-chosen, for reasons that moral agents recognize to be universally valid. Gilligan, on the other hand, associates autonomy with the independence and separateness of persons. Along with many feminist thinkers, she questions whether autonomy and caring relationships are compatible. This is a difficult issue, complicated in part because the concept of autonomy itself is in need of clarification. "Autonomy" has no univocal meaning in philosophical discussions of morality, and many of its uses are unanalyzed.

In the following sections I will present an account of autonomy that gives it a fundamental place in moral life without sacrificing either justice or care. Autonomy, as I will discuss it, originates in forms of interdependence emphasized in Rawls's account of the development of a sense of justice. Rawls's emphasis on love and friendship points the way to linking justice and care without sacrificing autonomy. Before turning to Rawls, however, some preliminary remarks about autonomy are in order.

AUTONOMY AND COMPETENCE

It is useful to begin with senses of "autonomy" that seem quite compatible with both justice and caring orientations in morality. Tom Hill, Jr. (1987), identifies three: 1) impartiality in reviewing and justifying moral principles; 2) the right to decide for oneself; 3) self-governance. Although not made explicit by Hill, each of these conceptions is related to the idea of *moral competence*. And it is this idea, I think, that best explains the importance of autonomy for morality.

Impartiality in reviewing and justifying moral principles requires us to detach ourselves from our particular likes, dislikes, biases, and commitments. This is, essentially, the universalizability requirement. As we have seen, Kohlberg confuses this requirement with the notion that one must be impartial at the level of particular decision making. Thus he thinks that Heinz should be as willing to steal the cancer-curing drug for a stranger as for his wife. However, the kind of impartiality Hill has in mind requires only that we not tailor our principles and practices to meet our particular concerns (as those of, for example, Michael Pritchard). There is no reason to suppose that we cannot justify principles and practices that allow or even require us within limits to be partial to ourselves, loved ones, friends, associates, and the like. In principle, there is no incompatibility between the kind of impartiality Hill advocates and care and compassion for particular persons or groups of persons.

What autonomy as impartiality requires of us is the capacity to transcend egocentricity when reflecting on moral principles and practices. That egocentricity is a barrier to moral competence is emphasized by cognitive-developmental theories such as Kohlberg's, and there is no reason to object to this. The account of how egocentricity is overcome, and the endpoint of such an account, does require careful analysis. This is a major burden of the Kohlberg and Gilligan chapters, which argue that critical reflection will not always take us to Kohlberg's stages 5 or 6.

The right to decide for oneself is also connected with the idea of moral competence. Hill points out that there can be no presumption that those who exercise their right to decide for themselves will decide as they should—either morally or prudentially. There does seem to be a presumption that those who are acknowledged to have this right also have the capacity to decide as they should. This does not imply that there is always (or ever) a correct choice. It implies only that, whatever range of acceptable choices we presume, the agent is capable of choosing responsibly within that range. If this capacity is denied, it is not clear what objection to paternalistic intervention is available. Emphasizing the right to decide for oneself may sound highly individualistic. In one sense, of course, it is. The individuality of each possessor of this right is respected, but this does not mean that individuals must decide independently of others, or that their decisions cannot reflect interdependence, care, or compassion.

The third sense of "autonomy" identified by Hill is the ideal of self-governance, which involves living one's life in ways consistent with maintaining personal integrity. Consider, first, the opposite of such a life: "People are not self-governing, in a sense, when their responses to problems are blind, dictated by neurotic impulses of which they are unaware, shaped by prejudices at odds with the noble sentiments they think are moving them. When we make decisions like this we are divided against ourselves. . . . There is no unified 'self' here to govern the decision" (Hill 1987, p. 136). Although not equating self-governance as an ideal with a unified personality as a general moral goal, Hill insists that "it is a morally worthy goal to try to face our important decisions with as few as possible of these self-fracturing obstacles" (1987, p. 136).

Such a view of autonomy, says Hill, does not take sides on the issue of whether a morality of rights and justice or a morality of care and compassion is to be preferred. Rather, he continues, the ideal of self-governance advocates facing "moral decisions with integrity and self-awareness" (1987, p. 137). Hill then qualifies his statement that the ideal of self-governance does not take sides on the justice/compassion controversy: "Or, perhaps better, if it favors either side, the ideal of autonomy for particular moral decisions urges us to face such problems with compassion: for I suspect that without compassion one can never really become aware of the morally relevant facts in the situations one faces. The inner needs and feelings of others are virtually always relevant, and without compassion one can perhaps never fully know what these are— or give them their appropriate weight" (1987, p. 137). Again, autonomy is linked with competence—this time through compassion. Certainly Gilligan would agree with this. Perhaps Kohlberg would as well, but, as we have seen, his account of moral development overplays the importance of justice and rights and underplays the importance of care and compassion. Interestingly, Rawls's account contains the seeds for linking autonomy to both justice and caring. It should prove helpful to return to his account.

AUTONOMY, SELF-REGARD, AND OTHERS

Autonomy is intimately related to our sense of dignity, particularly to self-respect and self-esteem. Gerald Dworkin points out that physically intrusive methods of changing people are generally objectionable because of the psychological need for maintaining "some realm of physical integrity which cannot be violated" (1976, p. 27). He adds that this is related to our concerns for privacy and dignity. As noted in Chapter 5, torture is perhaps the clearest example of using physical and psychological means for breaking down a person. Those who give in to torture often feel shame at their failure to maintain their composure. This shame typically involves a feeling of inadequacy and unworthiness, perhaps even a sense of having suffered a lowering or loss of dignity. In addition to any broken bones (physical disintegration), there is a sense of a loss of autonomy or self-control (psychological disintegration). Insofar as autonomy is an essential feature of one's identity as a person, invasions of autonomy threaten one's integrity, or wholeness.

Such invasions of autonomy do make an essential reference to others. It is at the hands of and in the eyes of the invaders that one suffers shame. It may also be in the eyes of other real or imagined observers that one experiences this shame. These examples, however, focus on others as threats to maintaining autonomy and positive self-regard. Others are also needed to nurture and sustain positive self-regard (self-respect and self-esteem).

John Rawls characterizes self-respect and self-esteem as including one's sense of his or her own value ("his secure conviction that his conception of his good, his plan of life, is worth carrying out") and confidence in the ability to fulfill his or her intentions (1971, p. 440). This sense of self-worth is, for Rawls, a primary good: "Without it nothing may seem worth doing, or if some things have value for us, we lack the will to strive for them. All desire and activity becomes empty and vain" (1971, p. 440). Obviously children's social environment is critical in developing their self-respect and self-esteem. At some point, respect for their integrity, or wholeness, must include respect for their autonomy. Deprived of opportunities to make, carry out, and reflect on decisions and commitments, children will have their autonomy thwarted. An important source of self-respect and self-esteem will be undermined, resulting in an impoverished personal integrity, or wholeness.

Still, with its emphasis on bodily and personal integrity, this account may seem too individualistic. It may seem that the separateness and independence of persons is emphasized at the expense of intimate, interdependent relationships among persons. Again, however, Rawls is instructive. If the maintenance of self-respect and self-esteem is essential to personal integrity, then autonomy is only one aspect of that integrity. Rawls also emphasizes the importance of positive relationships with others: being accepted and encouraged by others; being loved by others (for example, parents); and developing bonds of friendship. In fact, each of these is seen by Rawls to play an essential role in developing self-confidence that is necessary for effective autonomous functioning.

Instead of viewing autonomy in highly individualistic ("atomistic") terms, we could view it as fitting into a framework of strong social interdependence. This interdependence is as much a feature of the identity (or integrity) of persons as their bodies and autonomy. Thus a radical alteration of a person's social relationships can profoundly affect a person, even to the point of leaving him or her feeling "shattered" or "broken." In some cases, for example, a betrayal of trust could be as personally damaging as a physical beating.

Connections between the development of autonomy and caring for others receive additional emphasis in Rawls's psychological account of the development of a sense of justice. As we have seen, the first two levels of his account are grounded in reciprocal love, friendship, and trust. Although marked by heteronomous acceptance of parental injunctions, peer pressure, and authority, the socialization process described by Rawls ties the development of autonomy to increased sensitivity to the actual needs and interests of others, as distinct from one's own. That is, the development of autonomy is connected to the overcoming of egocentricity.

For Rawls, moral autonomy flourishes at his third level, that of principles of justice. Here one accepts principles of justice, not because of parental authority, the desire for social approval, or from deference to the given social and legal order, but because one is able rationally to discern

for oneself the merits of these principles. Principles of justice are principles that rational persons, deprived of the opportunity to tailor their
choice of principles to their special interests, would accept as principles
for evaluating the basic structure of our social and political institutions.

This view is inadequate insofar as it suggests that moral autonomy is
operative only in regard to principles of justice. However, bearing in
mind Hill's distinction between the impartial examination of practices
and the question of whether those practices themselves must endorse
impartiality, the inadequacy can be remedied. Moral judgments among
loved ones, friends, and associates do not have to be concerned only
with justice, and, insofar as they are amenable to impartial examination,
their justifications do not depend on their flowing from principles of
justice.

Still, linking autonomy with the idea of justification as Rawls does
suggests another problem. Moral autonomy on this view is subject to
certain restrictions. It is bound by what we might expect rational persons
to find mutually acceptable when each reasons from a position of equality and is prevented from tailoring the result to his or her special interests. This approach has the virtue of respecting the moral agency and
personal integrity of each person, but how can we reason autonomously,
one might ask, and yet be bound by such constraints?

AUTONOMY AND RATIONAL CONSTRAINTS

How can autonomous thinking be subject to constraints and at the same
time exhibit self-determination or self-regulation? To see how it is possible, let us briefly consider how autonomy might be exercised in a nonmoral area such as mathematics. Students who rely exclusively on their
teachers or classmates for answers are not solving mathematics problems
on their own. A mark of autonomous mathematical thinking is figuring
out problems for oneself. Still, some methods must be used, and not just
any method will do. These methods are not merely subjective "inven-
tions." If they are reliable, it should be possible for others to use them
too. In short, autonomous thinkers in mathematics understand and can
successfully employ methods of reasoning that are publicly sharable
with others who are competent in mathematics.

Most of us are not very autonomous when it comes to mathematics,
partly because few of us study mathematics beyond rather elementary

levels and also because high level mathematics is beyond the reach of most of us. Since most of us do not have to make complicated mathematical judgments, and, more importantly, since most of us do not have to take responsibility for making or not making such judgments, it is not a serious problem. There are, we hope, enough mathematical experts around to handle for us the more complex problems that have some bearing on our lives. In any case, perhaps we should say that most of us enjoy only relative autonomy in mathematics and that it is more an intuitive than theoretical matter. For most of us, our understanding of addition, subtraction, multiplication, and division is largely intuitive, even though partly the result of instruction and practice. Without attributing anything more than this to those who exercise mathematical skills, we can still distinguish those who are more autonomous from those who are less so. Some are better at explaining their solutions than others, some are more adept than others at coming up with answers on their own, some are more dependent than others in checking their work by using alternative methods, and so on. Yet once we get beyond elementary mathematical operations, most of us get lost rather quickly.

However, in moral matters we are less likely to defer to expertise, at least about the strictly moral.[2] Most of us do seem to be capable of being quite autonomous in our everyday moral thinking, even if we often fail to exercise this capacity.[3] As I have already indicated, most of us resent not being respected as autonomous in regard to making everyday moral and value judgments. Resistance to paternalistic treatment begins rather early in childhood and intensifies as we move into adulthood. This resistance is grounded in the conviction that we are competent to decide for ourselves. And insofar as others do regard us as morally competent, we are held responsible for our actions.

Moral autonomy includes competence to make responsible moral evaluations and decisions. Such competence requires rational and affective capacities that enable us to understand and take into consideration how what we do is likely to affect others, to reason impartially, and to reflect on the meaning of, rationale for, and possible applications of moral principles and rules. As Arthur Kuflik puts it:

> Just as someone who is incapable of mathematical reasoning is incapable of grasping for himself the validity of an important proof, so also someone who is incapable of moral reflection—that is, of thinking impartially, empathetically, and the like—is incapable of appreci-

ating for himself the validity of various principles of right and justice. . . . It is worth noting that respect for moral autonomy does not necessarily reflect the view that what is morally right is a matter of "purely subjective" preference. (1984, pp. 273-74)

This is not to say that moral reasoning can be as precise and as conclusive as mathematical reasoning but that there is such a thing as moral reasoning and that rational criteria for moral appraisal are available to those who are morally autonomous. It is because such rational constraints on moral reflection are available that we can speak of moral autonomy (as self-*regulation*) at all.[4]

I offer no elaborate account of the rational constraints involved in moral autonomy, but I will sketch out in very broad strokes some of the constraints I find plausible. I begin with the notion that whatever is morally justifiable is capable of public defense. Private preference is not to be confused with justification. The idea that moral justification is public has many supporters. For example, Kurt Baier (1958) insists that this is an essential feature of a moral point of view. John Rawls (1971) tries to justify fundamental principles of justice by requiring unanimous agreement among rational persons who reason from an initial position of equality without being able to take advantage of their special situations. Sissela Bok (1978) examines the justification of lies by subjecting them to a "test of publicity"—a procedure that appeals to what would be agreed to by a representative, reasonable group of persons engaging in open discussion of the pros and cons of such lies. Bernard Gert (1988) attempts to derive a set of moral rules by relying on the idea of "public advocacy."

What might we expect the outcome of public deliberation about morality to be? Gert plausibly argues that rational persons would be forced to publicly advocate moral rules, such as do not kill, harm, disable, cheat, or break promises. They would also agree that such rules can at times justifiably be broken—but not without good reason. Also characteristic of these rules is that they are not self-interpreting, either in regard to their meaning or the circumstances in which exception may be taken to them. They cannot be treated in a "mechanical" manner. What constitutes killing may seem clear enough in most instances (although we might have some doubts about whether letting someone die is a form of killing). What constitutes harm is more problematic; it requires an understanding of what matters to others—which is often obscured by egocentric thinking as well as the lack of empathic thinking.

One form of cheating is lying. As Sissela Bok argues in detail, those who are prepared to lie typically fail to appreciate fully the perspectives of those to whom lies are told (or others who will be affected by those lies). But the justification of lies requires that all relevant perspectives, including that of the liar, be taken into account. Again, egocentric thinking, even when well intentioned, is an obstacle.

The requirement that moral justification is essentially a public rather than private matter is a requirement of *reasonableness*. A reasonable person is rational—but not merely rational. Such a person must also exhibit qualities of fair-mindedness, respect for others, compassion, and concern for others. As Frank Sibley puts it:

> If I desire that my conduct shall be deemed *reasonable* by someone taking the standpoint of moral judgment, I must exhibit something more than mere rationality or intelligence. To be reasonable here is to see the matter—as we commonly put it—from the other person's point of view, to discover how each will be affected by the possible alternative actions; and, moreover, not merely to "see" this (for any merely prudent person would do as much) but also to be prepared to be disinterestedly *influenced*, in reaching a decision, by the estimate of these possible results. I must justify my conduct in terms of some principle capable of being appealed to by all parties concerned, some principle from which we can reason in common. (1953, p. 557)

Note again that although reasonable people appeal to principles that they are prepared to share with others, it does not mean that partiality to loved ones, friends, or associates is ruled out. The requirement of disinterestedness insists only that these principles apply impartially to all. That is, others may be partial to loved ones, friends, or associates, too. Those who are reasonable in this way are morally autonomous in all three senses identified by Hill. They are capable of impartially evaluating moral principles and practices, they have a right to decide for themselves, and they are capable of self-governance in ways consistent with personal integrity.

However, while rationality is clearly a fundamental aspect of moral autonomy, Bernard Gert (1988) is also quite right in insisting that it cannot be shown that it is necessarily irrational to be immoral. It certainly is not always irrational to act in ways that cannot be publicly advocated. Even if morality "pays" much of the time, it cannot be shown that it always does. It seems that, from the standpoint of motivation, morality must rely on more than the desire to be rational. Here, as Hill suggests, compassion, sympathetic concern, and caring for others all play a fundamental role.

Thus, rather than maintain that moral autonomy and caring for others are incompatible, it seems that they are complementary. Without agreeing with Hume that "reason is, and ought to be, the slave of the passions," we can agree that morality depends on moral sentiments. Cognitive development without the development of moral sentiments is not enough for moral autonomy, as the psychopath so sadly illustrates. Once again then, it can be concluded that, far from there being any incompatibility between moral autonomy and caring, the former requires the latter.

The implications this requirement has for Hill's first sense of "autonomy" should be noted here. Although an autonomous person is capable of impartially reviewing and justifying moral principles, this is not done from a standpoint detached from fundamental moral dispositions. That is, impartiality, fair-mindedness, respect for persons, and sympathetic concern for others are not themselves suspended. Since these dispositions are integral to moral justification, they will not themselves be subjected to critical review from a morally neutral standpoint. We might say that they are *confirmed* rather than justified or proven. As Reid might put it, what they express seems "self-evident," in the sense that no more basic reason can be given in their support, and they seem to be presupposed in all moral reasoning.

AUTONOMY AND MORAL AGENCY

I have tried to show that moral autonomy is related to moral competency, which itself involves a blend of rationality and concern for others. Any moral theory that holds people morally accountable must find a significant place for moral agents, according them whatever degree of competency that is commensurate with the responsibilities ascribed to them. I offer no comprehensive, unified theory myself, being skeptical both of the possibility of and need for such a theory. Instead, I will devote the rest of this chapter to a consideration of problems I think moral agency poses for one of the perennial candidates for a comprehensive, unified theory: utilitarianism.

It is often claimed that utilitarianism cannot provide a plausible account of the special obligations we have to others—for example, those arising from promising or contracting. The typical utilitarian response is to point out that these special obligations arise in the context of commonly accepted rules and practices, and that the observance of these rules and participation in these practices serve the general utility. Act- and rule-utilitarians may disagree about just how these rules and practices should be regarded, but either would likely acknowledge the utility of having people appeal to them in justifying what they do. Act-utilitarians often accuse rule-utilitarians of rule worship, but this does not mean that they have no respect for rules. They are simply opposed to blind obedience, especially when it is evident that compliance has counter-utilitarian consequences.

The apparent advantage of allowing utilitarians to appeal to rules is that this seems to take away much of the thrust of the attack of deontologists such as H. A. Prichard (1912) and W. D. Ross (1930). Deontologists say that promises should be kept because to promise is precisely to incur an obligation voluntarily. Utilitarians can agree; they can point out that the utility of the practice of promising depends on its participants taking the practice seriously, which requires taking the attitude that promises are to be kept unless there are clearly overwhelming considerations of utility ruling against this. This means that, by and large, promises should be kept because of what it is to promise, but it must always be remembered that the ultimate sanction for this is its general utility.

Countless utilitarians have argued for something like this. I do not intend to challenge the claim that promising can be sanctioned by utilitarianism. Instead, I will put a new wrinkle into the discussion. My question is this: Even if there are utilitarian reasons for having a practice like promising, what reason can be given for holding that any particular individual ought to be regarded as a full-fledged agent in such a practice? Such an agent would be capable of, among other things, making binding promises. My question is not answered simply by explaining what the practice of promising is. To see this, it will be helpful to consider this question in the context of games.

In general, it is one thing to state the rules and goals circumscribing the actions of participants in a game, and it is quite another to indicate who should or should not be allowed to participate. Certainly having the capacity to play the game is a relevant consideration. It may also be necessary for those who want to participate to stand in some special relationship to the other participants (for example, as a friend, classmate, or neighbor). Or there might be some stated eligibility rules. However, the rules of the game do not usually specify who shall or shall not be allowed to play. If a stranger picks up a bat used in a neighborhood baseball game and insists on batting, the participants might rightly refuse to allow it, even though it is not specified by any rules of the game and even though the stranger's participation would not violate any rules of the game.

Suppose someone claims that he or she has wrongly been barred from participating? What kind of moral appeal would be relevant? If there are some eligibility rules, perhaps an appeal to them could be made. These rules, in turn, could be appraised in terms of their general utility. Yet what if no such stated rules exist, and the neighborhood children are simply unfairly discriminating against a certain child? In this case a more direct appeal to utility would be in order. Thus, one might argue that such discrimination has counterutilitarian consequences. Of course, since this is not a principled objection to discrimination as such (in that utility could indicate the opposite), there is at least a theoretical worry that the charge of discrimination will be dismissed as indecisive.

Rather than examine utilitarian attempts to get around this worry, I wish to widen my inquiry. Suppose we talk now, not of games, but of less narrowly circumscribed practices. In the case of promising, one can appeal directly to the fact that a promise was made in claiming that a promisor should do what was promised. The promisor voluntarily incurred an obligation by promising, but what qualifies one as a promisor?

If we focus on adults, it may be difficult to see what is being asked. What could be more familiar than adults incurring obligations by promising? If we turn to children, it is immediately obvious that we do not uniformly regard children as agents in the practice of promising. Very small children are not regarded as promisors at all. Even if a two-year-old says, "I promise," we do not regard this as voluntarily incurring an obligation. And we plainly restrict the range of things about which even older children can promise or contract. A three-year-old might promise to pay a playmate ten dollars for a one-dollar toy, but this is not regarded by adults as a binding promise. Legal limits are placed on the age one must be to incur certain financial responsibilities by contracting.

It is not difficult to see that utilitarian reasons might be given why children of certain ages should not be regarded "of age" in many respects. But at what point should adults acknowledge that a child can determine for himself or herself certain special obligations to others? A utilitarian might say, at the age at which greater utility is likely to result from acknowledging this. Unlike in law, morality does not specify an age at which one acquires the capacity to make binding promises. There is no general rule at all concerning when the transition should be acknowledged to occur—other than that it should occur when the child is sufficiently mature to understand and appreciate the significance of having such a moral capacity. Yet do we really have any idea whether acknowledgment of this capacity at such a time is likely to lead to the enhancement of general utility? It would seem that, for all we know, in at least some instances greater utility would result from waiting a little longer.

What is troubling about utilitarianism here is that it implies that, if it could be shown that greater utility would result from denying that a reasonably mature child has the capacity to make binding promises, denial would be justified. Child rearing provides us with endless examples of children who complain that they are "of age" but that their parents, or others, do not treat them as if they are. At least some of these complaints seem warranted. It is implausible to suppose that these complaints are based on the claim that being accorded full moral status will promote the greatest good for the greatest number. (That there is no good reason why they should be concerned about the general utility in insisting on this status will be argued shortly.)

Of course, it is to be expected that children learn to accept certain responsibilities prior to any conversion to utilitarianism. As Hare and others point out, it is not only those who are professed utilitarians who should do what is likely to promote utility. Utilitarianism prescribes actions which can be done for nonutilitarian reasons. Children might well be required to do things prescribed by the principle of utility even if they are incapable of understanding utilitarian theory. In fact, a utilitarian might claim, it is very doubtful that anything like moral education would be possible if children were required to do things only after they could fully understand the ultimate justification for doing them. Socialization might be so long delayed as to be permanently obstructed.

Yet at some point children do grow up, and at least the more philosophically inclined ask just the sorts of questions about the foundations of morality that utilitarians do. We might expect utilitarians in their response to be forthcoming in explaining the true reason why people should be regarded as full-fledged moral agents. I will outline a plausible line of resistance to this purported reason, not offered as a knockdown "disproof" of utilitarianism—utilitarians can reject this view without fear of self-contradiction—but as an alternative, one that I believe is preferable to an exclusively utilitarian outlook.

Imagine that Harold has just "come of age" in regard to being able to reflect on the foundations of morality.[5] Although unfamiliar with utilitarian theory, he regards himself as a full-fledged moral agent. He is told by a utilitarian that the ultimate basis for being regarded by others as fully responsible for what one does is that this action is likely to promote the greatest good for the greatest number. The criteria for full moral agency are set out in terms of what will most likely enhance general utility. This implies, admits the utilitarian, that the criteria could vary if, in fact, utility would be better supported by doing so. However, he assures Harold, this is very unlikely.

All of this strikes Harold as misguided. He believes others should regard him as fully responsible because he is, in fact, competent to accept and act in accordance with adult responsibilities. He replies that he really has no idea whether his being regarded in this way is likely to promote the greatest good for the greatest number, but he sees no need to determine this in order to ascertain that he is qualified to be regarded as fully responsible.

Harold points out that the utilitarian's attempt to convert him to utilitarianism makes sense only on the assumption that he already is fully responsible. He can hardly be expected to accept the utilitarian theory unless he is already regarded morally competent. This need not, in itself, disturb the utilitarian, but Harold goes on to say that it is unreasonable for him to accept any moral theory that does not have a principled objection to others not regarding him as fully responsible. He believes this presents a problem for utilitarianism because it seems possible, at least in principle, that a situation could arise in which there would be a utilitarian justification for not regarding a fully responsible person as morally competent. He mentions the film *Suddenly Last Summer* (based on a Tennessee Williams play), in which a doctor has to decide whether to perform a lobotomy on a fully sane and competent young woman in order to acquire desperately needed funds for a hospital, funds that will otherwise be unobtainable. The young woman knows something about a wealthy widow's son that the widow wants kept secret. The widow offers the doctor a huge sum of money to perform the surgery, which allegedly will render the young woman harmless, though not unhappy.

At this point the utilitarian claims that there is an ambiguity in Harold's use of "regard" when he insists that any acceptable moral theory must regard him as fully responsible. In the lobotomy example the only sense in which the young woman would not be regarded as fully responsible is that she would be *treated* as if she were not responsible. But this is quite consistent with the doctor *believing* she is fully responsible, and in that sense she still would be regarded as fully responsible.

Although Harold agrees that there is some point in making this distinction, he does not believe it really meets the issue. His point is that the warrant for judging that someone is morally responsible is grounded in the moral competence that person has, rather than in considerations of utility. Furthermore, Harold says, this nonutilitarian basis of responsibility places moral constraints on how a person should be treated. Just as the basis of responsibility is nonutilitarian, so is the basis of these moral constraints. Even if it were agreed that in some extraordinary situations utilitarian considerations might justify treating a responsible person as if she were not, it would still be necessary to have these utilitarian considerations *outweigh* nonutilitarian, moral considerations. Yet utilitarianism denies that there are any nonutilitarian, moral considerations.

What constraints should the acknowledgment of a person's moral agency place on anyone? Consider a negative approach to this question. If someone were to treat Harold as if he were not fully responsible, Harold would likely react with resentment, or indignation. This reaction would be grounded in his sense of dignity; it is moral anger at the lack of respect from others. The Kantian flavor of this way of characterizing Harold's reaction is intentional. One of the virtues of Kant's moral theory is that the derivation of Kant's most fundamental principle, the categorical imperative, is already grounded in the idea of respect for persons, rather than (as with the principle of utility) respect for persons being only contingently derivable from it (Kant 1788).

Let us return now to the practice of promising. What reason should be given for saying that anyone should be acknowledged as a full participant in such a practice? Well, what is implied by the judgment that Harold cannot make binding promises? Such a judgment seems to imply that he lacks the competence to determine for himself certain special moral obligations to others that most people are assumed to have.

Harold might again regard the denial that he can make binding promises as an affront.

It might well be true that in practice the principle of utility can never plausibly be used to deny Harold's capacity to make binding promises. Nothing here turns on whether or not this is so. Rather, the point in considering Harold's reaction to others denying his capacity is to show that he would not argue on utilitarian grounds that his moral capacity to make binding promises should be respected. His resentment points to another ground—namely, his belief that he is fully competent to incur special obligations to others by promising. He believes it is not necessary to call on the principle of utility to sanction either his capacity to make binding promises or the special obligations he incurs when he exercises that capacity. He regards his competency quite sufficient grounding for both. Utilitarian arguments concerning his moral capacity and its exercise are at best unnecessary—at worst they present a potential obstacle to the kind of respect he believes his status as a moral agent warrants.

Some utilitarians might reply that Harold's view rests on a fundamental misunderstanding. Utilitarianism, they say, is a theory about the foundations of morality. It is no objection to utilitarianism that ordinary people like Harold do not appeal to the principle of utility when demanding that they be acknowledged as full-fledged moral agents. It will be recalled from Chapter 2 that Hare maintains that there are good utilitarian reasons for children to be raised with settled moral dispositions that make no direct appeal to utility.

However, this utilitarian move comes at the price of holding that most moral agents are ignorant of the most basic reason why they should be acknowledged to be moral agents. Harold has a reason for insisting that he should be accorded this status. Contrary to what he thinks, this reason is not fundamental. Those few who understand utilitarianism at its deepest and most subtle level grasp the most fundamental reason. Thus we return to the worry raised in Chapter 2 that utilitarianism has a rather condescending view of ordinary moral agents.

If Harold sees this, he must make a choice. On the one hand, he can side with that select group of utilitarian theorists and admit that, up until now, he has been mistaken about why he should be acknowledged to be a moral agent. Nearly everyone else continues to be mistaken—and this is the way it should be. On the other hand, he can cling to his conviction that his moral standing is grounded in his competence, not in more distant considerations of general utility. This conviction is part of his sense of himself as a moral agent—and an expression of his personal integrity. The question of whether utilitarianism takes personal integrity seriously enough is the major concern of Chapter 11.

11
Utilitarianism and
Personal Integrity

Although aware of the relativity of all the various life-styles which have given meaning to human striving, the possessor of integrity is ready to defend the dignity of his own life-style against all physical and economic threats. For he knows that an individual life is the accidental coincidence of but one life with but one segment of history; and that for him all human integrity stands or falls with the one style of integrity of which he partakes.
—*Erik Erikson*, Childhood and Society

Integrity is not a conditional word. It doesn't blow in the wind or change with the weather. It's your inner image of yourself, and if you look in there and see a man who won't cheat, then you know he never will. Integrity is not a search for the rewards of integrity. Maybe all you ever get for it is the largest kick in the ass the world can provide. It's not supposed to be a productive asset. Crime pays a lot better. I can bend my own rules way, way over, but there is a place where I finally stop bending them. I can recognize the feeling. I've been there a lot of times.
—*John MacDonald*, The Turquoise Lament

In the last two chapters I have tried to articulate two fundamental ideas that are grounded in respect for personal integrity. Chapter 10 proposes that it is moral competence rather than contribution to overall utility that warrants an individual's status as a full-fledged moral agent. Chapter 9 argues for a sphere of morality from which interpersonal reproach is excluded. The discussion there is restricted to circumstances in which personal decisions and commitments do not conflict with what Urmson calls "rock-bottom, basic duties." The grounding of such duties is impersonal, in the sense that they are minimal moral requirements that apply to anyone. The sphere of personal morality discussed in Chapter 9 also has an impersonal grounding—namely, universalizable respect for personal integrity.

However, there are complications. On the one hand, there are moral perspectives that require more from us than fulfilling "rock-bottom, ba-

sic duties." Utilitarianism is a clear instance. Even when moral requirements issuing from considerations of utility do not conflict with self-
imposed personal "oughts," their grounding is different. On the other
hand, broader concerns for personal integrity raise fundamental questions about the reasonableness of moral requirements that seem to go
against the grain of one's personal integrity.

Of course, if we begin from a utilitarian perspective, it will seem to us
that the basic problem is determining to what extent that perspective can
accommodate our more personal values. From a developmental point
of view, it is clear that attaining such a perspective is at best a moral
achievement rather than a given. So, one might ask how an impersonal,
utilitarian perspective can reasonably make claims on us in the first
place.

Viewing this perspective as individual moral agents, we can see the
problem of integrating our sense of ourselves as moral agents with personal values that give meaning and coherence to our lives. Many of these
more personal values are firmly in place before we can reasonably be expected to be able to take into account the demands of an impersonal
moral perspective such as utilitarianism. These personal projects, commitments, and attachments constitute an important part of our sense of
ourselves, or personal integrity.

Among contemporary philosophers, Bernard Williams (1973) has
taken the lead in questioning the reasonableness of impersonal, utilitarian demands that may require us to abandon or seriously alter projects,
commitments, or attachments that are essential to our personal integrity.
They are what give our lives meaning or point; and without them, Williams holds, neither morality nor anything else will be taken seriously. It
is morality that must be accommodated to personal integrity, rather than
the reverse. The place of impersonal moral values in our lives is thus
posed as a problem rather than as a settled matter.

These issues resist confident resolution. I believe Thomas Nagel is
right in holding that morality must find a place for both personal and impersonal practical reasoning (1986, p. 189). He is also right in emphasizing that precisely what place should be reserved for each is "a problem
of real life and not just of philosophical theory" (1986, p. 189), as we
know from our own experiences. Any plausible moral theory should
raise discomfort at some point for those of us who, knowing we could as-
sist starving or destitute people, nevertheless spend money on amenities
that contribute to the kind of personal life we want to live. As Nagel says,

"This is true not only of purely impersonal moralities like utilitarianism or other consequentialist views. Provided a morality admits substantial agent-neutral reasons arising from the interests of others, it will face this problem even if it also grants significant weight to agent-relative reasons of autonomy and obligation" (1986, p. 190).

Without pretending to offer a resolution of this unavoidable problem, this chapter will focus on problems that the more demanding impersonal moral theories such as utilitarianism pose for personal integrity. I begin with Bernard Williams's trenchant attack on utilitarianism as not being able "to make sense, at any serious level, of integrity" (1973, p. 82).

UTILITARIANISM AND INTEGRITY

Williams presents two examples to clarify his contention that utilitarianism has special problems with integrity. The first is that of George, a pacifist in need of work. George is offered a job in a laboratory that does research on biological and chemical warfare. He knows that if he refuses the job, it will go to someone who would very enthusiastically undertake such research. The second example is that of Jim, who stumbles onto an execution in a remote South American village. Jim is told that, as an honored guest, he will be permitted to shoot one of twenty (presumably innocent) Indians who are lined up to be shot. The remaining nineteen will be released. But if Jim refuses, Pedro will shoot all twenty.

On Williams's view, the utilitarian thing to do in each case calls for considerable personal compromise. He thinks it would be unreasonable to require George to take the job and give up his pacifism, even if it would prevent someone else from zealously pursuing research George finds fundamentally objectionable. This would be an unwarranted threat to George's integrity.[1] Yet, Williams contends, this is precisely what utilitarianism seems to require. Although Williams agrees with the utilitarian view that Jim probably should shoot one Indian to spare the nineteen, he thinks that the utilitarian way of deriving that conclusion fails to do justice to the importance of Jim's integrity in deliberating about such a situation.[2]

Although Williams spends little time explaining what he means by 'integrity,' it is clear that he is not restricting himself to moral integrity. He mentions projects, commitments, and personal relations that are, in some sense, "what we are all about." No doubt some of these are importantly related to our sense of ourselves as moral agents, but they go beyond this. They are what give our lives meaning, purpose, or point. If they are shattered, so are we. These projects, commitments, and personal relations form what is, in some sense, an "integral whole," a personal integrity of which moral integrity is only a part. As Spencer Carr puts it, Williams is concerned with "the harmonious integration of persons: their acts, convictions, projects, and feelings (at least)" (Carr 1976, p. 243).

How does this apply to George, the pacifist? Carr offers the following analysis: "Rather than having George's action follow especially from his projects, utilitarianism puts his projects on the same footing with those of others. In so doing, it makes it possible for George's actions to be determined more by the projects of others than by his own. This would separate George's actions from his projects, rendering his total personality less integral—that is, robbing him of some degree of personal integrity" (1976, p. 244).

Carr's response to this is in the form of a dilemma. Imagine a utilitarian offering advice to George. If George does not follow the advice, his integrity will remain intact. On the other hand, if George follows the advice, either he will do so while retaining his nonutilitarian convictions, or he will be converted to utilitarianism. If he retains his nonutilitarian convictions, his integrity will be adversely affected. Carr says this is trivial—anyone loses integrity by allowing another to determine one's choice against his or her principles. If he is converted to utilitarianism, the problem of integrity will vanish, for his most basic project then will be utilitarian. In response to the claim that having our obligations determined by the actions of others results in a loss of integrity, Carr points out that we often do find that our obligations are determined in this way. Yet it is not clear why this must compromise one's integrity. Besides, if one is a utilitarian, there can be no projects more important than the utilitarian one.

Given only these possibilities, it seems that Williams's concern about integrity dissolves. But suppose George falls somewhere between simply caving in to his utilitarian advisor while retaining his feelings, on the one hand, and becoming fully converted to utilitarianism, on the other hand. That is, suppose that George retains his basic convictions and feelings, while at the same time finding himself somewhat attracted to utilitarianism. Is a mutual accommodation possible? According to both Williams and Carr, such accommodations are not always possible. Williams's view is that, if George retains his pacifist convictions, the utilitarian perspective will strain against them and will, to that extent, alienate him from them. Carr concedes this but challenges its moral significance: "It seems, in fact, that we are pulled in two directions here. On the one hand we have a tendency to admire a person who sticks to what we are here calling moral feeling. But we also tend to sympathize with the person who wrestles with these feelings and has the courage, as we might say, to act against them" (1976, p. 245). Thus, while there may be some loss of personal integrity, it is not clear that there is any loss of moral integrity.

Even Williams acknowledges that there may be circumstances in which one must act against one's moral feelings. He agrees with utilitarians that Jim should shoot one of the Indians. However, Williams's rationale can be distinguished from utilitarianism. We can distinguish preventing a disaster from promoting the greatest good, even though the latter may entail the former, as in the case of Jim. Williams emphasizes that there is a vital difference between outcomes produced by *my* doing something and outcomes produced by *someone else* doing it (1973, p. 94).[3] An idea closely connected to the value we place on integrity is that "each of us is specially responsible for what *he* does, rather than for what other people do" (1973, p. 99). This does not mean that our obligations are never determined more by what others do than by what we do. Williams's agreement with utilitarianism that Jim should shoot one of the Indians indicates this. Rather, Williams's point seems to be that utilitarianism is committed to what is, in effect, a depersonalized conception of agency.

The ideal utilitarian agent, Williams seems to think, is someone who can regard his or her own projects and commitments as if they were someone else's, someone who aspires to view matters from an absolutely impartial point of view—*sub species aeternitatis*. This view is essentially that of the classical impartial spectator theory as applied to utilitarianism. It is aptly summarized by John Rawls:

Endowed with ideal powers of sympathy and imagination, the impartial spectator is the perfectly rational individual who identifies with and experiences the desires of others as if these desires were his own. . . . On this conception of society separate individuals are thought of as so many different lines along which rights and duties are to be assigned and scarce means of satisfaction allocated in accordance with rules so as to give the greatest fulfillment of wants. . . . The correct decision is essentially a question of efficient administration. This view of social cooperation is the consequence of extending to society the principle of choice for one man, and then, to make this extension work, conflating all persons into one through the imaginative acts of the impartial sympathetic spectator. Utilitarianism does not take seriously the distinction between persons. (1971, p. 27)

Of course, this is only a hypothetical, ideal model. No actual person could hope to achieve this perspective. But it is toward such a perspective that a utilitarian is to aspire and against which one judges the adequacy of one's actual concerns and commitments.

With this in mind, let us return to Jim's predicament. Although agreeing that Jim should shoot one Indian to save the remaining nineteen, Williams objects to the way in which utilitarianism arrives at this conclusion. The basic objection seems to be that, from a utilitarian point of view, whatever reluctance Jim might have to shooting the Indian is merely self-indulgent squeamishness. This characterization of his reluctance is unsettling because "we are partially at least not utilitarians, and cannot regard our moral feelings merely as objects of utilitarian value" (1973, p. 103). Williams explains that our moral relation to the world is, in part, constituted by such feelings and by our sense of what we can or cannot "live with." Utilitarianism alienates us from these feelings by asking us to view them impartially, as might be done by a third person whose aim is to maximize good consequences in general.

Despite Williams's attempt to avoid advocating self-indulgence, J. J. C. Smart's reply to Williams repeats the charge: "From the utilitarian point of view Williams' insistence on the preservation of one's integrity does seem to be an egotistical one" (1977, p. 133). What needs to be clarified is why favoring the integrity of an individual at the expense of maximizing good consequences is not simply an endorsement of self-indulgence. This in turns requires further clarification of the role Williams thinks personal integrity should have in practical deliberation.

At the outset it is important to differentiate the following three notions from one another: (1) being motivated primarily by the thought that doing such-and-such is good *for me*; (2) doing something that is, in fact, good for me, without the fact that it is good for me being a primary motivation for my doing it; (3) doing something that indicates that I have certain basic projects, commitments, or concerns. It seems clear that (1) (be-ing motivated primarily by the thought that something is good for me) can at times be self-indulgent. However, it is much harder to sustain the charge of self-indulgence when (2) (self-regarding motivation) is not con-spicuous. So we must ask whether, in particular cases, (3) (doing some-thing that indicates I have certain basic projects, commitments, or con-cerns) is best assimilated to (1) or (2).

Williams's point seems to be that, from a utilitarian point of view, inso-far as pursuing my projects or commitments is assimilated to (1) and it falls short of utilitarian ends, a charge of self-indulgence will be leveled, since my attention is focused more on how *my* well-being is affected by having those projects or commitments than on that to which I am sup-posedly committed. However, when (2) is combined with (3), it is harder to make a charge of self-indulgence stick. Even if my projects and com-mitments are otherwise misdirected, the fact that they are good for me does not by itself show that I am being self-indulgent.

Still, if we are required to evaluate our projects and commitments from a utilitarian perspective, often it will seem that we are self-indulgently fa-voring our own cases. That is, (3) will be assimilated to (1). Williams's ex-ample of the drowning wife illustrates this.[4] A husband has to choose be-tween saving his wife or a total stranger from drowning. Assuming Alex loves and is committed to Betty, we would expect him unhesitatingly to try to save her. His personal integrity is involved to the extent that his identity is bound up with his love for and commitment to her. Still, inso-far as he unhesitatingly tries to save her, he is acting for her sake, not for the sake of preserving his own integrity, or wholeness. This is so despite the shattering effect her drowning would have on him—and despite the fact that the particular urgency of his acting on her behalf is grounded in the special relationship *he* has to Betty.

There are various ways in which Alex might be alienated somewhat from his love for and commitment to Betty. Even focusing on the fact that Betty is his wife can cause difficulties. If he entertains the thought that husbands are justified in preferring their wives over strangers, this in-volves, as Williams puts it, "one thought too many." Even the thought that Betty is *his* wife and not just *someone's* wife (whose husband hap-pens to be Alex) is not direct enough. What is fundamental for Alex is that it is *Betty* who is drowning. Knowing that she is his wife helps us understand his special concern for her, but that is not how we would ex-pect him to put it to himself.

Suppose Alex has given some prior thought to what he would do if he were ever to find himself in a circumstance like this, and a utilitarian chain of thought flashes before him. From a *sub species aeternitatis* perspective, he reasons, it must be acknowledged that the stranger is probably loved by someone else, too, perhaps by even more people than Betty is. The stranger's suffering and loss of life is just as serious to him as Betty's suffering and loss of life is to her. Others may suffer as much, if not more, from the stranger's death as from Betty's death. From a utilitarian point of view, there is a further factor that might swing the balance in favor of Alex's saving Betty. He will suffer more from the realization that he could have saved Betty, but did not, than he will from the realization that he could have saved the stranger, but did not. Regardless of whether Alex's dispositions here are rationally grounded from a *sub species aeternitatis* perspective, they must be counted as relevant in any utilitarian calculation.[5]

Yet, notice what happens if it is the anticipation of this extra suffering that swings the balance for Alex in favor of saving his wife. The crucial factor now is not that Betty is in need of help; it is that *he* will suffer more if he does not save her, but saves the stranger instead. Insofar as this explains his action, he is acting more from self-regard in saving Betty than if he were to save the stranger. It also means that he is not acting primarily from love of and commitment to Betty—the very relationship said to be a fundamental part of his personal integrity, or wholeness.

The problem is not with what utilitarianism ultimately commends. It seems to pose a threat to Alex's integrity even as it approves his saving Betty because of the kinds of thoughts it injects into his deliberations.[6] However, it might be objected that the drowning wife example is rather special and limited. Given the intimate relationship between Alex and Betty, Williams seems to be denying the appropriateness of Alex engaging in any moral deliberation at all when Betty's life is at stake. We might wonder if anything can be learned about moral integrity from this example, but variations on it can bring moral integrity into the picture.

Suppose three people are drowning, Betty and two strangers. Alex cannot swim, but he can throw a life jacket in either of two directions. If he throws it to Betty, she will be saved. If he throws it in the other direction one stranger will be saved, and there is some real possibility that she can reach the second one in time to help. If Alex hesitates for a moment of moral reflection, would we say that he has entertained "one thought too many"? If so, we could add a third stranger, or some children, who could be saved. At some point, we should concede that moral deliberation is appropriate.

Williams's concern with utilitarianism (and other forms of impersonal morality) is not that moral deliberation becomes appropriate at some point or other but that utilitarianism seems to find it appropriate at virtually any point. Alex's deciding to rescue Betty for utilitarian reasons seems to threaten to undermine a fundamental part of the relationship, even if there are utilitarian reasons pulling against rescuing her. It is appropriate for Alex to wonder if he is morally justified in saving Betty at the expense of several other lives being lost. However, only if he is a utilitarian will he conclude that deciding he is morally justified in saving her requires him to calculate that greater utility is (somehow) served by doing so. It is just this utilitarian way of looking at the situation that Williams thinks invites charges of self-indulgence and at the same time threatens to alter the feelings Alex has for his wife.

Variations on Jim's plight pose similar problems. Suppose Jim were assured that the twenty Indians would be saved if Pedro could shoot Jim instead. We readily understand Jim's reluctance to accept such a proposition—even if he were quite certain that the Indians would be spared. Here Jim would be weighing his own life against that of the twenty Indians. Given that extreme self-sacrifice is called for, from a utilitarian point of view, a "self-indulgent" refusal might be permitted, or at least excused.

But suppose Jim stumbled on the scene with his wife, Joan. He is told that if Joan is shot without his resistance, the twenty Indians will be spared. If Jim views this offer from a utilitarian perspective, but nevertheless resists, he will either find self-serving, utilitarian reasons for resisting, or he will resist his utilitarian conscience. In the latter case, his partiality to Joan will appear to him as self-indulgence, however understandable psychologically. Assuming Jim loves Joan, it is an unfortunate consequence of the utilitarian outlook that the differences between refusing to be killed and resisting a loved one's being killed are so small. (Another variation reveals how great a difference there might be. If Jim were firmly convinced that if he or Joan were shot, the twenty Indians would be spared, he might offer himself in place of Joan.)

Leaving aside examples involving loved ones, Williams is convinced that utilitarianism poses problems for moral integrity. Concern for one's moral integrity can easily dissolve into an obsession with one's "moral purity." When placed in a utilitarian framework, the examples of Jim and

George raise this worry, since moral integrity is at issue in both cases. If either Jim's or George's refusal is seen as acting for the sake of protecting their moral integrity, self-indulgence may surface. Williams suggests that, to avoid seeing integrity as a reflexive form of self-indulgence, it is preferable not to view integrity as a virtue:

> In saying that, I do not mean that there is not all that much to be said for it, as one might say that humility was not a virtue. I mean that while it is an admirable human property, it is not related to motivation as the virtues are. . . . It is rather that one who displays integrity acts from those dispositions and motives which are most deeply his, and has also the virtues that enable him to do that. Integrity does not enable him to do it, nor is it what he acts from when he does so.
>
> If that is right, we can see why integrity, regarded as a virtue, can seem to smack of moral self-indulgence. For if it is regarded as a motive, it is hard to reconstruct its representation in thought except in the objectionable reflexive way: the thought would have to be about oneself and one's own character, and of the suspect kind. (1981, p. 49)

Thus far, all of the problems utilitarianism poses for integrity concern the impact of utilitarian thought on deliberation. Two moves can be made by utilitarians at this point. First, they can "bite the bullet" and insist that utilitarian reflection should be a fundamental part of ordinary deliberation. There may be occasions when the kind of integrity Williams values is knocked askew by alienating us somewhat from our moral feelings and personal affections, but this simply shows that integrity has less value than many of us think. Such a move acknowledges the problem but concludes that it is not significant enough to constitute a serious criticism of utilitarianism. This seems to be J. J. C. Smart's response.

A second move is to argue that utilitarianism is not primarily a theory about how ordinary agents should deliberate. This view concedes that, for the most part, utilitarian reflection is not a part of ordinary moral deliberation. Our basic projects, commitments, and concerns are seldom a product of utilitarian reflection. Not only is this so, it is just as it should be. Utilitarianism, on this view, is best understood as a theory about the criteria that should be used in determining whether courses of conduct, policies, institutions, and so on are as they should be, which is quite distinct from saying that anyone should actually employ these criteria in their everyday deliberations (Hare 1981; Railton 1984).

Hare, for example, argues that it is a very good thing from a utilitarian point of view that people typically develop dispositions which make it difficult to conscience shooting one Indian to save twenty. By and large, the ordinary, nonutilitarian responses we have to situations are quite serviceable, but there are times when it is desirable for us to move to a more critical level of moral thought. Here a direct consideration of utilitarian criteria will be appropriate. It also may be discovered that these criteria, in special circumstances, strain against widely held moral feelings. According to Hare, it will happen rather infrequently and even then primarily because the moral dispositions of "well brought-up" persons are well suited for ordinary rather than extraordinary circumstances. There is great utility in this being so. Our ability to determine what, in a particular circumstance, is likely to bring about the most good is generally unreliable. Steady nonutilitarian dispositions are more reliable in this regard, and they also provide a firmer basis for interpersonal relationships that depend on cooperation. Thus, it is understandable and desirable that Jim would have great difficulty deciding to shoot an Indian.

Hare has little sympathy with "desert-island" counterexamples to utilitarianism. Since our basic moral dispositions are formed in more ordinary circumstances, we should not expect them to be well suited for extreme cases that have an air of unreality about them. It may be objected that Williams's example of Jim the explorer has such "desert-island" features. After all, how likely is it that we would ever encounter such a situation, especially one where all the variables that naturally concern us are so carefully controlled (for example, the assurance that the other Indians will not be shot anyway)?

Still, sometimes thought-experiments about the extraordinary are instructive. Consider a scene from John Fowles's novel *The Magus* (1977), a much richer, more unsettling example than Jim and the Indians. Maurice Conchis recalls the World War II German occupation of the small Greek island village where he was mayor. Island guerrillas have killed four German soldiers. Wimmel, the German officer in command, has ruled that for every German killed on the island, twenty Greek inhabitants will be executed. Two guerrillas have been captured and subjected to cruel torture, but they refuse to provide information about the other guerrillas.

Wimmel tells Conchis that if he, as mayor, executes the two guerrillas, the eighty hostages will be spared; otherwise they all will be executed. Conchis recalls:

> I said, "I am not an executioner."
> The village men began to shout frantically at me.
> He looked at his watch, and said, "You have thirty seconds to decide."
> Of course in such situations one cannot think. All coherence is crowded out of one's mind. You must remember this. From this point on I acted without reason. Beyond reason. (1977, p. 431)

It is not clear from the narrative that Conchis actually does act entirely without reason. It is clear that he is in the grip of irresolvable internal conflict and horror. His first decision (about which he says, "I have no choice") is to carry out the execution. When he pulls the trigger several times only empty clicks are heard. Wimmel explains, "It is strictly forbidden for the civilian population to possess loaded weapons." Conchis then realizes that he is expected to beat the two guerrillas to death with the rifle. His initial resistance is met with a threat to his own life. He sets himself to bludgeon one of the guerrillas but "left a fatal pause of a second to elapse." Finally, he defiantly refuses—in the face of his own execution and the derision of the eighty hostages and the onlooking villagers. Conchis and the eighty hostages are summarily shot, but somehow he survives to tell the story and bear its moral wounds.

Perhaps this is the sort of example Williams has in mind when he says there are some circumstances so morally monstrous that sanity requires suspension of moral deliberation. However, an especially steely-willed utilitarian might say, even here there is a lesser evil to be chosen. This may be true. Hare's archangel could tell. Still, as Hare points out, we are not archangels—either in powers of discernment or capacity for retaining composure in the face of such terror and revulsion. In a case such as this it seems that no moral theory will afford one comfort or easy conscience.

Despite the enormity of the situation, however, there is evidence of integrity in the form of courage and steadfastness. It can be seen in the refusal of the two guerrillas to talk and in their defiant attitude to the end. It also can be seen in Conchis even as he changes his course of action. Throughout the confusion he remains steadfast in doing what he thinks is right. Interestingly, however, this is so as much when he is in a possibly utilitarian mode while trying to save the hostages as when he joins the guerrillas in shouting for freedom. Adherence to principle—utilitarian or otherwise—in such circumstances clearly requires the kind of inner strength that is a mark of integrity.

We can imagine things going otherwise. Wimmel told Conchis that he would be spared if he cooperated, that he would not be included in the group of eighty hostages. Conchis expressed relief for a moment. If, subsequently, he had acted as he did (attempting to shoot the guerrillas) because he was spared, or in the hope of being spared, it would have shown a lack of integrity. That is, if all morally creditable motives vanished in the face of Wimmel's threats and temptation, so would Conchis's integrity. But Conchis is not portrayed as losing his integrity. He had good reason to believe that if he did not cooperate with Wimmel, he would be executed along with everyone else. This is the choice he ultimately made, and it required moral courage. He was willing to sacrifice his life rather than perform an abominable act. Yet the perhaps more utilitarian choice—that of shooting the guerrillas—also required courage.

Utilitarians like Hare and Smart might admire the courage of Conchis when, in such a desperate moment, he pulled the trigger. Could they admire the courage he displayed in his ultimate refusal? I should think so. Smart, for example, says that there are good utilitarian reasons for rearing children so that they will not easily sacrifice a few for the many. Miscalculation, overzealousness, and hard-heartedness are common enough.

If utilitarians do insist that the principle of utility is to be understood primarily as providing criteria for determining the acceptability of conduct, policies, and institutions rather than as a deliberative principle, it is not clear how Williams can sustain his charge that utilitarianism "cannot hope to make sense, at any serious level, of integrity." However, he might make two replies. First, from the standpoint of moral deliberation, the power and distinctiveness of utilitarianism shrinks almost to the point of vanishing. There is a real question of *for whom* utilitarianism is to serve as a moral theory.

Second, even if utilitarianism allows a significant place for respecting personal integrity, it is not clear that it does so for the most appropriate reasons. Respect for personal integrity is granted only by indirection, either as an acknowledged means to greater good or as a dispensation, a concession to the inevitability of our having nonutilitarian based projects, commitments, and affections. To repeat a theme from Chapter 2, this has an air of condescension. The typical moral agent remains largely ignorant of morality at its most fundamental level—the level of criteria for assessing the moral appropriateness of the ways in which we live our lives.

Before we agree with the view that ordinary moral agents are ignorant in this way, powerful reasons for accepting it should be provided. Clearly more is needed than showing that utilitarianism, too, can find a place for respecting personal integrity. Williams links personal integrity with those projects, commitments, and concerns that give our lives meaning and point. Furthermore, as Williams points out, having certain nonutilitarian based projects and commitments is, for nearly all of us, a condition for our being moral agents at all. This is where our moral world begins. Utilitarianism, like other impersonal moral perspectives, tries to extend our concerns beyond the merely parochial, but this should be done in a way that does not lose sight of the inherent importance that projects, commitments, and concerns have for moral agents. Attempting to derive that importance from a *sub species aeternitatis* perspective seems to put things the wrong way around. From the outset, our moral agency is bound up with our personal integrity. It is from here that the importance of viewing matters *sub species aeternitatis* must be explained if it is to be made credible to moral agents. Moral agents are likely to view with some caution any account that threatens to subvert their personal integrity. If the only way to avoid that threat is to suppose that moral agents will seldom have any use for such an account, it is not clear that we should take comfort in it. A more direct grounding of the importance of personal integrity seems preferable. Samuel Scheffler tries to provide that in his *Rejection of Consequentialism* (1982). We will now turn to his account.

AGENT-CENTERED PREROGATIVES

Scheffler defends two basic claims. First, moral agents are not always required to do what there is good reason to believe will produce the best state of affairs. Second, moral agents are always permitted to do what there is good reason to believe will produce the best state of affairs. The first claim is defended in terms of what Scheffler calls an *agent-centered prerogative*. Each of us has personal concerns and commitments with a significance for us that an impersonal calculation of the best state of affairs does not adequately represent. The second claim denies that there are *agent-centered restrictions* against trying to bring about the best state of affairs. Together, these two claims permit but do not require us to accept and act on utilitarian principles.[7]

Scheffler argues that personal integrity should be acknowledged to be relevant in moral deliberation independently of its contribution to overall utility. According to him, utilitarianism attaches moral weight to personal concerns and commitments in strict proportion to their weight in an impersonal ranking of overall states of affairs. Utilitarianism might make a "consequentialist dispensation to devote more attention to one's own happiness and well-being than to the happiness and well-being of others" (Scheffler 1982, p. 15).[8] But such a dispensation does not attach *moral* weight to personal concerns and commitments as *mine*. An agent-centered prerogative, on the other hand, attaches independent moral weight to the personal point of view.

From an impersonal, utilitarian point of view, my concerns and commitments do not necessarily carry any more moral weight than anyone else's. If I am allowed to favor my own concerns and commitments, it is only because this will contribute to the best state of affairs overall. But Scheffler says the function of an agent-centered prerogative is "to deny that the permissibility of devoting energy to one's projects and commitments depends on the efficacy of such activity as an instrument of overall benefit" (1982, p. 17). Although utilitarianism and one's personal point of view might favor the same actions, the supporting reasons for those actions are quite different.

Unlike Williams, Scheffler does not think that utilitarianism systematically undermines personal integrity. Scheffler's defense of utilitarianism on this score is essentially the same as Spencer Carr's: "But if someone *wants* to bring about the best state of affairs, either out of a supererogatory willingness to sacrifice his own projects or because bringing about the best *is* his project, there is no reason from the standpoint of personal integrity to forbid that. Such a person is surely not alienated 'from his actions and the source of his action in his own convictions'" (Scheffler, p. 22). However, Scheffler's agent-centered prerogative is designed to provide agents with a protected zone for personal integrity that is in no way dependent on its overall utility. Still, this is not an unlimited protected zone. One cannot, in the name of personal integrity, claim liberty to do just anything; and one must guard against having personal integrity collapse into egoism. Neither of these is what Scheffler has in mind (1982, pp. 17–19, 22).

What is the perspective that moderates the tension between utilitarianism and one's personal point of view? Utilitarianism cannot adequately represent the significance I want to attach to my personal concerns and commitments, but, as Scheffler himself warns, my wants may be excessive. Personal perspectives can be unacceptably egocentric or even egoistic. The potential excesses of both utilitarianism and one's personal point of view must be restricted. Yet utilitarianism cannot restrict one's personal point of view, since one's personal point of view is permitted to take exception to utilitarian ends. One's personal point of view alone cannot restrict the claims of utilitarianism, since personal wants may be excessive.

Unfortunately, Scheffler never carefully articulates what this moderating perspective is. He assures us that agent-centered prerogatives are not egoistic, but he says that "it is not part of this investigation to address the question of why, ultimately, such a prerogative *ought not* to take an egoist form" (1982, p. 70). Still, Scheffler is confident that he has provided a principled rationale for agent-centered prerogatives, and that it has no implications for agent-centered restrictions. Further, he asserts that he can find no principled rationale whatsoever for agent-centered restrictions.

What is Scheffler's principled rationale for agent-centered prerogatives? It cannot be merely the fact that personal concerns and commitments naturally originate independently of utilitarian concerns. This would include objectionably egoistic and egocentric concerns and commitments, too. Furthermore, Scheffler is not claiming that only *he* has an agent-centered prerogative. All of us have. Thus, agent-centered prerogatives must be sanctioned from some sharable perspective, but it cannot be from the impersonal perspective of the best state of affairs overall, the utilitarian perspective.

An attractive alternative is to advocate a principle of respect for personal integrity. Such a principle, although impersonal, values more than states of affairs; it values personal agency as well. Thus, although satisfying the principle might be compatible with producing the best state of affairs overall, it is an entirely contingent matter. What is not contingent is that agents are permitted, within limits, to favor their own concerns and commitments.[9]

If something like a principle of respect for personal integrity provides the principled rationale for Scheffler's agent-centered prerogatives, does it also provide a principled rationale for some agent-centered restrictions? I will now try to show that it does. For illustrative purposes, and because Scheffler himself discusses it, I will consider promising.[10] However, similar remarks could be made about contractual relations generally, as well as about many other special, moral relations. Scheffler discusses promising in just two places, and then only in footnotes (1982, pp. 22-23, 85). This is surprising, since utilitarian treatments of promising have been challenged so frequently by critics.

An agent, Harold, can voluntarily incur an obligation by making a promise. This promise, says Scheffler, is binding on him, *unless* the outcome would be better if he broke it. Although Harold may exercise his agent-centered prerogative and keep the promise even if more good would come from breaking it, it is only permissible, not a moral requirement. In contrast, nonutilitarians such as Ross and Prichard insist that the prospect of somewhat better consequences resulting from breaking the promise rather than keeping it does not override the obligation to keep it. We need not say that everyone who makes promises agrees with this. It is enough that most people do view promises this way.

Suppose Harold wants to give his word that he will not break his promise even when somewhat more overall good would result. Would Scheffler say that Harold may not use his agent-centered prerogative in this way? He will concede that Harold is not required to break his promise in order to bring about more good. But Harold is saying more than this—that he accepts the idea that he ought not to break his promise even when more good would result. This does not mean that Harold's position is absolutist. He might agree that promises may be broken in order to avoid especially bad consequences or even that there are times when the prospect of exceptionally good consequences could justify breaking a promise. It seems that for Scheffler, Harold's agent-centered prerogative may not be used to incur an obligation to refrain from trying to maximize good consequences by breaking the promise—even if Harold wants to commit himself to that. Such an agent-centered restriction apparently lacks a principled rationale.

However, it does seem that there is a principled rationale here—viz., Harold's exercise of his autonomy. Part of Scheffler's defense of his agent-centered prerogative is that it provides a protected zone for one's personal agency. One aspect of this is that a limit is placed on one's responsibility (1982, p. 19). Equally important is being able to determine, through voluntary action, some of one's moral relations with others, which Scheffler allows to a limited extent in the case of promising. But it seems an arbitrary restriction to say that, while one is permitted to keep promises even when more good could come from breaking them, one is not able voluntarily to incur obligations to do the same. It cannot be objected that Harold's willingness to incur obligations in this way is idiosyncratic. Moral communities have rather settled moral practices, and promising is one of them. Utilitarians acknowledge its utility. Rule-utilitarians even acknowledge the importance of having a rule requiring that a promise be kept even when more overall good would result from its being broken.

Moral practices are not established by individual fiat. Individual agents grow up in communities with well-established moral practices, and most spend their entire lives in such communities. Yet Scheffler says virtually nothing about this. Within communities moral agents are interdependent, and moral demands are made on one another that are based to some extent on mutually accepted rules, practices, and expectations. Very little of this makes a direct appeal to an impersonal consideration of the best state of affairs overall.

To see more clearly how the principled rationale for agent-centered prerogatives can provide a basis for agent-centered restrictions, it is necessary to take a closer look at one's personal point of view. Although Scheffler continually refers to the importance of personal concerns and commitments, he spends remarkably little time discussing how these concerns and commitments are viewed by those who have them. Scheffler's agent-centered prerogative is characterized in terms of what is permitted, but this does not mean that agents themselves regard their concerns and commitments in terms of what is permissible. From the perspective of impersonal respect for personal integrity, it is permissible for Harold, by promising, to commit himself to a course of action that falls short of utilitarian ends. From Harold's perspective, however, once the commitment is made, it is not merely permissible for him to pursue that course of action. It is morally required, and he regards keeping his word as a matter of integrity.

Consider a different perspective. David promises Harold he will repay his loan of $500 by December. Harold plans to buy a new car in December, but he will need his $500 in order to do so. However, moved by a campaign for improving the local library, David donates $300 to the library fund in late November. As a result, he can repay only $200 to Harold in December. Does Harold have any basis for moral complaint?

Suppose David defends himself by saying, "I know I promised. But it seemed to me that I could do more good by giving to the library. I'll be able to pay you the $300 in January. Then you can get your car. If the library drive had not reached its goal by the end of November, the project would have been abandoned." Harold could argue with David's claim that his $300 was crucial to the library drive, or that more overall good would have resulted from the full return of the loan. He would be more likely to argue that David *promised* to repay the money and that he ought not to have given it to the library—at least not without asking Harold. In effect, David took it upon himself to dispense Harold's $300 without his consent.

Perhaps the case could be described in such a way that David's action, from an impersonal standpoint, clearly did have the best outcome overall. However, that should not obscure the source of Harold's complaint. As I am presenting his view, he is not complaining that David has failed to understand what really would have had the better outcome; rather, he is countering with a different principle. He is not offering a utilitarian argument for saying that David should have kept his promise. He is claiming that David should have kept his word, even if more good might have resulted from David giving the money to the library. It is not that Harold could never recognize a legitimate reason for not repaying the loan on time; it is just that *this* reason is not good enough.

We can imagine circumstances in which Harold might be more open to David's reasoning. Suppose, for example, David tells Harold at the outset that he will repay the money by December—unless he can accomplish more good by breaking the promise. If Harold agrees to lend the money under these conditions, he might not have a complaint (assuming he agrees with David's assessment of the importance of the library fund). The main point is that most people who make promises do not make clear to the promisee that they will keep their promises unless more good can come from breaking them. Most people to whom promises are made do not understand such promises either. Scheffler's case is not helped much by supposing that Harold and David see promising differently from most.

Let's turn now to David's agent-centered prerogative. Is it Scheffler's view that David can promise to repay Harold by December, but that he has no obligation to do so if he can accomplish more good by breaking the promise? It would seem so. But what about *Harold's* agent-centered prerogative? Must Harold agree that, when he lends money to David, David may justifiably break his promise if he can do more good by doing so?

If Scheffler's answer is no, then Harold will be able to insist that there is an agent-centered restriction on David. If he answers yes, then lending money places people in a much more vulnerable position than most would find acceptable. It seems that Scheffler's view lacks a principled rationale for ruling out such agent-centered restrictions. Common practice and reasonable expectations seem to support agent-centered restrictions in regard to promising (and contractual relations generally). Scheffler might reply that these examples can be accommodated within utilitarianism. Impersonal consideration of optimal outcomes can recognize the utility of restrictions on promising, but since this is impersonal calculation, it is not agent-centered.

There is a serious problem with such a reply; it could be made against agent-centered prerogatives. As pointed out earlier, utilitarianism can evaluate practices by using utilitarian criteria without thereby advocating that agents themselves use utilitarian principles in their actual deliberations. Utilitarianism can acknowledge the importance of agents favoring their own projects and commitments just because they are theirs. There is a sense, then, in which utilitarianism can allow for an agent-centered prerogative of sorts, thus providing considerable room for personal integrity.

As we have seen, Scheffler's reply is that, even if utilitarianism does not actually undermine personal integrity, the moral weight to be attached to personal integrity does not derive *exclusively* from an impersonal consideration of optimal, overall outcomes. The personal point of view carries independent moral weight. If this is so, the same can be said of agent-centered restrictions that result from the exercise of agent-centered prerogatives, as in the case of Harold.

AGENT-CENTERED RESTRICTIONS

I have argued that, through promising, contracting, and the like, the exercise of agent-centered prerogatives can give rise to moral restrictions. However, Scheffler might reply that this argument leaves a much larger point untouched. Nonutilitarians typically claim that, quite independently of voluntarily incurring obligations by promising, there are circumstances in which moral agents *ought* to refrain from trying to maximize the good. Scheffler denies that this is so. For Scheffler, an agent-centered prerogative might permit refraining, but it cannot require it. It seems the most we can say is that an agent has the prerogative of adopting a strictly personal attitude that he or she ought to refrain from maximizing. This would, however, be the nonuniversalized "ought" discussed in Chapter 9. Scheffler need not challenge this, but he objects to the view that there is an interpersonal "ought" that entails nonutilitarian moral restrictions. He might concede that promising is a special case. In general, he might still insist, there are no such restrictions.

If anything turns on actual outcomes, it will be exceedingly difficult to show that there are any agent-centered restrictions of the sort Scheffler is denying here. For any putative example of a restriction that conflicts with utilitarian ends, a utilitarian might attempt to show that, all things considered, utilitarianism requires such a restriction as well. Just as the exercise of agent-centered prerogatives cannot be shown decisively to permit something that actually conflicts with utilitarian ends, agent-centered restrictions might not yield such conflicts either. The crucial differences for Scheffler are not over *outcomes* but over the underlying *grounding* of the restrictions. Agent-centered restrictions, like agent-centered prerogatives, have a nonutilitarian grounding, regardless of whether they actually require anyone to act in ways that conflict with utilitarian ends.

To support his denial of agent-centered restrictions, Scheffler asks us to consider the following kind of situation. A favorite candidate for a nonutilitarian restriction is that innocent persons should not be harmed. A moral agent, A1, finds that if she fails to harm a certain person, P1, five other persons will inflict similar harms on five other innocent persons. Scheffler asks what nonutilitarian rationale might be offered for saying that A1 ought not to inflict harm on P1. If it is wrong to violate a certain restriction, R (harming the innocent), how can it be wrong to violate R in order to prevent five similar violations of R?

It is difficult to know how to respond to this example. In some respects it is similar to Williams's example of Jim the explorer. In that situation we were asked to compare Jim's shooting one Indian with Pedro's shooting nineteen. From an impersonal point of view, clearly it is worse for one person to kill nineteen innocent persons than one. As Williams himself admits, a nonutilitarian would be hard pressed to condemn Jim for shooting one Indian to prevent nineteen others from being shot.[11]

Scheffler's example may be better designed to test out Williams's idea that "each of us is specially responsible for what *he* does, rather than for what other people do" (1973, p. 99). His example is less extreme in two respects. First, it focuses on harming rather than killing. Second, each agent is imagined to bring about similar consequences rather than one (Pedro) victimizing many more. Scheffler asks, if it is wrong to violate restriction R, why is it wrong for one person to violate R in order to prevent five others from similarly violating R?

Framing this in the abstract may lead us to oversimplify matters, so let us fill in some details. Adam wants to join one of the local teen gangs. The gang grabs six younger children and drags them into a back alley. As part of his initiation rites, Adam is told that he must bloody one of the children's noses. If he fails to, five gang members will bloody the noses of five remaining children. Would it be wrong for Adam to bloody the child's nose?

The first thing to notice about this example is that the precise number of victims is not crucial (Darwall 1986, p. 300). Suppose we say that it would not be wrong for Adam to bloody the nose of one child in order to prevent the bloodying of thirty other children. It does not follow that we must say the same if the number is changed to five. A nonutilitarian need not be an absolutist about such matters in order to defend the idea of agent-centered restrictions. The basic question is whether it makes any difference in this kind of situation who causes the harm. I believe it does.

To see why, it will be helpful to reduce the number of parties in the example. Adam is told that if he does not bloody little Eddie's nose, Bruno will bloody little Timmy's nose. Thus, either Adam or Bruno will violate the restriction against harming the innocent. It seems obvious that here the similarity ends. In fact, the circumstances of Adam and Bruno are very different. Adam is being asked to use Eddie merely as a means to an end—actually two ends, to pass the initiation test and to prevent little Timmy from getting his nose bloodied. Adam should also ask whether the gang is respecting his moral agency by deliberately placing him in a circumstance where he must choose between harming an innocent child or simply standing by while someone else does.

However we should characterize Bruno's circumstance, clearly it is different. His refusal to bloody Timmy's nose will not result in Adam bloodying Eddie's. He would not be bloodying Timmy's nose in order to prevent Adam from bloodying Eddie's, nor would he be doing it in order to pass the initiation rites. In short, although we are asked to consider Adam and Bruno's violating the same restriction, a more complete description of their respective circumstances reveals that their proposed actions are not equivalent.

In general, there is nothing inevitable about anyone's nose being bloodied here, whether we imagine five bloodied noses or only one. Deliberate action is required, regardless of who does it, or how many do it. Thus there is reason for saying that it would be wrong for Adam to bloody little Eddie's nose. It would also be wrong for Bruno to bloody little Timmy's nose. This does not mean that there is nothing for Adam to do but wash his hands of the entire affair. He should try to convince Bruno not to hit Timmy.

Suppose, now, that Adam refuses to hit Eddie and urges Bruno not to hit Timmy. Just as Bruno is about to bloody Timmy's nose, the police arrive on the scene and stop the proceedings. From a consequentialist point of view, we can say that it is best that Adam refused, for now no one has a bloody nose. We can imagine two ways in which Adam might explain why he refused:

(a) "I kept hoping Bruno wouldn't really do it, or that someone would come along. But if I'd done it, that would have settled it. Someone would have had a bloody nose."

(b) "I didn't know if Bruno would really go through with it, or if someone might come along. But *I* wasn't about to go along with anything like that. It's just wrong to bloody little kids' noses like that. What'd they ever do to deserve that? It would have been terrible if Bruno bloodied Timmy's nose, but that would have been *his* responsibility, not *mine*."

While (a) makes no appeal to Williams's notion that "each of us is specially responsible for what *he* does, rather than for what other people do," (b) does. And it seems to be a perfectly reasonable remark for Adam to make in these circumstances.

It might still be asked, how far can such a view be pushed? Suppose we go back to the first version. If Adam does not bloody little Eddie's nose, five gang members will bloody the noses of five other children. Adam refuses. Bruno bloodies Timmy's nose, and the remaining little children all begin to cry. The offer is repeated. Would it be wrong for Adam to bring the whole matter to a close by bloodying Eddie's nose? This makes it more difficult for Adam. Worse, he is quite certain that no one will show up in time to prevent what will surely follow if he continues to refuse.

At some point Adam may give in—if not in this case, in a suitably cruel alternative. Yet this does not undermine Williams's point. Even granting that there is a point at which we cannot reasonably fault Adam for harming one innocent to prevent similar harms to others, he is specially responsible for what he does in a way that he is not responsible for what others do. If he bloodies the nose of an innocent child, he is responsible for having done that. If Bruno bloodies the nose of an innocent child, Adam is not responsible for having done *that*, even if he is responsible for not having *prevented* him from doing it.

Resistance to being manipulated or bullied into violating moral restrictions—even when this will prevent even more violations—is something we should expect from persons with moral integrity. There are utilitarian reasons for saying this, as terrorist tactics amply illustrate. This is one of the reasons it is difficult to determine if there are any actual situations in which agent-centered restrictions conflict with utilitarian ends. It is more a problem in determining just what utilitarianism requires of us than in providing nonutilitarian grounds for agent-centered restrictions.

Stephen Darwall argues that, to provide a principled rationale for nonconsequentialist (and, thereby, nonutilitarian) agent-centered restrictions, an "inside out" approach is required (1986). We should not proceed, as utilitarians do, from valued states of affairs to the importance of developing and sustaining moral integrity, or an "outside in" approach. It will fail to account for the independent importance maintaining one's moral character should have for a moral agent.

Darwall suggests following the lead of Butler and Kant by working toward a theory of conduct from a theory of moral character, thus reversing the procedure of utilitarianism. Butler and Kant share the view that those subject to the demands of morality have a moral capacity the exercising of which "is both essential to good character and constitutive of moral integrity" (Darwall 1986, p. 310). This capacity is a kind of competence. According to Darwall, it has basically four elements: the capacity a) to be aware of motives and reasons that might move us to act; b) to reflect on the idea of someone acting on a given reason or principle; c) to be able to evaluate morally someone's acting on such a reason or principle; and d) to regulate one's own conduct in accordance with such evalu-ations. The exercise of this competence is a fundamental responsibility of moral agents and enables them to be, as Butler puts it, "a law unto themselves."[12]

Darwall notes that the Butler/Kant approach to morality is agent-centered from the very outset, beginning with the idea that each of us is responsible for maintaining our own integrity. Noting our standing as moral agents, Butler says, "Our constitution is put in our power. We are charged with it; and therefore are accountable for any disorder or viola-tion of it" (Butler 1730, cited in Darwall, p. 311). This supports Williams's idea that "each of us is specially responsible for what *he* does, rather than for what other people do." This does not mean that we have no re-sponsibilities that result from what others do or fail to do. Nor does it mean that we can insulate ourselves from others by refusing ever to alter our projects or commitments in light of circumstances for which we bear no special responsibility for creating.

Of course, Williams is concerned with more than moral integrity. As Nagel reminds us, we cannot avoid having to wrestle with the problem of deciding to what extent personal desires should be modified in light of more impersonal moral demands. Conceding this should not lead us to dismiss the idea that personal integrity, as such, provides grounds for agent-centered restrictions as well as prerogatives.

12
Why Be Moral?

And though it is allowed that, without a regard to property, no society could subsist; yet according to the imperfect way in which human affairs are conducted, a sensible knave, in particular incidents, may think that an act of iniquity or infidelity will make a considerable addition to his fortune, without causing any considerable breach in the social union and confederacy. That *honesty is the best policy*, may be a good general rule, but is liable to many exceptions; and he, it may perhaps be thought, conducts himself with most wisdom, who observes the general rule, and takes advantage of all the exceptions.
—*David Hume*, Enquiry Concerning the Principles of Morals

No man would allow him to be a man of honour, who should plead his interest to justify what he acknowledged to be dishonourable; but to sacrifice interest to honour never costs a blush.
—*Thomas Reid*, Essays on the Active Powers of Man

A QUESTION OF INTEGRITY

It may be unfashionable today to talk about "a man of honour," or even a "principle of honour." But when Thomas Reid uses these expressions, what he has in mind is familiar enough to us. He is talking about moral integrity. He is also expressing the view that when morality conflicts with other considerations, morality should prevail. Contemporary philosophers refer to this as the *overridingness* of morality.

Of course, those who share this view of morality do not necessarily agree about what morality requires from us. They agree about the importance of morality rather than its content. Also, this view does not imply that moral reasons for doing or not doing something always override nonmoral reasons for doing the opposite. For example, a moral reason for being in my office at 3:00 P.M. would be that a student made an appointment to meet me at that time. A nonmoral reason for not keeping the appointment would be that I have received a last minute invitation to

225

meet with a famous visiting professor whose research is of great interest to me. That meeting is also at 3:00 P.M., and there is no way to reach the student in time to change the appointment. I have an obligation to meet the student. I do not have an obligation to meet with the visiting professor—even if it is my only opportunity to do so. Barring further complications, it seems that a nonmoral reason (wanting to meet with the professor) can override a moral reason (the obligation to meet the student).[1]

However, if a moral reason is overridden by a nonmoral reason, how can it be claimed that morality is overriding? The answer is that morality itself can allow for exceptional circumstances such as the one just described. A reasonable moral point of view acknowledges that moral obligations are not everything, and it will not insist that moral reasons of that sort must override all other reasons we have for doing this or that. The overridingness of morality need require only that one's conduct be limited to what is morally acceptable. That is, one should not choose immoral or morally objectionable courses of action over those that are morally acceptable.

This approach seems to be what Reid has in mind when he objects to someone "who should plead his interest to justify what he acknowledged to be dishonourable." Only if it can plausibly be claimed that it would be "dishonourable" for me to break the appointment is the overridingness thesis challenged. Reid himself explains in more familiar terms what he means by a "principle of honour." This expression, he says, "is only another name for what we call a regard to duty, to rectitude, to propriety of conduct. It is a moral obligation which obliges a man to do certain things because they are right, and not to do others because they are wrong" (1788, p. 587). Thus, as long as my breaking the appointment is not morally objectionable, I will not be acting contrary to Reid's "principle of honour."

It might be thought that "honour" connotes rank or class. Reid explicitly rejects this: "Men of rank call it *honour*, and too often confine it to certain virtues that are thought most essential to their rank. The vulgar call it *honesty, probity, virtue, conscience*. Philosophers have given it the names of *the moral sense, the moral faculty, rectitude*" (1788, p. 587). Reid uses several expressions to capture what he has in mind. He does not confine himself to just one moral motive. Instead, he appeals to a rather inclusive set of reasons for action. However, they form a constellation that seems best characterizable as one's moral integrity.

It is no coincidence that Reid should talk about moral integrity and the overridingness of morality in the same context because, for him, moral integrity requires one to regard morality in this way. Although many philosophers today maintain that we should regard morality as overriding, this view is seldom discussed in terms of its implications for moral integrity,[2] particularly in typical philosophical discussions of the question, "Why be moral?"

"Why be moral?" has proven to be an especially vexing question for those who want to hold that morality should be overriding when it conflicts with other considerations, such as self-interest. If one gives moral reasons for being moral, one is charged with circular reasoning. The natural alternative to giving moral reasons is to appeal to self-interest. Then one is faced with the following problem: If the ultimate sanction for being moral is self-interest, then if it ever is in one's self-interest not to be moral, no good reason can be given for being moral. Thus morality cannot, in such a circumstance, be shown to be overriding. As Kai Nielsen says, "We just have to make up our minds which point of view we wish to take. . . . *at this point* we just choose and there can be no reasons for our choice" (1989, p. 181).

I will try to show that there is a way around the problem. I will not try to show that everyone has a good reason to be moral even if this conflicts with self-interest. In line with the views developed in Chapter 3, what I have to say here will not touch those who lack moral concerns, such as psychopaths, but few of us are psychopaths, nor are we egoists. This observation is important, since the typical philosophical adversary of morality in discussions of "Why be moral?" is the egoist. How this distorts the approach we should take to the question will be addressed shortly.

I will not attempt to show that it would be *irrational* to decide against morality, for it need not be, but I will argue that it is *reasonable*, and therefore supportable with good reasons, to side with morality when conflicts arise. Furthermore, I will argue that, for those with moral integrity of the sort commended by Reid, there is no vicious circularity in answering "Why be moral?" with moral reasons. In fact, insofar as we think it important that people have such moral integrity, it is just the sort of response we should encourage in moral education.

All of us find ourselves from time to time in situations where we are tempted to go against our moral principles. These may occasion our asking whether our principles are too demanding or too restrictive, or whether they really do apply in the present circumstance. Careful reflection might convince us that our moral principles are quite acceptable—and that they do, indeed, require us to do something that we otherwise do not want to do. What is at issue, then, is whether we should abide by our principles, even granting their acceptability.

Reid's view is that we should, and that anyone with moral integrity (that is, any "man of honour") would agree. What does such a view entail, and what reason is there for accepting it? When Reid claims that a "principle of honour," or moral principle, is "superior in dignity" to a principle of self-interest (1788, p. 587), he cannot mean that moral reasons are motivationally superior to reasons of self-interest. Often they are not. Nor is Reid concerned that those who pursue their true self-interest will violate acceptable moral principles. In fact, he is convinced, like Butler, that, properly understood, morality and self-interest never really conflict—at least not in the long run. Reid's point seems to be that, insofar as any issue between them could in principle arise, morality must be accorded superiority over reasons of self-interest. What he seems to be most concerned about is how we are disposed toward morality, regardless of whether another point of view commends the same actions. More specifically, he focuses on the esteem we have for those who do accord superiority to moral reasons. Evidently, for Reid, the superior dignity ascribed to a "principle of honour" is also ascribed to those who abide by that principle.

One of the virtues of Reid's passage quoted at the outset of this chapter is that, by emphasizing the different reactive attitudes we have to departures from morality and self-interest, it suggests what is at stake in resisting the subordination of morality to self-interest. As I hope to make clear, the importance of resisting the subordination is bound up with our concern for self-respect, as well as respect for others. Reid reminds us of two very different kinds of attitude we can have about relationships between self-interest and conduct (1788, p. 587). On the one hand, we can feel *pity* for someone who pays too little regard to self-interest, perhaps for someone who is unhappy and listless as a result of wasting talents or opportunities. On the other hand, we might feel *indignation* at someone who pays too much regard to self-interest—for example, by being self-indulgent at the expense of others.

Indignation at another's excessive self-regard is not necessarily aimed at the unqualified pursuit of self-interest (egoism), for at least two reasons. First, it is not only the complete egoist who arouses our indignation. More likely, it is someone who, while often genuinely concerned about others, occasionally acts from self-interest at the expense of others. Second, it is at least conceivable that a complete egoist would never give others cause for indignation. Whether this would happen depends on the extent to which an egoist might believe that self-interest requires acting at the expense of others. Fear or lack of imagination, for example, can stand in the way of taking advantage of others. Also, we might consider the egoistic hermit who withdraws from society in the belief that nothing can be gained from associating with others. Such an egoist might be so miserable and lonely that only pity rather than indignation is evoked.

Reid might say that egoistic hermits, for all their self-regard, pay too little regard to what is in their self-interest. Yet he would not be satisfied with a perspective that commends only enlightened self-interest. For, insofar as this perspective is deliberately adopted and consistently adhered to, there can be no basis for indignation at what would otherwise be regarded as wrongs that we do to each other. At most, we could wrong ourselves, not others. Indignation would give way to regret at doing less than the best one can do for oneself. Wronging others would be reinterpreted as foolish or unwise behavior (insofar as this behavior works against the self-interest of the agent).

When self-interest and morality are compared, it is often assumed that the comparison must be between a completely egoistic point of view and morality. However, it is more likely that those asking "Why be moral?" are not purely egoistic. All of us are at times tempted to allow self-concern to override our moral concerns, even if we would never seriously consider allowing it always to happen. Of course, to admit this liability is not to justify giving in to it. What is needed is a reason for not giving in to it. If one's basic appeal is to a "principle of honour," it needs to be shown that this appeal can be given reasonable support even in the face of the challenge of those who ask why they should be moral.

Kai Nielsen's discussions of this challenge are very helpful,[3] and I will examine them in some detail. Although I believe they ultimately fail satisfactorily to answer the questions they pose, they do clearly and effectively articulate the challenge.

FRAMING THE QUESTION

Nielsen points out that the question "Why be moral?" can have more than one meaning. To avoid confusion, he suggests that it should be divided into two questions: (1) "Why should people be moral?" and (2) "Why should I be moral?" (1989, p. 172). Nielsen says it is important to separate these questions because it is so often assumed that an adequate answer to the first is also an adequate answer to the second. He maintains that once these questions are distinguished it becomes clear that reasons showing why people should be moral are inadequate to show why I, a particular individual, should be moral.

Nielsen is convinced that Kurt Baier's (1958) discussion of "Why be moral?" is marred by the failure to distinguish these two questions. He seems satisfied that Baier, inspired by Hobbes, has shown why people should be moral. Baier's answer to (1) is that if people are not moral, social chaos will result even if everyone tries to follow a principle of enlightened self-interest; So, it is necessary that people commit themselves to a moral (as distinct from purely egoistic) point of view. If Nielsen agrees with Baier so far, why does he not agree that Baier has shown why any particular individual ought to be moral?

Nielsen answers that although Baier might be right in saying that social chaos would result from everyone's following a principle of enlightened self-interest, possibly some individuals (such as Hume's sensible knave) could do so without this result. In the face of such a possibility, a given individual might ask, "Why should *I* be moral if it is more advantageous for me not to be?" Once the question is put in this way and apart from anything that further reflection might show is in one's self-interest, Nielsen claims that there is really nothing more to be said. The individual must simply decide what to do. Thus, Nielsen goes to great lengths to show that an individual is in fact less likely to be happy not being moral than we might at first glance think.

Of course, it is understandable that those who do their part would be upset with those who make an exception of themselves at the expense of others. To the "plain man" who says one should be moral because "it is wicked, evil, morally reprehensible not to be moral," Nielsen replies that the question has been misunderstood: "A clear-headed individual could not be asking for a *moral* justification for being moral. This would be absurd. Rather he is asking the practical question: why should people be bound by the conventions of morality at all?" (1989, p. 173).

Baier tries to answer this question from a standpoint that would be acceptable to everyone, but Nielsen rejects his appeal to "the best reason *sans phrase*." Not interested in the best thing to do for all concerned, "the individual egoist could still legitimately reply to Baier: 'All of what you say is irrelevant unless realization of the greatest total good serves *my* best interests. When and only when the reasons for all involved are also the best reasons for me am I personally justified in adopting the moral point of view'" (Nielsen 1989, p. 179).

It should be noted that in the space of a few pages Nielsen's "clear-headed individual" has become an "individual egoist." The question "Why should I be moral?" is now cast into the mold of the perennial battle of Egoism vs. Morality. Why the egoist is chosen to speak for those who ask why they should be moral is never explained and will be questioned shortly. It should also be noted that Nielsen concedes far more to the egoist than that egoism can be advocated without lapsing into logical inconsistency or incoherence, the common criticisms of egoism. He is giving it an aura of respectability. It is "legitimate" (not merely logically consistent) for the egoist to insist that he or she is "personally justified" in adopting a moral point of view when and only when it serves self-interest.

Of course, whatever Nielsen means by *personally* justified, he does not mean *morally* justified. He agrees with John Hospers (1961) that *if* we are reasoning from a moral point of view, it is perfectly correct to say that one should be moral "because it is right." Hospers shows that "from the moral point of view 'Because it's right' must be a sufficient answer"; but he also shows "how it cannot possibly be a sufficient answer from the point of view of self-interest or from the point of view of an individual challenging the sufficiency of the whole moral point of view, as a personal guide for his actions. It seems that we have two strands of discourse here with distinct criteria and distinct canons of justification. We just have to make up our minds which point of view we wish to take. . . . *at this point* we just choose and there can be no reasons for our choice" (1989, p. 181). The passage is both puzzling and complex. It is best to discuss it in two parts: (a) why "Because it's right" cannot be a sufficient answer from the point of view of self-interest; and (b) why it cannot be sufficient from the point of view of an individual challenging the sufficiency of the moral point of view.

In regard to (a), there is one sense in which Nielsen and Hospers are clearly right. If morality and self-interest ever do conflict, self-interest alone cannot show that we always ought to be moral. Butler's and Reid's theological views assure them that a true conflict can never arise. However, in the absence of theological assurances, it seems highly implausible to suppose that conflicts never arise.

We need to ask what relevance "the point of view of self-interest" has to the question "Why should I be moral?" If the questioner is completely egoistic, or on the edge of becoming so, then obviously the unqualified commendation of morality will not be convincing. Yet most of us are not completely egoistic, nor are we on the edge of becoming so. Nielsen apparently agrees, so it is not clear why he thinks it is relevant to have his "individual egoist" ask, "Should I become moral and give up my individual egoism or shall I remain an egoist?" (1989, p. 176).

By putting the question this way, Nielsen significantly shifts the burden of the argument. Since he acknowledges that most of us are not seriously contemplating the adoption of a thoroughgoing egoistic point of view, a better question might be, "Should I suspend, for the moment, my moral scruples and act as an egoist would?" The differences between these two questions are considerable. Nielsen's "individual egoist" asks why he or she should *acquire* moral scruples. The second question asks why one should *consistently adhere to* the moral commitments one already has. Given that the "individual egoist" cannot fairly be said to represent those who ask why they should be moral, it seems more appropriate to understand "Why should I be moral?" in the manner of (b)—that of challenging the sufficiency of the moral point of view, but from the standpoint of those already committed to some extent to that point of view.

In fact, despite the attention he devotes to the "individual egoist," Nielsen seems most concerned about the challenges to morality posed by his students. He describes a typical student's questioning: "He *feels* that he should be moral, but is he somehow being duped? He wants a *reason* that will be a good and sufficient reason for his being moral, quite apart from *his* feelings or attitudes about the matter. He does not want to be in the position of finally having to decide, albeit after reflection, what sort of person to strive to be" (1989, p. 186). Clearly this is not an "individual egoist" asking whether to continue being egoistic. He is someone, call him Mark, who does have moral commitments but wonders whether they have any rational foundation. Furthermore, it is not clear what his position would be if he were convinced that there is no rational foundation for his moral commitments. It requires further argument to show that this belief would render him capable of *deciding* what kind of person to strive to be. Nielsen may be underestimating the grip that our moral feelings, attitudes, and dispositions have on us. It seems more plausible to suppose that, for most, such a belief would make it easier occasionally to act contrary to one's moral convictions, or occasionally to alter one's moral convictions themselves. But this is a far cry from adopting the standpoint of a thoroughgoing egoist.

It is important to notice that Mark's questioning of morality does not imply that he has *found* it wanting in rational grounding. That might be concluded upon investigation, but initially he simply raises the question. Also, Mark's question leaves open the possibility that he will quite appropriately conclude that the very best reasons for adopting the point of view he is challenging are the very reasons for acting that are commended by that point of view.[4]

Nevertheless, Nielsen seems antecedently so convinced that moral reasons cannot be shown as sufficient for answering "Why should I be moral?" that he devotes most of his time to trying to show that being moral is more in our self-interest than we might think. Dismissing the "plain man" as having nothing of relevance to offer, Nielsen never does give moral reasons for being moral a fair hearing, at least in part because of a mistaken assumption. He assumes that when the "plain man" answers the question "Why should I be moral?" with moral reasons, he has confused the question with a *request for* moral reasons for being moral.[5]

If this assumption were correct, then we should also assume that anyone answering "Why should I be moral?" with reasons of self-interest thinks (mistakenly) that the question is a request for an answer in terms of self-interest. The question is really asking for the best reasons for being moral, as well as some assessment of their sufficiency for answering the challenge to morality, leaving open whether the best answer will turn out to be reasons commended by a moral point of view, reasons of self-interest, or reasons of some other kind. Nielsen quite rightly insists that "should" in "Why should I be moral?" does not *mean* "morally should," but it does not follow that the question cannot be answered in terms of moral reasons.

Unfortunately, Nielsen simply drops any further consideration of moral reasons and turns to reasons of self-interest. Yet if moral reasons are antecedently ruled out, perhaps reasons of self-interest should be ruled out as well. (In effect, Hume does this when he says "reason is, and ought to be, the slave of the passions." Of course, this leaves us with the problem of determining the force of "ought to be.") To see why reasons of self interest should be ruled out, we must consider what assumptions must be made when we offer reasons of self-interest as reasons for being moral.

To answer "Why should I be moral?" by maintaining that it is in my self-interest to be moral assumes that considerations of self-interest do provide me with good reasons for acting one way rather than another. It may seem obvious that considerations of self-interest do provide us with good reasons for acting, but most people think that moral reasons do, too, and moral reasons have been ruled out. Suppose we ask, "Why is the fact that it is in my self-interest to be moral a good reason for being moral?" If appeals to self-interest are relevant to "Why should I be moral?" we must assume that there is an answer to this question as well.

A utilitarian might argue that if we act in truly self-interested ways, it will ultimately promote the greatest good for the greatest number; we will be guided by what Adam Smith calls "an invisible hand." This would subordinate reasons of self-interest to general utility. However, it is likely that few would think it necessary to subordinate reasons of self-interest to utility or any other value in order to feel justified in asserting that considerations of self-interest do provide us with good reasons for acting. That is, a more common view would be that reasons of self-interest are in and of themselves good reasons for acting one way rather than another.

Can this common view be proven true? Is it in need of proof? Although these questions may be important, it is not necessary to answer them for appeals to self-interest to be relevant to "Why should I be moral?" If reasons of self-interest do provide us with reasons for acting, appeals to self-interest are relevant—even if it cannot (or need not) be proven that they do. What is important here is that Nielsen assumes (as most do) that they do. He makes no attempt to justify his assumption. This seems perfectly acceptable but, parity of reasoning should allow moral reasons the same initial status. Either moral reasons do provide us with good reasons for acting one way or another, or they do not. If they do not, then they are not relevant in answering "Why should I be moral?" If they do, then they would seem to be as relevant as reasons of self-interest. The real issue turns on the question of whether moral reasons in and of themselves provide us with good reasons for doing one thing rather than another.[6] By disallowing moral reasons at the outset, Nielsen prevents us from giving them a full hearing. Reasons of self-interest are allowed to dominate the discussion by default, and Nielsen proceeds as if only they provide us, in and of themselves, with reasons for acting one way or another.

Nielsen's account is therefore biased in favor of reasons of self-interest, but this bias might be rectified in two ways. The first is to disallow *both* reasons of self-interest and moral reasons. Unfortunately, this would virtually bring the discussion to an end, as any other kinds of reasons would seem to be subject to the same objection. Hence, it would no longer be clear just what "Why should I be moral?" is asking for, or why it should be of any concern to us. Again, this is the kind of stalemate Hume's account of reason threatens to bring about.

The second way is to give moral reasons equal billing with reasons of self-interest, at least to the extent that each gets a full hearing. Presumably, when someone says that one should be moral because it is right, he or she has something more in mind than, "I (morally) should be moral because it is morally right to be moral." That is, presumably a fuller characterization of morality is available that will help us understand why someone might commend being moral to us. Nielsen never allows the "plain man" or the philosopher to say what that might be.

APPEALS TO CONSCIENCE

We can now explain the predicament of Nielsen's student. Mark *feels* he should be moral, but he wants a *reason* for being moral. Whether or not Mark should conclude that he has been "duped" into feeling he should be moral, on Nielsen's view it seems he should conclude that no reason can be given why he should feel as he does. Still, he knows that how he feels affects his happiness. Insofar as he is rationally self-interested, he will consider the fact that he does have such feelings when calculating what is most conducive to his personal happiness. Personal happiness, it seems, is the rational guide at this point. As Mark begins his reflections he will realize that, through conditioning, social interaction, and moral training, he has various susceptibilities to feel guilty, have compassion for others, desire their happiness, and so on. That is, psychologically speaking, he is not completely egoistic; and this is reflected in his moral principles. Thus it is misleading for Nielsen to construe Mark's query about why he should be moral as equivalent to the egoist's question, "Should I become moral and give up my individual egoism or shall I remain such an egoist?"

Although Mark is not completely egoistic, this does not mean that he has sufficient reason or motivation to do whatever he thinks is right. Perhaps to a large extent he will be so motivated without giving any special thought to his personal happiness. Of course, being motivated in this way does not necessarily mean he is doing what can be rationally commended as such. But reflection might show that, given his susceptibilities to various feelings and concerns, he would be less happy if he ignores them. That is, it is rational for him to take them seriously.

Even if Mark might not at this particular moment want to do what he thinks is right, reflection might show that in the long run he will be happier if he does it anyway. For example, he may avoid guilt feelings, so in this case, he would have sufficient reason for doing what is right. Nielsen assumes that, for most of us at least, reflection will show that considerations of personal happiness nearly always commend doing what is right. Our interpersonal concerns and commitments are too deeply rooted to be ignored. Furthermore, reflection on human nature shows that, as social creatures, we do not find our happiness enhanced by completely egoistic attitudes. Finally, there is always the threat of being caught taking advantage of others, and there may be residual guilt feelings (however irrational they might seem to an egoist).

Nielsen thinks all of this shows that considerations of personal happiness go some way in commending doing what is morally right, but his optimism is tempered by the realization that personal happiness might not be served by doing what is right in certain exceptional circumstances. Here we can see how strikingly different Nielsen's and Reid's perspectives are. Nielsen has us consider a situation in which an individual who is contemplating doing something he acknowledges is morally wrong (1) is unlikely to be caught; (2) is unlikely, as a result, to develop habits leading to punishment; and (3) is free from qualms of conscience. Nielsen says it might make an individual in such a situation happier not to act morally. To support his point, he presents several examples in which an individual might, all things considered, be happier doing what he or she thinks is morally wrong. What follows from this? Nielsen's answer is that, although the consistently selfish person is not likely to be very happy, these examples show that "for *limited patterns of behavior*, no decisively good reasons can be given to some individuals that would justify their doing the moral thing in such a context" (1989, p. 192).

Is there really nothing more that can (or should) be said? Consider again the three conditions that supposedly leave us in this situation. The individual is unlikely to get caught or to develop bad habits. These are, of course, self-interested concerns. The third condition is that the individual will be free from qualms of conscience. Although we might expect conscience to provide a significant link to some sort of concern about others for their own sake, Nielsen considers conscience only insofar as it affects its *possessor's* happiness. Yet why shouldn't the individual say, "I know my conscience wouldn't bother me if I were to do this. But I also know that it would be wrong, and my conscience *should* bother me. So, I won't do it." Nielsen would not deny that one could say this, but he would insist that there is no *good reason* to say it in such a circumstance.

It may not be irrational to regard one's conscience in this way, but it is important to examine the implications it would have for one's moral integrity. If I take my conscience into consideration only insofar as it is likely to affect my happiness, I seem to stand in a peculiarly *external* relationship to my conscience, and, consequently, to my moral commitments. On this view, I regard my conscience as a convenient guide to what is likely to lead to my happiness or unhappiness. Even when my conscience is not itself directly concerned with my happiness, I know that acting contrary to its dictates may make me unhappy. If my unhappiness will result only from guilt feelings (and not, say, from being caught), I might regard my conscience in that situation as a nuisance—but something I must take into account nevertheless. If, as in the situations imagined by Nielsen, my conscience will not bother me and I will not otherwise suffer unhappiness, I no longer have any good reason to refrain from what I *acknowledge* to be morally wrong.

This is in striking contrast to Reid's "man of honour." The kind of person Reid has in mind is committed to moral principles in such a way that knowingly to violate them would be to do what is "dishonourable." Whether acting contrary to one's "principle of honour" would result in feelings of guilt is not Reid's primary concern. That could be expected to be the usual result for a person with moral integrity, but these feelings themselves are not to be understood as the basis for acting one way rather than another. For Reid, the basis for acting is the "principle of honour" itself—that is, the rightness or wrongness of what is being contemplated. It is the direct commitment to that principle that marks one a "man of honour" and thus manifests one's moral integrity.

AN EGOCENTRIC TRAP

The fundamental shortcoming of approaching "Why be moral?" exclusively from the perspective of *my* personal happiness is that it is *egocen-*

tric. No attempt is made to take directly into account how different the perspectives of *others* might be—especially those who might be wronged. Very small children are incapable of understanding the extent to which the perspectives of others differ from their own. Though no doubt capable of understanding these differences better than small children, Nielsen's individual "I" does not acknowledge that there is good reason to accommodate one's perspective to be sharable with others. Or, if one does, it is only to the extent that one believes it will affect personal happiness. It is only another way of saying that the individual "I" fails to acknowledge the full relevance of the fact that the perspectives of others are significantly different.

This will be seen as a failure only from a perspective that transcends egocentricity. Consider how Nielsen frames the question "Why should I be moral?" Once the egocentric perspective is transcended, the same question could be rephrased, "Why should he or she (the individual 'I') be moral?" Nielsen's focus on the individual "I" does not permit the transition from first- to third-person perspective. Surely, however, there is a perspective that does permit this transition, a perspective in which one respects the fact that others, too, have a point of view that has as much warrant for being given a hearing as one's own. What this perspective depends on is, as Thomas Nagel says, "a recognition of the reality of other persons, and on the equivalent capacity to regard oneself as merely one individual among many" (1970, p. 3).

Although an egocentric perspective does in some sense recognize the reality of others, it does not permit regarding oneself as merely one individual among many—at least not in the sense intended by Nagel. The perspective Nagel commends is intuitively expressed in the question "How would you like it if someone did that to you?" He says, "The essential fact is that you would not only *dislike* it if someone else treated you in that way; you would resent it. That is, you would think that your plight gave the other person a reason to terminate or modify his contribution to it, and that in failing to do so he was acting contrary to reasons which are plainly available to him" (1970, p. 83). Here we are reminded of Reid's view. What remains to be shown is that in order for there to be a rational basis for the resentment of which Nagel speaks, one must adopt a perspective that also provides good reason for feeling indignation at the wrongs done to others as well as oneself. (Of course, if it is the agent in question who has perpetrated the wrong, we would expect feelings of guilt rather than indignation.)

It is true, as Nagel himself points out, that a thoroughgoing egoist would not resent how he or she is treated by others, even though the treatment can be disliked. Yet it must be recalled that Nielsen's student is not an egoist; and he is certainly not prepared to give up moral reasoning entirely, even if occasionally he might find it tempting to do so. The kind of resentment Nagel refers to is directed against the egocentricity of others in its insistence that others have good reason not to treat one in certain ways. As we have seen in Chapter 5, this is also an expression of one's self-respect. The price of the reasonableness of that resentment is that one must oppose one's own egocentricity as well. Insofar as one has reason to resent certain ways that one is treated, one also has reason not to wrong others—even though wronging them might occasionally lead to greater personal happiness. The fact that feelings of guilt may be absent in exceptional circumstances is strictly irrelevant.

Given the importance of self-respect, Nielsen's student can have a rational basis for experiencing resentment, but it is rationally grounded in a perspective that opposes his egocentric predilections as strenuously as those of others. It does not follow that Mark will be motivated by this kind of consideration, which, however, does not negate its rationality. There may be situations in which Mark has to decide whether to be moral when acting otherwise seems to promise personal gain, or at least seems to be more expedient. A good reason for being moral is available, the same reason he would appeal to in resenting being wronged by someone else. It is grounded in respect for persons, which is presupposed by the reasonableness of one's resentment.

It is true that nothing I have said shows that it would be irrational for an individual egoist, an egocentric individual, or a psychopath to resist this perspective. I have said only that it is rational to accept it and, therefore, that it is not based solely on feelings devoid of rational grounding. It is not a condition of rationality that a rationally grounded perspective must render alternative perspectives irrational, especially when, as in the case of Mark, one already has commitments that clash with alternative perspectives.

This last comment needs elaboration. It is important to know what kinds of commitments and concerns are held by those who ask why they should be moral. It is unrealistic, as well as unnecessary, to expect people to detach themselves entirely from their commitments and concerns when reflecting on this question. Insofar as "Why be moral?" is a practical question, it arises in a context of potential conflict between one's moral principles and other concerns one might have. Apart from the commitments and concerns that underlie the potential conflict, the question is of only theoretical interest.

Certainly Nielsen's student raises the question as a matter of practical concern. Mark must decide which of his commitments and concerns are most important. We should not assume that his decision must be predicated on what will contribute most to his happiness for there to be good reasons for deciding one way rather than another. Such an assumption would mean that there would be no room for Mark to ask himself *whose* happiness (or interests, rights, and so on) should be regarded as most relevant to his decision.

If Mark decides that he should do what he thinks is morally right, even when he might personally stand to gain from doing otherwise, it does not follow that he is merely doing his "duty for duty's sake." He is doing what he thinks is right for the sake of others, who, like himself, object to being treated as if their perspectives count for nothing when others are deliberating about whether to wrong them. Thus, he will be acknowledging that the interests of others, too, must be taken into account and be given their due. He has reason to want such recognition from others. Yet he cannot reasonably demand it unless he is willing to reciprocate that recognition.

MORAL EDUCATION

The issue of how we should approach the question "Why be moral?" is important for moral education. If indeed we do think it is important and desirable that persons come to regard moral considerations as overriding, we should be concerned to use the most appropriate means for achieving that end. There is considerable empirical evidence that once children are able to appreciate the reasons given, the method of "induction" is the most effective means of encouraging moral development (Hoffman 1970; Damon 1988). This method consists of giving reasons to children for acting in certain ways (in contrast to merely threatening or punishing them). As Baier points out in his objection to adopting enlightened self-interest as a policy, it is important that people be seriously committed to moral values. Thus children need to be brought "inside" morality, accepting the reasonableness of moral reasons as such, rather than just as a means to personal happiness. As Reid might put it, they have to be encouraged to accept "principles of honour" as such.

Nielsen and Baier agree that *within* the moral point of view moral reasons are supreme and overriding. However, the implication of Nielsen's analysis is that, although it is important that people be encouraged to accept the moral point of view, a "clear-headed" individual should be able to see that this point of view is based on a convenient social myth. The moral point of view insists that there is good reason for an individual to be moral even when there might be something to be gained from doing otherwise. Apparently, this is the myth that we must foist on children. We must convince them that acting at the expense of another is in itself a reason for not so acting, quite apart from considerations of self-interest or expediency. If *we* are "clear-headed," we can see that there is really no good reason for anyone to believe it.

Put so baldly, the myth seems to reveal a deep cynicism in the attitude of a "clear-headed" individual. He or she can see no real reason for respecting persons as such, but he or she does see reason to convince *others* that they have good reason to respect persons in this way. Others are to be respected by a "clear-headed" individual insofar as this contributes to personal happiness or insofar as he or she, quite arbitrarily it seems, decides to respect them.

Although Nielsen's student *feels* he should be moral even at the expense of some personal gain, he *is* being "duped." It is not that only dupery could convince him that he should do what morality requires. Nielsen agrees that for the most part there is good reason for Mark to do what morality requires. The dupery concerns the *reasons* he has been led to accept for doing what morality requires. Mark has been duped to the extent that his feelings, not to speak of his integrity, reveal that he has been led to believe that the best reason, and a rationally sufficient reason, for being moral is itself a moral reason. However, if what I have argued is right, morality need not be grounded in such dupery—at least for those who do get beyond egocentricity. Reid's "man of honour" can have good reason to regard a "principle of honour" as overriding, even when self-interest or expediency pull in a different direction.

Consider a college student, Amy, taking her first ethics course. Amy has grown up believing that moral reasons are overriding. She is taking an ethics course because she wants to get clearer about fundamental moral questions. When her professor asks the class "Why be moral?" Amy answers: "If I'm not moral, I might cause harm to others; or I might treat them unfairly, violate their rights, or fail to respect them. I guess the basic thing is that it just isn't right." The professor then makes the standard reply:

> Professor: That might be a good answer from the moral point of view, Amy. But you are giving moral reasons for being moral. That's not what I was asking for. It really begs the question. You have to step outside the moral point of view and ask why you should be moral.
>
> Amy: But how can I do that? And, besides, why do I have to?
>
> Professor: Well, let me put it this way. I ask myself "Why be moral?" If I have my wits about me, I am not asking "What moral reason or reasons have I for being moral?" Rather, I am asking, "Can I, everything considered, give a reason sufficiently strong—a non-moral reason clearly, for my always giving an overriding weight to moral considerations, when they conflict with other considerations, such that I could be shown to be acting irrationally, or at least less rationally than I otherwise would be acting, if I did not give pride of place to moral considerations?" (Nielsen 1989, pp. 286–87)[7]
>
> Amy: I'm not sure I understand what you are saying. But I'll admit that sometimes I'm tempted to do what I know is wrong. And, of course, I'm not perfect. But when I do what I know is wrong, I feel guilty later and tell myself I shouldn't have done it. I can't say I think I've been irrational, but I don't think I've acted on the best reasons.
>
> Professor: Consider the clever egoist. Of course, he'll be careful not to tromp over others in wild and indiscriminate ways. But he's quite prepared to act immorally when he sees it is to his advantage; and it's naive to suppose that this will result in unhappiness or harm to himself. We need to beware of those moralizing moralists—those keepers of the true faith—who read their own sentiments into all humankind and conclude that all immoralists must be unhappy. (Nielsen 1989, p. 284)
>
> Amy: But I'm no clever egoist. So why do I have to worry about what might make such a person happy or unhappy? I don't know if I've even ever met such a person. I do know that when I see people selfishly acting at the expense of others—and that includes me—I get upset and all the more determined to do what I think is right.
>
> Professor: That's fine, Amy. I'm not suggesting that you act otherwise. But if we are going to be through and through tough-minded

and not be taken in by mythologies, we will conclude that, in the last analysis, we must just decide to act in one way or another without having reasons sufficient to show that one course of action rather than another is required by reason. (Nielsen 1989, p. 295)[8]

At the end of the semester, Amy is invited to visit the home of Mandy, one of her classmates. They try to reconstruct the discussion of "Why be moral?" Amy adds: "I don't think acting moral is 'required by reason'—whatever that means. People who act immorally aren't necessarily irrational or crazy. When the professor said we just have to decide one way or the other, he really confused me. I agree that I have to decide what to do in specific situations. But when he said that, I thought, 'It seems to me that somehow I've already decided what kind of person I want to be, and it's nothing like the clever egoist.' I wanted to say something more, but then I got even more confused. I couldn't ever remember *deciding* what kind of person I wanted to be—so how did I get to be like I am?"

As Mandy is about to comment, their conversation is interrupted by loud voices from another part of the house. Mandy's younger brother, Amoral Andy, has just burst triumphantly into the kitchen with an armful of groceries and an announcement for his father.

Andy: Wow, this is my lucky day! I went to the store with the $10 bill you gave me. I bought $6.80 worth of groceries, and I got $13.20 in change!

Father: The cashier must have made a mistake. He probably thought you gave him a $20 bill. You should return the $10.

Andy: Finders keepers, losers weepers.

Father: Come on, Andy. It's not right to keep it, and you know it.

Andy: Right, schmite. Why should I do what's right?

Father: Because it's *right*, that's why.

Andy: What kind of reason is that? "You should do what's right because it's right." Sounds like a big circle to me.

Father: Look, it's dishonest, and you know it. Don't get cute with me!

Andy: Hey, everyone's dishonest at least once in a while. People cheat on their income taxes. My friends would keep the money. Businesses just rip off people anyway. Why should I be honest if everyone else is dishonest?

Father: Everyone isn't dishonest. Besides, even if they are, that doesn't make it right. You should be honest because that's the right thing to do.

Andy: Oh, the big circle again!

Father: Think about the cashier. What's going to happen when he finds out he's $10 short at the end of the day. Either he'll have to put in his own $10, or he'll get in big trouble with his manager. He might even lose his job.

Andy: That's his problem. Maybe he'll learn to be more careful next time. Anyway, everyone has to look out for number one. I'll bet he'd keep the money if he were me. Why should I be any different?

Father: Because it's not fair—and it doesn't become fair just because others might do the same.

Andy: Fair, schmair. Why should I be fair? If everyone's unfair, I'd be a fool to be fair. Besides, no one at the store will know where the money went.

Father: Don't exaggerate. Everyone isn't unfair. Anyway, look at it this way. How would you feel if you were the cashier?

Andy: I suppose I'd feel lousy. But it's a lousy world. That's just the way it goes sometimes.

Father: But you're not doing anything to help that. Even if I agree that it's a "lousy world," it's not right for you to add to it.

Andy: It's not right? There you go again.

Father: I don't understand you, Andy. We've tried to bring you up with the right values. Where have we gone wrong?

Andy: Not another one of your guilt trips, Dad! It won't work. Look, I know you and Mom have tried your best. But you're so old-fashioned. People don't think the same as in "the good old days." Times are changing. You're just trying to pin *your* values on me.

Father: That's not fair. There are good reasons for my values—good reasons for you and me.

Andy: Don't go philosophical on me, Dad. You got your values from your parents, and they got theirs from their parents. It's all pretty conservative stuff—and very relative.

Father: That seems like a rather superficial view—and a convenient one, too, if I might say so. What you need is a good ethics course next year when you go to college. Then you'll see that there's a lot more to this. Ask Mandy and Amy.

How will Andy do in his ethics class? If he has Amy's professor, he will no doubt impress him as having a better understanding of "Why be moral?" than Amy. It seems ironic that, among equally intelligent and reflective students, those lacking in moral concern may fare better in ethics courses than those with strong moral commitments.

It is not merely ironic; the professor's remarks are based on Chapter 14 of Nielsen's *Why Be Moral?* (1989). However, Nielsen concludes his article by conceding that he finds his reflections depressing: "I detest, as much as any of you, such lack of moral integrity as one finds in immoralism" (1989, p. 299). This, he says, fortifies his resolve to do his best to "bring about a world in which genuine moral community will become possible and the class of immoralists . . . will wither away or at least dwindle with the social circumstances not being so conducive to their flourishing" (1989, p. 299). He adds that there "must be a pervasive attitude of disinterested caring for all human life (and perhaps for all sentient creatures)—the smallest as well as the greatest of us" (1989, p. 300).

Suppose this "moral revolution" were successful. How would members of the moral community view the question "Why be moral?" Since there would be no immoralists or amoralists left, would there be any point in imagining that the question is being posed by such persons? But, such persons aside, there would still be occasions on which the question could arise. It is not only immoralists and amoralists who are tempted to do what they regard to be wrong, and there may be moments of doubt. In such moments, how should these doubts be handled? If Nielsen is right, no answer outside of morality will suffice. If Reid is right, no such answer is needed—at least not for a "man of honour."

Nielsen sums up his position:

I have been concerned to argue that reason (human intelligence and understanding) without the collaboration of *moral sentiment* does not require that moral reasons be taken as overriding. . . . *Morality requires commitment here, not still further understanding.* Though this is not at all to say or to suggest that the moral commitment must be blind or without understanding. . . . But it is also true that nothing has been unearthed called the "point of view of reason" which would adjudicate matters here. . . . Reason doesn't decide here. (1989, p. 299)

If by the "point of view of reason" we are to understand, with Hume, a point of view detached from moral sentiments and any other concerns the absence of which would render us irrational, Nielsen is right, but his point is quite limited. Such a "point of view of reason" is not the actual point of view of anyone, with the possible exception of the psychopath. Once we consider the points of view of real people, however, matters look quite different. If real people do accept "the moral point of view," they do regard moral reasons as overriding, and it is an expression of their integrity that they insist, when pressed, that the best reasons for being moral are moral reasons.

Nielsen might object that when one asks "Why be moral?" one cannot be asking for moral reasons for being moral. This is true enough. However, although one might not be directly asking for moral reasons, it still can be appropriate to give them. The question "Why be moral?" can be construed in either of two ways here: (1) What are the best reasons for being moral? (2) In the face of challenges, why should one opt for morality? The answer to either question can be in terms of moral reasons, and it is important for those with moral integrity to answer in such terms.

Even if Nielsen's "moral revolution" were accomplished, there would still be the problem of bringing children into the moral community. If Amoral Andy were not amoral through and through, but only "testing the waters," what kinds of considerations should be offered to bring him "into the fold"? If his father were to appeal to Nielsen's "point of view of reason" and offer nonmoral reasons for being moral, he would surely fail. All attempts to provide "external" justifications of morality are bound to fall short of the mark — for two reasons. First, they will do so for the reasons Nielsen gives. Stripped of moral sentiments, "reason" will not come down decisively in favor of morality. Second, such attempts divert attention from the moral integrity of those seeking an answer and, thereby, detract from the integrity of morality itself.

Of course, the "moral revolution" is not here. This is the source of Nielsen's depression and his moral resolve. Given this state of things, how should the question "Why be moral?" be handled? My suggestion is that it first be considered from the standpoint of those who, as a matter of practical concern, raise it. For whom is "Why be moral?" likely to be a practical question, and under what circumstances? It is likely to be a question for virtually any reflective person, child or adult, at some time or other. Yet, philosophical discussions of the question typically convert the questioner into a tough-minded egoist, immoralist, or amoralist. The fundamental assumption that seems to be made is that answers that would be unsatisfactory for such tough minded inquirers would (and should) also be unsatisfactory for more ordinary inquirers — those who, while not totally lacking in moral integrity, may be struggling with their own moral confusion and uncertainty.

Answering "Why be moral?" with moral reasons cannot be fairly characterized as saying simply, "I should be moral because it is immoral not to be moral." Most college students, for example, do not begin their introductory ethics courses with a clearly worked-out understanding of competing ethical theories, or a clearly articulated "moral point of view." Nor do they typically have well-worked-out views about whether morality is "relative" or "absolute." If they are reflective, they will have many questions, including the question "Why be moral?" At the same time, most will have some firm moral convictions, and they will have some sense that morality should be taken seriously.

As students develop a clearer and fuller understanding of what morality involves, what they have in mind when they give moral reasons for being moral will also be more developed. When, at the end of the semester, Amy insists that moral reasons be given for being moral, presumably she can say more than, "I should be moral because it is immoral not to be moral." Assuming that "the moral point of view" now has more determinate meaning for her, she is in a position to spell out in some detail what being moral requires and why it is important. That her account will be from "the inside" need not detract from the informativeness and significance of what she says to herself or those who might be willing to listen to what she has to say. "It's immoral to be immoral" is, indeed, unhelpful. However, pointing out what morality consists in and why challenges to it should be resisted is not a simple task—even for the most committed Amys. They should be encouraged to undertake this task in ways consistent with their integrity and with minimal distractions from the mythical egoists, immoralists, and amoralists that philosophers throw in their way.

What of Hume's sensible knave? Hume's own answer is to appeal to those of us who, resisting the promise of material gains, draw moral strength from our own integrity: "Inward peace of mind, consciousness of integrity, a satisfactory review of our own conduct; these are the circumstances, very requisite to happiness, and will be cherished and cultivated by every honest man, who feels the importance of them" (1777, p. 283). As for the sensible knave's desire to be the exception to the rule,

Hume says that "if a man think that this reasoning much requires an answer, it will be a little difficult to find any which will to him appear satisfactory and convincing. If his heart rebel not against such pernicious maxims, if he feel no reluctance to the thoughts of villainy or baseness, he has indeed lost a considerable motive to virtue" (1777, p. 283).

On this matter, Reid and Hume agree—with a significant qualification. Reid's basic objection to the knave's conduct is that it is unjust, or unfair, since it takes advantage of the cooperativeness of others. Since Hume supposes the knave can do this without causing "any considerable breach in the social union and confederacy," Reid thinks Hume cannot really sustain his appeal to integrity.

For Hume, justice is an *artificial* virtue whose value is derivable from its social utility, but, Reid wonders, if the knave's conduct does not detract from social utility, how can Hume sustain his charge of "villainy and baseness"? Not sharing Hume's view that justice depends on social utility for its moral importance, Reid appeals directly to justice as a *natural* virtue. For Reid, concern for justice develops independently of, and prior to, concern for social utility. In "a man of honour" concern for justice is a matter of principle. Thus Reid insists: "Ask the man of honour why he thinks himself obliged to pay a debt of honour? The very question shocks him. To suppose that he needs any other inducement to do it but the principle of honour, is to suppose that he has no honour, no worth, and deserves no esteem" (1788, p. 587).

As should be clear enough by now, I am more sympathetic to Reid than Hume on this matter. Nevertheless, for both, the answer to the sensible knave comes from *within* morality. Neither is concerned to make external appeals. This, I believe, is as it should be.

Notes

CHAPTER 1. INTRODUCTION

1. If comparisons between logical and moral judgment were to be carried further, inductive rather than deductive logic would provide a more promising area. Since virtually all nontrivial, moral generalizations have exceptions, inferences from moral premises to conclusions will be more like inductive than deductive inferences. For example: "You promised John you would do the work for him. Promises (generally) ought to be kept. So, you ought to do the work for him." However, I am less interested here in inference patterns as such than in the general idea that we have both logical and moral sensibilities in which we may have warranted confidence, so I will press inference comparisons no further.

CHAPTER 2. ON BECOMING A MORAL AGENT

1. I rather weakly say "suggests" since some of Burnyeat's later comments seem to allow reason a modest role in even the initial phases of moral development.

2. See, for example, the extensive publications of Matthew Lipman's Institute for the Advancement of Philosophy for Children, Gareth Matthews's *Philosophy and the Young Child* (1980) and *Dialogues with Children* (1984), as well as my own *Philosophical Adventures with Children* (1985).

3. For serious worries about encouraging children to think philosophically about morality, see Joseph Flay, "Can Children Do Moral Philosophy?" in Matthew Lipman and Ann Margaret Sharp, eds., *Growing Up with Philosophy* (Philadelphia: Temple University Press, 1978, pp. 145-57). Many of Flay's worries are drawn from his interpretation of Aristotle. For more optimistic accounts see the essays by Evans, Martin, Katzner, Benjamin, Diller, Lipman and Sharp, and Hare in the same volume.

4. Shakespeare's *Troilus and Cressida*, II, ii, 166 f. This is cited by David Ross in his translation of Aristotle's *Nicomachean Ethics* (Oxford: Oxford University Press, 1980), p. 3.

5. Page references are to the Hildesheim, Gekorg Olms Verlagsbuchandlung reproduction of the 1895 Edinburgh edition of Reid's *Philosophical Works*, vol. 2,

with notes by Sir William Hamilton. *Essays on the Active Powers of the Mind* was first published by Reid in 1788. Cited passages are from Essay 3, "Of the Principles of Action," and Essay 5, "Of Morals."

6. This does not mean that philosophical thinking has no role to play in Reid's account. "Moral philosopher" and "metaphysician" presumably, for Reid, refer to a relatively small number of persons who invest considerable time in reading, writing, or talking about philosophical matters—typically in ways not readily accessible to the ordinary person, at least not without considerable effort. In Reid's eighteenth-century Scotland this required familiarity with, for example, the writings of such philosophers as Plato, Aristotle, Joseph Butler, Francis Hutcheson, David Hume, and Adam Smith—not to speak of metaphysicians such as Descartes, Locke, Berkeley, Spinoza, and Leibniz.

It is a mistake to think that one must be a moral philosopher or metaphysician in that sense in order to engage in philosophical thinking. It is not just mathematicians who engage in mathematical thinking, nor is it only philosophers who engage in philosophical thinking. Equally significant here, as the recent writings of Matthew Lipman, Gareth Matthews, and many others amply illustrate, children are quite capable of philosophical reflection.

7. It might be objected that, strictly speaking, this is not so. It is true that geometric systems are usually thought of as deductive, whereas utilitarian systems are not. What Reid is emphasizing is the hierarchical arrangement characteristic of both, with subsidiary rules being derivable from, and dependent on, a higher principle. Whether the derivations are deductive or not is not essential to Reid's point, so, though the analogy is somewhat loose, it is suggestive. I will adopt his usage for convenience in referring to the contrast he wishes to draw.

8. More importantly, this more piecemeal approach is compatible with the notion that there simply is no comprehensive, coherent moral system to be grasped. The unavailability of such a system, however, would not imply moral chaos. It would indicate only that there are limits to the systematization of morality.

9. This is Burnyeat's rendering of Aristotle's *Nicomachean Ethics*, 1095b2–13.

10. For other rich examples of children's thinking about fairness, see the chapters entitled "Fairness" and "Reciprocity" in my *Philosophical Adventures with Children* (1985).

11. For criticisms of Hare's views of levels of moral thinking, see T. M. Scanlon, "Levels of Moral Thinking," and J. O. Urmson, "Hare on Intuitive Moral Thinking," in Douglas Seanor and N. Fotion, eds., *Hare and Critics* (Oxford: Clarendon Press, 1988). See also Hare's replies in the same volume.

12. This is nicely illustrated by one of Bernard Williams's examples ("Persons, Character, and Morality," in his *Moral Luck* [Cambridge: Cambridge University Press, 1981], pp. 17–19). A husband has the opportunity to save either of two people, but not both; one is his wife. If the husband were to try to "justify" saving his wife by appealing to a moral principle (utilitarian or otherwise), he would have, according to Williams, "one thought too many." Hare agrees with this, but he insists that utilitarianism can accommodate it. There is great utility in people

responding to the needs of loved ones without the mediation of, say, the principle of utility. Although the principle of utility provides the ultimate *criterion* for morally appropriate choice, it is not itself to be understood as a principle for the *decision making* of ordinary moral agents except, perhaps, in certain exceptional circumstances. Whether this avoids the problem of personal integrity posed by Williams will be considered in detail in Chapter 11.

13. This is only half of the full retributivist view. Typically retributivism includes the idea that, at least for some kinds of wrongdoing, the guilty ought to be punished. To say that only the guilty deserve to be punished does not strictly imply that wrongdoers should be punished. It implies that those who are punished should be guilty. Guilt is a necessary condition for deserving punishment. It may not be sufficient.

14. It should be noted that Hare's example is, strictly speaking, confined to a legal system. The retributivist intuition expresses a fundamental principle of not punishing the innocent, which has implications for legal systems that accept this principle. In fact, some who are not duly convicted of committing crimes may nevertheless have committed them. Whether a retributivist must insist that such persons, because innocent "in the eyes of the law," should not be punished is perhaps controversial. If a retributivist agrees with Hare that a system permitting punishment of those not duly convicted is a bad system, it will be for a reason different from Hare's utilitarian one. A retributivist will object to such a system on the grounds that it will open the door to punishing those who are actually innocent—that is, those who clearly do not deserve to be punished.

15. Further refinements are possible. Although an agent may have involuntarily or unintentionally caused harm, he or she could be held responsible for not having prevented such circumstances from arising (through drunkenness, for example). Reid includes culpable omissions within the range of the voluntary.

CHAPTER 3. ACCOUNTABILITY, UNDERSTANDING, AND SENTIMENTS

1. For an account of amorality that does not necessarily deny responsibility, see Milo (1984, chap. 3).

2. Whether psychopaths have moral rights is a more complicated matter. Jeffrie Murphy (1972) argues that they do not. I am not convinced that the psychopath's moral incapacity to enter into reciprocal moral relations with others removes all basis for the ascription of moral rights. This would imply that nonhuman animals, too, lack moral rights. Perhaps they do, but I will not address this controversy here.

3. This, I take it, is part of what Gilbert Ryle is trying to do in "On Forgetting the Difference between Right and Wrong" (1958). Also, as Richard Schmitt argues, this is a major concern of Martin Heidegger in *Being and Time*. See Schmitt (1969), especially chaps. 2 and 5, for an analysis of the concept of understanding that is very suggestive in this regard.

4. Consider Ruth in Fay Weldon's novel, *The Life and Loves of a She-Devil*, about

to embark on a journey of total vengeance against her husband and his mistress: "It takes a little time to become wholly she-devil. One feels positively exhausted at first, I can tell you. The roots of self-reproach and good behavior tangle deep in the living flesh: you can't ease them out gently; they have to be torn out, and they bring flesh with them" (1983, p. 48).

CHAPTER 4. REASON AND RESENTMENT

1. Strawson's reference to the "moral idiot" in this context suggests he agrees with this assessment of the accountability of the psychopath. See also his comments on moral understanding in *Skepticism and Naturalism: Some Varieties* (1985, p. 35). Although he does not specifically refer to the psychopath there, the implications of what he says for the psychopath's understanding of morality is clear.

2. Thus, Strawson argues that a *general* thesis of determinism will not undermine accountability, a complex issue that I will not address here. Much of Strawson's essay is an elaboration of this thesis. For helpful discussions, see Jonathan Bennett (1980) and Gary Watson (1988).

3. I am indebted to Jonathan Bennett for this observation.

4. Thus, as we shall see later, the psychopath presents a special problem for Reid. Neither he nor Hume seem to have seriously considered the possibility that there might be adult *human* beings entirely lacking moral sentiments. Hume does consider the possibility of rationally "superior beings" who lack our moral sentiments. As will be seen, one of the implications of this possibility is that Hume's and Reid's views are more similar than one might otherwise suspect.

5. The idea of justice Reid discusses here is not necessarily associated with property. For Hume, property is an essential aspect of justice; for him, the idea of justice is to some extent bound up with an understanding of social and political practices. Thus he thinks of justice as an *artificial* virtue. Reid, on the other hand, thinks of justice as a *natural* virtue. It is a more primitive moral notion, one which is later joined with human artifices and conventions. Still, underlying these artifices is a more basic, natural idea of justice.

6. In Chapter 7 I will argue that Lawrence Kohlberg's cognitive theory of moral development neglects the moral sentiments. I will suggest that an account of how resentment undergoes changes in moral development raises serious problems for Kohlberg's theory. Here I believe Butler, Reid, and even Hume have much to offer.

7. A nonretributivist perspective would approve punishment only if some good could be expected to result. Butler and Reid certainly recognize the good and bad tendencies of resentment. Although they give consequentialist reasons for regulating resentment (because of the harm and wickedness it may occasion), they do not try to justify the punishment associated with resentment in terms of its good consequences. For them, the desire for punishment that is an essential part of resentment is related to desert.

8. Would it have been preferable for Martin Luther King not to have been *an-*

gered by injustice, or for his followers not to have been *angered* by his assassination? If King permitted a tone of *indignation* in his speeches, was it a moral shortcoming on his part? For further discussion of the place of moral anger, see Bernard Boxhill (1976).

9. See, for example, Stanley Schachter (1964, pp. 49–80); Skinner (1953, chap. 10); and my "On Taking Emotions Seriously" (1976, pp. 211–32).

10. For further discussion of this point, see Mackie (1980, pp. 139–44).

11. Letter of March 16, 1740, printed in D. D. Raphael, ed., *British Moralists* (1969), vol. 2, pp. 110–11.

12. Compare this with what Hume says in his *Enquiries Concerning the Principles of Morals* (1777, p. 286): "Here therefore *reason* instructs us in the several tendencies of actions, and *humanity* makes a distinction in favour of those which are useful and beneficial."

CHAPTER 5. INTEGRITY, DIGNITY, AND JUSTICE

1. This view of dignity is related to Stephen Darwall's notion of "recognition respect," in contrast to "appraisal respect." See his "Two Kinds of Respect" (1977). A matter in need of further consideration is whether dignity is shared by all, regardless of how we might assess them morally. Do psychopaths have dignity? Jeffrie Murphy (1972) denies they have moral rights. Perhaps he would also deny that they have dignity. Later in this chapter I suggest that having a capacity for a sense of dignity is a plausible basis for attributing dignity to someone. Whether psychopaths have this capacity is open to question. However, a highly immoral person (as distinct from the amoral psychopath) can nevertheless have a sense of dignity. Such persons, I hold, should be regarded as having dignity. This still leaves open questions about the extent to which, and manner in which, they might appropriately be punished. That regard for dignity should impose some limits, however, will be illustrated later in this chapter with an example presented by Edmund Cahn (1962).

2. For example, Joseph Kupfer (1982) convincingly argues that lying involves *self-opposition*, an internal conflict resulting from saying aloud what one disbelieves. This, he argues, threatens the *integration* of the liar's personality.

3. Critics view Garver's analysis as going too far. See, for example, Joseph Betz (1977). I will not address the question of whether Garver's concept of violence is too inclusive. Instead, I will concentrate on his remarks suggesting important links between the ideas of violence and violation—and, ultimately, dignity and integrity.

4. This is not to say that surgery never involves damage, harm, or destruction. Malpractice does occur. Yet even when valued parts of the body are removed or destroyed, if we deem the surgery successful, we will say that, on the whole, the *person* is now better off than before.

5. The relationship between violence done to something and its integrity was first suggested to me by the late Gerald MacCallum in his unpublished paper "What Is Wrong with Violence?" The paper is discussed at some length by Terry Nardin (1973).

6. This idea is explored by John Rawls, who says, "shame springs from a feeling of diminishment of the self" (1971, p. 445). Rawls has been rightly criticized for conflating self-respect and self-esteem. See, for example, Laurence Thomas (1978). For certain purposes it is important not to refer to these two terms together. However, since shame may relate to either, I refer to them together while acknowledging their differences.

7. It is this description that leads Laurence Thomas (1978) to insist that self-respect and self-esteem are different. Even those who lack confidence in the ability to fulfill their intentions, or who lack a "secure conviction that [their] conception of [their] good, [their] plan of life, is worth carrying out" (Rawls 1971, p. 440) can have self-respect. Self-respect, unlike self-esteem, is not necessarily dependent on one's sense of accomplishment or achievement.

8. C. B. Macpherson (1962) attributes such a conception of persons to the political tradition from Hobbes through Locke. He calls this "possessive individualism." Recent feminist literature is quite critical of this highly individualistic notion of autonomy. It is a centerpiece in Carol Gilligan's celebrated *In a Different Voice* (1982). How we should understand autonomy in light of these criticisms will be discussed in Chapter 10.

9. Ellen Meiksens Wood (1973) contrasts two historical traditions of autonomy. One is the competitive model attributed to Hobbes, Locke, and (to some extent) Mill. The other is a more cooperative model attributed to Rousseau, Kant, and Marx. The interdependent features of autonomy will be explored in greater detail in Chapter 10.

10. See Michael Meyer, "Dignity, Rights, and Self-Control" (1989), for a recent attempt to ground rights in dignity.

11. For an important discussion of the distinction between "acting from" and "acting for the sake of," see Michael Stocker's "Values and Purposes: The Limits of Teleology and the Ends of Friendship" (1981).

12. Chapter 3 of Martin Benjamin's *Splitting the Difference* (1990) has a helpful discussion of various ways in which we might lack moral integrity.

13. This is a major theme in Fingarette's *Self-Deception* (1969). It should be pointed out that Fingarette does not restrict his discussion to *moral* integrity. For a comprehensive discussion of morality and self-deception, see Mike Martin's *Self-Deception and Morality* (1986).

14. Note the shift from "indignation" in the last paragraph to "resentment" here. Rawls refers to the anger we feel at wrongs others do to others as indignation, whereas it is resentment that we feel when we are ourselves wronged (1963, p. 299). Butler, on the other hand, refers to impartial resentment as indignation. As a moral sentiment, resentment for Butler is "indignation raised by cruelty and injustice . . . which persons unconcerned would feel" (1730, p. 75). As a kind of disinterested anger, this resentment, or indignation, can be addressed to wrongs

against oneself as well as others, which seems preferable to Rawls's more re-stricted view. Certainly the fixer's indignation is directed at wrongs both to him-self and others.

15. This is the question of whether we have "duties to ourselves." For a per-suasive case for giving self- and other-regarding considerations equal moral standing, see Judith Andre's "The Equal Moral Weight of Self- and Other-Regarding Acts" (1987).

CHAPTER 6. MORAL PSYCHOLOGY AND RESPECT FOR PERSONS

1. Although Rawls tailors his psychological principles somewhat to suit his concept of justice, he acknowledges that his theory of moral development draws extensively from the psychological theories of William McDougall, Jean Piaget, and, more recently, Lawrence Kohlberg (1971, p. 461).

2. Rawls does briefly mention how the principles of moral psychology might operate in a society based on utilitarian principles (1971, section 76). His discus-sion, again, seems to be confined to the notion of a well-ordered society; he never considers how these principles might operate in less than well-ordered societies.

3. It should be emphasized that I am referring here only to what *psychological* theories might tell us about the possibility of a Rawlsian ideally just society. It is quite possible that, even if psychological principles as such pose no serious ob-stacle to the establishment of such a society, there are other kinds of obstacles that effectively prevent its establishment (e.g., of a political or economic nature). Thus, to say that Rawls's principles of justice do not flout the principles of moral psychology is not to say that there is necessarily much likelihood of his ideally just society ever being realized.

4. I am not presupposing any precise meaning here for the expression "capac-ity for sympathy." I choose this expression primarily because Rawls does. For some purposes it might be preferable to speak variously of compassion, fellow-feeling, or care or concern for the well-being of others. The interrelationships of these notions and their significance for morality raise issues too complex to be dealt with here. For a helpful discussion of these matters, see Philip Mercer's *Sympathy and Ethics* (1972).

5. In addition to my own views, Deigh includes on the optimistic side writings by David A. J. Richards, David H. Jones, Bernard Boxhill, Barry Stroud, Herbert Morris, and Laurence Thomas. To this list could be added R. S. Peters, R. V. Han-naford, Nel Noddings, and Lawrence Blum, among others. Among psycholo-gists, Martin L. Hoffman and Carol Gilligan are particularly noteworthy.

6. This is an overriding theme of Laurence Thomas's *Living Morally* (1989). Also, linking parental love with respect for persons helps undermine the view that caring for others and respecting them are radically distinct. On this see Robin Dillon's "Care and Respect," *Explorations in Feminist Ethics: Theory and Practice,* ed. Eve Browning Cole and Susan Coultrap McGuinn (in press).

CHAPTER 7. COGNITION AND AFFECT
IN MORAL DEVELOPMENT

1. In his later writings Kohlberg acknowledges difficulty in clearly differentiating stages 5 and 6. However, the distinction between the third level (postconventional), the one in which they reside, and the other two levels is maintained.

2. This raises a very general question about the adequacy of Kohlberg's view that there are six stages. It seems clear that the cognitive abilities of adults at stages 1 and 2 are very different from young children at those stages. Can it plausibly be said that the reasoning of adults and children at those stages is not significantly different? Kohlberg says that one of the distinguishing features of stages 5 and 6 is that, at this level, meta-ethical thinking is possible, but it would seem that adults at stages 1 and 2 are also capable of meta-ethical thinking. Should we not say that, in addition to children's stages 1 and 2, there are adult stages 1 and 2?

Yet even putting it this way would be misleading. Clearly children as well as adults develop sophisticated ways of determining what is in their self-interest. Although there are obvious differences between *very* young children and adults, differences are much less marked between, say, the self-interested thinking of an eight-year-old and an adult. The clever thinking involved in "learning the ropes" in regard to self-interest is well under way even before adolescence. Thus if critical, self-interested thinking is well under way in childhood, why not say the same about critical, moral thinking? Again, Fullinwider's (1989) observations about learning moral conventions are well taken. (See Chapter 2.)

3. For a recent summary of the findings of Hoffman and others, see William Damon, *The Moral Child* (1988), especially chap. 2, "Empathy, Shame, and Guilt: The Early Moral Emotions."

4. See also Robert Hannaford, "Moral Reasoning and Action in Young Children" (1985) and Laurence Thomas, *Living Morally* (1989). For a good critique of Piagetian assessments of children's cognitive abilities, see Margaret Donaldson, *Children's Minds* (1979) and Gareth Matthews, *Philosophy and the Young Child* (1980).

5. Notice that, although the absence of reciprocation can inhibit concern for others, the presence of reciprocation may not be sufficient to generate acceptance of a broad enough principle of respect for persons. Thus, the criticism of Rawls in Chapter 6 still holds.

CHAPTER 8. CARING AND JUSTICE
IN MORAL DEVELOPMENT

1. The terminology is actually Kohlberg's. In *Psychology of Moral Development* (1984), he variously refers to Gilligan's "ethic of care," "ethic of responsibility,"

and "ethic of personal responsibility" and seems to treat these expressions equivalently. For convenience, I will refer to Gilligan's perspective as an "ethic of care." Kohlberg's contrasting perspective will be referred to as his "ethic of justice."

2. Kohlberg's reply can be found in various parts of *Psychology of Moral Development* (1984). For a sampling of the extensive attention given to Gilligan's writings, see Eva Feder Kittay and Diana T. Meyers, eds., *Women and Moral Theory* (1987); Owen Flanagan and Kathryn Jackson, "Justice, Care, and Gender: The Kohlberg-Gilligan Debate Revisited" (1987); Lawrence Blum, "Gilligan and Kohlberg: Implications for Moral Theory" (1988); and Jonathan Adler, "Particularity, Gilligan, and the Two-Levels View: A Reply" (1989).

3. Whether Gilligan has really shown that Kohlberg slights women's moral perspectives is not an issue I will take up here. Although this aspect of her research has received a great deal of critical attention, nothing I explore in this chapter requires a resolution of the controversy.

4. For a related criticism, see Adler (1989). He employs Hare's (1981) two level view of morality discussed in Chapter 2. However, unlike Hare, he does not assume that critical morality (level 2) is utilitarian. Nor does he suggest that critical morality may discover that intuitive level thinking (level 1) is radically separate from critical morality.

5. This appeared in the *Daily Hampshire Gazette* (Northampton, Mass.), July 25, 1985.

CHAPTER 9. PERSONAL MORALITY

1. See, for example, Marcia Baron's "Kantian Ethics and Supererogation" (1987, pp. 237–62). Baron develops a Kantian notion of imperfect duty as an alternative to the supererogatory. However, it is clear that this is not a juridical notion.

2. That Urmson had this broader class of action in mind all along is evident in the closing pages of "Saints and Heroes." For example, see p. 205 of that article.

3. Still, as Baron (1987) shows, it is not necessary to restrict the notion of duty in this way.

4. I am speaking here of the example as presented by Urmson, not of the historical Francis. That is, I am treating the example of Francis as if Urmson intended it to be taken in the same way as the other examples of supererogatory action he presents. None of those examples makes any assumptions about particular religious convictions or special commitments made to others.

5. Here I am thinking of, for example, Tom Hill's "Servility and Self-Respect" (1973) and his "Self-Respect Reconsidered" (1982). See also Gilligan's *In a Different Voice* (1982).

6. This does not mean that they must be *openly* reproachful. Nor does it mean that they must be severely reproachful—only that they have a somewhat critical attitude toward those who fail to do what they ought.

7. For convenience I will refer to Urmson's examples in terms of "supererogation," even though he has since expressed regret at having used that expression.

My use of the expression is not intended to assume that there must be a special place in morality for the supererogatory as such. See, for example, Marcia Baron's (1987) thoughtful attempt to avoid making a special place for it.

8. I am not suggesting that this is an explicitly and self-consciously articulated attitude. Often it is not.

9. Michael Clark, "The Meritorious and the Mandatory," *Aristotelian Society*, n.s., vol. 79(1978/9): pp. 22–33.

CHAPTER 10. AUTONOMY, REASON, AND SENTIMENTS

1. It should be noted that Dworkin has recently modified much of what he said in "Autonomy and Behavior Control" (1976). He no longer equates "substantive independence" and "substantive autonomy," thus allowing for the possibility that autonomy and interdependence are compatible. See his *Theory and Practice of Autonomy* (1988). However, his earlier view is representative of those who suspect that autonomy and interdependence are incompatible and therefore merits discussion.

2. This is deliberately hedged. For example, issues of distributive justice may require the expertise of economists for resolution. Still, this does not mean that economists have moral expertise in regard to moral principles, even if economic expertise is required in applying them to society.

3. I use the vague expression "everyday moral thinking" in contradistinction to, for example, policy-making at governmental and institutional levels or the complexities of implementing such policies.

4. As will be apparent shortly (and as emphasized in earlier chapters) these rational constraints are not merely rational—whatever that might mean. The constraints are rational in the sense that only rational beings are capable of understanding and applying them. However, there is no claim that all imaginable rational beings accept them. Recall the earlier chapters on Reid and Hume. I am not saying that it is necessarily irrational to reject the rational constraints embraced by moral autonomy.

5. The name "Harold" occurs to me here because the view espoused has been inspired by reflecting on H[arold] A. Prichard's classic "Does Moral Philosophy Rest on a Mistake?" (1912). I do not suggest that Prichard says anything like this, but it does seem to me that Harold's view captures some of the spirit of Prichard's essay. Harold's view is also inspired by my reading of H. L. A. Hart's "Are There Any Natural Rights?" (1955) and Wesley Hohfeld's *Fundamental Legal Conceptions* (1919). Hart's reference to a right that enables us voluntarily to incur special obligations seems to me to be a moral analogue to Hohfeld's conception of "legal power." Just as the latter notion ascribes legal competence to those with legal powers, the former ascribes moral competence to those who have the right voluntarily to incur special obligations. However, the analogy is imperfect, and a useful analysis is beyond the scope of anything that can be attempted here.

CHAPTER 11. UTILITARIANISM
AND PERSONAL INTEGRITY

1. Unfortunately, this example is more complex than Williams seems to realize. Taking the job conflicts with George's moral integrity, but his moral integrity is only a part of his overall personal integrity. Since he has had difficulty finding work in his field, turning down the job may conflict with his personal integrity because it may mean giving up his career in biological research. If we think of that career as one of George's basic "projects," he is faced with a choice that may inevitably alter his personal integrity. For the example to be useful, Williams must assume that George's moral integrity takes precedence over this particular project. The conflict is obscured somewhat by Williams's characterization of George's commitment to pacifism as a "project." Evidently he intends this term to have a very broad reference—including moral commitments as well as jobs, careers, and nonmoral endeavors.

2. Of course, we need to know much more about the circumstances in order to be sure that utilitarianism requires Jim to shoot an Indian. However, since Williams is not contesting this conclusion, we can presume that the fuller story would rule out worries such as Pedro shooting the remaining nineteen anyway.

3. For the need to qualify such a claim in important ways, see Nancy Davis, "Utilitarianism and Responsibility" (1980). See also John Harris, "Williams on Negative Responsibility and Integrity" (1974).

4. This example is taken from Williams's "Persons, Character and Morality" (1981, esp. pp. 117–19). Although Williams does not discuss this example in terms of integrity, there are strong parallels with his explicit examples. However, it should be noted that this is an example in which personal, but not necessarily moral, integrity is at stake. The examples of George and Jim focus more obviously on moral integrity. Finally, the target of Williams's criticism in the drowning wife example is not merely utilitarianism but impersonal morality in general.

5. Another consideration favoring Betty could enter in. If she knows that Alex is in a position to help her, but he goes for the stranger instead, she may feel let down or betrayed in her dying moments. This, too, must be considered relevant from a utilitarian point of view, regardless of how rationally grounded such feelings are. However, suppose that Betty does not realize that Alex could save her, but the stranger knows Alex could save him. The stranger's anguish or disappointment at being ignored will have to be thrown into the calculations. To simplify, I will suppose that neither is aware that Alex is in a position to save either.

6. Whether this can fairly be said of all forms of utilitarianism will be considered shortly.

7. Throughout this chapter I will refer to utilitarianism rather than consequentialism. "Consequentialism" is the broader term, as it includes less than maximizing views as well as maximizing utilitarian views. I am interested primarily in what Scheffler has to say about utilitarianism. No distortion of his meaning should result from using the narrower term here.

8. Although his agent-centered prerogative offers an alternative rationale for individuals favoring their own projects and commitments, Scheffler does not

fully articulate what that rationale is. This weakness has been pointed out by Stephen Darwall (1984) and Shelly Kagan (1984). In what follows I will outline a principled rationale which will also provide the basis for criticizing Scheffler's denial of agent-centered restrictions.

9. These limits need to be spelled out carefully. Here I offer only a few qualifications. The principle of respect for personal integrity need not be the only moral principle, and it need not be absolute. For example, it could sometimes be overridden by overwhelmingly bad consequences that could result from strict adherence to it. It is not my intent to suggest that there is only one fundamental moral principle; nor is it my intent to rank fundamental moral principles in the abstract. My suggestion is only that a principle of respect for personal integrity can be an independent moral principle, not reducible to or derivable from any other.

10. For an account of the paradoxical implications of Scheffler's views about promising, see George Harris (1989). Harris's critique, like mine, emphasizes the *interpersonal* features of promising and personal relations. Other critiques of Scheffler's claim that agent-centered prerogatives are independent of agent-centered restrictions include Larry Alexander (1987) and Stephen Darwall (1984).

11. Again, we must assume that worrisome variables are tightly controlled. We must be assured that the other Indians will be shot if Jim does not shoot one, that they will be spared if he does, and so on.

12. As Darwall points out, the phrase is from Paul's *Letter to the Romans* (2: 14), which provides the background for Butler's Sermons 1 and 2 (1730).

CHAPTER 12. WHY BE MORAL?

1. Bernard Williams says that morality encourages the idea that only an obligation can override an obligation (1985, p. 180). This example, then, is an exception to that idea, but I do not think it is an objection to morality—only to an unduly narrow conception of morality.

2. A notable exception is D. Z. Phillips and H. O. Mounce's *Moral Practices* (1969), especially chaps. 3 and 4.

3. References will be to two chapters of Nielsen's *Why Be Moral?* (1989). Chap. 8, "Why Should I Be Moral?" was originally published in *Methodos*, 15 (1963), and it has been widely anthologized. Chap. 14, "Why Should I Be Moral?— Revisited," was originally published in *American Philosophical Quarterly*, 21, 1984.

4. For an elaboration of this point see my article "On 'Should I Be Moral?' A Reply to Snare" (1976).

5. This seems to be Nielsen's (1989) view in chap. 8, "Why Should I Be Moral?" However, in chap. 14, "Why Should I Be Moral? Revisited," he seems to correct the assumption.

6. This point is well made by Dan W. Brock in his "Justification of Morality" (1977). See especially p. 76.

7. Various passages from chap. 14 of Nielsen (1989) are incorporated in this imaginary dialogue.

8. Notice the gap between having to *just decide* what to do and having one's decision *required by reason*. If the latter expression implies that acting otherwise is acting *irrationally*, too much is being demanded. As I have already claimed, one can have good reasons for doing something even if not doing it is not irrational. In such a case one does not "just decide."

Selected Bibliography

Adler, Jonathan. 1989. "Particularity, Gilligan, and the Two-Levels View: A Reply." *Ethics* 100: 149–56.

Alexander, Larry. 1987. "Scheffler on the Independence of Agent-Centered Prerogatives from Agent-Centered Restrictions." *Journal of Philosophy* 84: 277–83.

Andre, Judith. 1987. "The Equal Moral Weight of Self- and Other-Regarding Acts." *Canadian Journal of Philosophy* 17: 155–66.

Aristotle. 1980. *Nicomachean Ethics*. Translated by W. D. Ross. Oxford: Oxford University Press.

Arrington, Robert. 1979. "Practical Reason, Responsibility, and the Psychopath." *Journal for the Theory of Social Behavior* 9: 177–93.

Austin, J. L. 1961. *Philosophical Papers*. Edited by J. O. Urmson and G. J. Warnock. Oxford: Oxford University Press.

Baier, Kurt. 1958. *The Moral Point of View*. Ithaca, N. Y.: Cornell University Press.

Baron, Marcia. 1987. "Kantian Ethics and Supererogation." *Journal of Philosophy* 84: 237–62.

Benjamin, Martin. 1990. *Splitting the Difference: Compromise and Integrity in Ethics and Politics*. Lawrence: University Press of Kansas.

Bennett, Jonathan. 1980. "Accountability." In *Philosophical Subjects*, edited by Zak Van Straaten, pp. 14–47. Oxford: Oxford University Press.

————. 1989. "Two Departures from Consequentialism." *Ethics* 100: 54–66.

Betz, Joseph. 1977. "Violence: Garver's Definition and a Deweyan Correction." *Ethics* 87: 339-51.

Blum, Lawrence A. 1980. *Friendship, Altruism and Morality*. London: Routledge and Kegan Paul.

————. 1988. "Gilligan and Kohlberg: Implications for Moral Theory." *Ethics* 98: 472–91.

Bok, Sissela. 1978. *Lying: Moral Choice in Public and Private Life*. New York: Pantheon.

Boxhill, Bernard. 1976. "Self-Respect and Protest." *Philosophy and Public Affairs* 6: 58–69.

Brock, Dan W. 1977. "The Justification of Morality." *American Philosophical Quarterly* 14: 71–78.

Burnyeat, M. F. 1980. "Aristotle on Learning to Be Good." In *Essays on Aristotle's Ethics*, edited by Amelie Rorty, pp. 69-92. Berkeley: University of California Press.

Butler, Joseph. (1730) 1970. *Butler's Fifteen Sermons*. Edited by T. A. Roberts. London: Society for Promoting Christian Knowledge.

Cahn, Edmund. 1962. *The Sense of Injustice*. Bloomington: Indiana University Press.

Carr, Spencer. 1976. "The Integrity of a Utilitarian." *Ethics* 86: 241–46.

Clark, Michael. 1978/9. "The Meritorious and the Mandatory." *Aristotelian Society*, n.s. 79: 23–33.

Cleckley, Hervey. 1976. *The Mask of Sanity*. 5th ed. St. Louis: C. V. Mosby.

Damon, William. 1988. *The Moral Child*. New York: Free Press.

Darwall, Stephen. 1977. "Two Kinds of Respect." *Ethics* 88: 36–49.

_____. 1984. "Samuel Scheffler: *The Rejection of Consequentialism*." *Journal of Philosophy* 81: 223–24.

_____. 1986. "Agent-Centered Restrictions From the Inside Out." *Philosophic Studies* 50: 291–319.

Davis, Nancy. 1980. "Utilitarianism and Responsibility." *Ratio* 22: 15–35.

Deigh, John. 1982. "Love, Guilt, and the Sense of Justice." *Inquiry* 25: 391–416.

Dillon, Robin. In press. "Care and Respect." In *Explorations in Feminist Ethics: Theory and Practice*, edited by Eve Browning Cole and Susan Coultrap McGuinn.

Donaldson, Margaret. 1979. *Children's Minds*. New York: Norton.

Duff, Anthony. 1977. "Psychopathy and Understanding." *American Philosophical Quarterly* 14: 189-200.

Dworkin, Gerald. 1976. "Autonomy and Behavior Control." *Hastings Center Report* 6: 23–28.

_____. 1988. *The Theory and Practice of Autonomy*. New York: Cambridge University Press.

Dworkin, Ronald. 1977. *Taking Rights Seriously*. Oxford: Oxford University Press.

Edel, Abraham. 1969. "Humanist Ethics and the Meaning of Human Dignity." In *Moral Problems in Contemporary Society*, edited by Paul Kurtz, pp. 227–40. Englewood Cliffs, N. J.: Prentice-Hall.

Erikson, Erik. 1963. *Childhood and Society*. 2d ed. New York: Norton.

Feinberg, Joel. 1970. *Doing and Deserving*. Princeton, N. J.: Princeton University Press.

Fingarette, Herbert. 1967. *On Responsibility*. New York: Basic Books.

_____. 1969. *Self-Deception*. London: Routledge & Kegan Paul.

Flanagan, Owen, and Jackson, Kathryn. 1987. "Justice, Care, and Gender: The Kohlberg-Gilligan Debate Revisited." *Ethics* 97: 622–37.

Flay, Joseph. 1978. "Is Ethics for Children Moral?" In *Growing Up with Philosophy*, edited by Matthew Lipman and Ann Sharp, pp. 145–57. Philadelphia: Temple University Press.

Fowles, John. 1977. *The Magus*. Boston: Little, Brown & Co.

Friedman, Marilyn A. 1986. "Autonomy and the Split-Level Self." *Southern Journal of Philosophy* 24: 19-35.

_____. 1987. "Autonomy in Social Context." In *Proceedings of the Second International Conference of the North American Society for Social Philosophy*, edited by James Sterba and Creighton Peden. New York: Edwin Mellen Press.

_____. 1989. "Friendship and Moral Growth." *Journal of Value Inquiry* 23: 3–13.

Fullinwider, Robert. 1989. "Moral Conventions and Moral Lessons." *Social Theory and Practice* 15: 321–38.

Garver, Newton. 1970. "What Violence Is." In *Philosophy for a New Generation*, edited by James A. Gould, pp. 352–64. New York: Macmillan.

Gert, Bernard. 1988. *Morality*. New York: Oxford University Press.

Gilligan, Carol. 1982. *In a Different Voice: Psychological Theory and Women's Development*. Cambridge, Mass.: Harvard University Press.

Haksar, Vinit. 1965. "Aristotle and the Punishment of Psychopaths." In *Aristotle's Ethics*, edited by James J. Walsh and Henry Shapiro, pp. 80–101. Belmont, Calif.: Wadsworth.

Halfron, Mark. 1989. *Integrity: A Philosophical Inquiry*. Philadelphia: Temple University Press.

Hallie, Philip. 1979. *Lest Innocent Blood Be Shed*. Kansas City, Mo.: Harrow.

Hannaford, Robert. 1985. "Moral Reasoning and Action in Young Children." *Journal of Value Inquiry* 19:85–98.

Hare, R. M. 1963. *Freedom and Reason*. New York: Oxford University Press.

_____. 1981. *Moral Thinking*. New York: Oxford University Press.

Harris, Errol. 1966. "Respect for Persons." In *Ethics in Society*, edited by Richard DeGeorge. New York: Anchor Books.

Harris, George. 1989. "A Paradoxical Departure from Consequentialism." *Journal of Philosophy* 86: 90–102

Harris, John. 1974. "Williams on Negative Responsibility and Integrity." *Philosophical Quarterly* 24: 265–73.

Hart, H. L. A. 1955. "Are There Any Natural Rights?" *Philosophical Review* 64: 175–191.

_____. 1986. "Who Can Tell Right from Wrong?" *New York Review of Books*, 17 July, pp. 49–52.

Hill, Tom, Jr. 1973. "Servility and Self-Respect." *Monist* 57: 87–104.

_____. 1982. "Self-Respect Reconsidered." In *Respect for Persons*, edited by O. H. Green, pp. 129–37. New Orleans: Tulane University Press.

_____. 1987. "The Importance of Autonomy." In *Women and Moral Theory*, edited by Eva Feder Kittay and Diana T. Meyers, pp. 129–38. Totowa, N. J.: Rowman and Littlefield.

Hobbes, Thomas. (1651) 1960. *Leviathan*. Oxford: Basil Blackwell.

Hoffman, M. L. 1970. "Moral Development." In *Carmichael's Manual of Child Psychology*, vol. 2, edited by P. A. Mussen, pp. 261–369. New York: Wiley.

_____. 1976. "Empathy, Role-Taking, Guilt, and the Development of Altruistic Motives." In *Moral Development and Behavior*, edited by Thomas Lickona, pp. 124–143. New York: Rinehart & Winston.

Hohfeld, Wesley. 1919. *Fundamental Legal Conceptions*. New Haven, Conn.: Yale University Press.

Hospers, John. 1961. *Human Conduct: An Introduction to the Problems of Ethics*. New York: Harcourt Brace Jovanovich.

Hume, David. (1740) 1888. *A Treatise on Human Nature*, edited by L. A. Selby-Bigge. Oxford: Clarendon Press.

_____. 1969. "Letter to Hutcheson, March 16, 1740." In *British Moralists*, vol. 2, p. 111, edited by D. D. Raphael. Oxford: Oxford University Press.

_____. (1777) 1975. *Enquiries Concerning Human Understanding and Concerning the Principles of Morals*. 3rd ed. Edited by Paul Nidditch. Oxford: Clarendon Press.

Jaksa, James, and Pritchard, Michael S. 1988. *Communication Ethics: Methods of Analysis*. Belmont, Calif.: Wadsworth.

Kagan, Jerome, and Lamb, Sharon. 1987. *The Emergence of Morality in Young Children*. Chicago: University of Chicago Press.

Kagan, Shelly. 1984. "Does Consequentialism Demand Too Much? Recent Work on the Limits of Obligation." *Philosophy & Public Affairs* 13: 249-54.

Kant, Immanuel. (1788) 1957. *Foundations of the Metaphysics of Morals*. New York: Liberal Arts Press, Bobbs-Merrill.

Kekes, John. 1983. "Constancy and Purity." *Mind* 92: 499-518.

Kittay, Eva Feder and Meyers, Diana T., eds. 1987. *Women and Moral Theory*. Totowa, N. J.: Rowman and Littlefield.

Kohlberg, Lawrence. 1973. "The Claim to Moral Adequacy of a Highest Stage of Moral Judgment," *Journal of Philosophy* 70: 630–46.

_____. 1981. *The Philosophy of Moral Development: Essays on Moral Development*, vol. 1. San Francisco: Harper & Row.

_____. 1984. *The Psychology of Moral Development: Essays on Moral Development*, vol. 2. San Francisco: Harper & Row.

Kuflik, Arthur. 1984. "The Inalienability of Autonomy." *Philosophy & Public Affairs* 13: 271–98.

Kupfer, Joseph. 1982. "The Moral Presumption Against Lying." *Review of Metaphysics* 36: 103–26.

Lipman, Matthew. 1988. *Philosophy Goes to School*. Philadelphia: Temple University Press.

Lipman, Matthew; Sharp, Ann; and Oscanyan, Frederick. 1980. *Philosophy in the Classroom*. 2d ed. Philadelphia: Temple University Press.

Lynd, Helen Merrill. 1958. *On Shame and the Search for Identity*. New York: John Wiley & Sons.

McCord, William, and McCord, Joan. 1965. *Psychopathy and Delinquency*. New York: Grune & Stratton.

MacDonald, John. 1973. *The Turquoise Lament*. New York: Lippincott.

_____. 1985. *The Lonely Silver Rain*. New York: Fawcett Gold Medal.

McFall, Lynne. 1987. "Integrity." *Ethics* 98: 5–20.

MacPherson, C. B. 1962. *The Theory of Possessive Individualism*. Oxford: Oxford University Press.

Mackie, J. L. 1980. *Hume's Moral Theory*. Boston: Routledge & Kegan Paul.

Malamud, Bernard. 1966. *The Fixer*. New York: Farrar, Straus & Giroux.

Martin, Mike. 1986. *Self-Deception and Morality*. Lawrence: University Press of Kansas.

Marx, Karl. (1844) 1966. "Alienated Labor." In *Political Man and Social Man*, edited by Robert Paul Wolff. New York: Random House.

Matthews, Gareth. 1980. *Philosophy and the Young Child*. Cambridge, Mass.: Harvard University Press.

————. 1984. *Dialogues with Children*. Cambridge, Mass.: Harvard University Press.

————. 1987. "Concept Formation and Moral Development." In *Philosophical Perspectives in Developmental Psychology*, edited by James Russell, pp. 175–90. Oxford: Basil Blackwell.

Mercer, Philip. 1972. *Sympathy and Ethics*. Oxford: Oxford University Press.

Meyer, Michael. 1989. "Dignity, Rights, and Self-Control." *Ethics* 99: 520–34.

Milo, Ronald. 1985. *Immorality*. Princeton: Princeton University Press.

Morris, Herbert. 1976. *On Guilt and Innocence*. Berkeley: University of California Press.

Murphy, Arthur. 1965. *The Theory of Practical Reason*. LaSalle, Ill.: Open Court.

Murphy, Jeffrie. 1972. "Moral Death: A Kantian Essay in Psychopathy." *Ethics* 82: 284–98.

Nagel, Thomas. 1970. *The Possibility of Altruism*. Oxford: Oxford University Press.

————. 1979. *Mortal Questions*. Cambridge: Cambridge University Press.

————. 1986. *The View from Nowhere*. Oxford: Oxford University Press.

Nardin, Terry. 1973. "Conflicting Conceptions of Political Violence." In *Political Science Annual*, vol. 4, edited by Cornelius P. Cotter, pp. 75–126. Indianapolis: Bobbs-Merrill.

Nielsen, Kai. 1989. *Why Be Moral?* New York: Prometheus Books.

Peters, R. S. 1974. *Psychology and Ethical Development*. London: George Allen & Unwin.

Philips, Michael. 1987. "Reason, Dignity and the Formal Conception of Reason." *American Philosophical Quarterly* 24: 191–98.

Phillips, D. Z., and Mounce, H. O. 1969. *Moral Practices*. London: Routledge and Kegan Paul.

Piaget, Jean. (1932) 1965. *The Moral Judgment of the Child*. New York: Free Press.

Postema, Gerald. 1983. "Moral Responsibility in Professional Ethics." In *Profits and Professions*, edited by Wade L. Robison, Michael S. Pritchard, and Joseph Ellin, pp. 37–63.

Prichard, H. A. (1912) 1949. "Does Moral Philosophy Rest on a Mistake?" In *Moral Obligation*. Oxford: Clarendon Press, pp. 1–17.

Pritchard, Michael S. 1976a. "On 'Should I Be Moral?' A Reply to Snare." *Canadian Journal of Philosophy* 6: 121–26.

————. 1976b. "On Taking Emotions Seriously: A Critique of B. F. Skinner." *Journal for the Theory of Social Behavior* 6: 211–32.

————. 1985. *Philosophical Adventures with Children*. Landham, Md.: University Press of America.

Railton, Peter. 1984. "Alienation, Consequentialism, and the Demands of Morality." *Philosophy & Public Affairs* 13: 134–71.

Rawls, John. 1963. "The Sense of Justice." *Philosophical Review* 72: 281–303.

————. 1971. *The Theory of Justice*. Cambridge, Mass.: Harvard University Press.

Reid, Thomas. (1788) 1895. *Essays on the Active Powers of the Mind* in *Philosophical*

Works, vol. 2, with notes by Sir William Hamilton. Hildesheim: Gekorg Olms Verlagsbuchhandlung.

Ross, W. D. 1930. *The Right and the Good*. Oxford: Oxford University Press.

Ryle, Gilbert. 1958. "On Forgetting the Difference between Right and Wrong." In *Essays in Moral Philosophy*, edited by A. I. Melden, pp. 147-62. Seattle: University of Washington Press.

Scanlon, T. M. 1988. "Levels of Moral Thinking." In *Hare and Critics*, edited by Douglas Seanor and N. Fotion, pp. 129-46. Oxford: Clarendon Press.

Schachter, Stanley. 1964. "The Interaction of Cognitive and Physiological Determinants of Emotional States." In *Advances in Experimental Social Psychology*, edited by Leonard Berkowitz, pp. 49-80. New York: Academic Press.

Scheffler, Samuel. 1982. *The Rejection of Consequentialism*. Cambridge: Cambridge University Press.

————. 1989. "Deontology and the Agent: A Reply to Jonathan Bennett." *Ethics* 100: 67-76.

Schmitt, Richard. 1969. *Martin Heidegger on Being Human*. New York: Random House.

Shweder, Richard A.; Turiel, Elliot; and Much, Nancy C. 1981. "The Moral Intuitions of the Child." In *Social Cognitive Development: Frontiers and Possible Futures*, edited by John H. Flavell and Lee Ross, pp. 288-305. Cambridge: Cambridge University Press.

Sidgwick, Henry. 1907. *The Methods of Ethics*. 7th ed. London: Macmillan.

Skinner, B. F. 1953. *The Science of Human Behavior*. New York: Macmillan.

Smart, J. J. C. 1977. "Benevolence as an Over-riding Attitude." *Australasian Journal of Philosophy* 55: 126-35.

Smith, Adam. (1759) 1976. *The Theory of the Moral Sentiments*. Indianapolis: Liberty Classics.

Smith, Robert J. 1984. "The Psychopath as Moral Agent." *Philosophy and Phenomenological Research* 45: 177-93.

Spiegelberg, Herbert. 1971. "Human Dignity: A Challenge to Contemporary Philosophy." *Philosophy Forum* 9: 39-64.

Stocker, Michael. 1976. "The Schizophrenia of Modern Ethical Theories." *Journal of Philosophy* 73: 453-66.

————. 1981. "Values and Purposes: The Limits of Teleology and the Ends of Friendship." *Journal of Philosophy* 78: 747-65.

Strawson, P. F. 1968. "Freedom and Resentment." In *Studies in the Philosophy of Thought and Action*, edited by P. F. Strawson, pp. 71-96. New York: Oxford University Press.

————. 1985. *Skepticism and Naturalism: Some Varieties*. New York: Columbia University Press.

Taylor, Gabrielle. 1985. *Pride, Shame, and Guilt*. Oxford: Oxford University Press.

Thomas, Laurence. 1978. "Morality and our Self-Concept." *Journal of Value Inquiry* 12: 258-68.

————. 1989. *Living Morally*. Philadelphia: Temple University Press.

Urmson, J. O. 1958. "Saints and Heroes." In *Essays in Moral Philosophy*, edited by A. I. Melden, pp. 198-216. Seattle: University of Washington Press.

————. 1988. "Hare on Intuitive Moral Thinking." In *Hare and Critics*, edited by Douglas Seanor and N. Fotion, pp. 161–69. Oxford: Clarendon Press.

Watson, Gary. 1988. "Responsibility and the Limits of Evil." In *Responsibility, Character, and the Emotions*, edited by Ferdinand Schoeman, pp. 256–86. Cambridge: Cambridge University Press.

Weldon, Fay. 1983. *The Life and Loves of a She-Devil*. New York: Ballantine Books.

White, Robert. 1963. "Ego and Reality in Psychoanalytic Theory," *Psychological Issues* 3: 3–203.

Williams, Bernard. 1973. "A Critique of Utilitarianism." In *Utilitarianism: For and Against*, edited by J. J. C. Smart and Bernard Williams, pp. 77–150. Cambridge: Cambridge University Press.

————. 1981. *Moral Luck*. Cambridge: Cambridge University Press.

————. 1985. *Ethics and the Limits of Philosophy*. Cambridge, Mass.: Harvard University Press.

Winch, Peter. 1972. *Ethics and Action*. London: Routledge & Kegan Paul.

Wittgenstein, Ludwig. 1953. *Philosophical Investigations*. Translated by G. E. M. Anscombe. New York: Macmillan.

Wood, Ellen Meiksens. 1973. *Mind and Politics*. Berkeley: University of California Press.

Index

271